OXFORD GARDENS

The contrasts of Oxford
A medieval lane in the Queen's College: a foil and complement to the
grand architecture of Gibbs's Radcliffe Camera and Hawksmoor's
All Souls.

OXFORD GARDENS

The university's influence on garden history

by
Mavis Batey

Scolar Press

To Keith

First published in 1982 by Avebury Publishing Company, Amersham, England.
© Mavis Batey, 1982. All rights reserved.

Reissued by Scolar Press, 1986

British Library Cataloguing in Publication Data:

Batey, Mavis
  Oxford gardens: the university's influence on
  garden history.
  1. University of Oxford   2. Gardens—Oxford
  (Oxfordshire)—History
  I. Title
  712'.7'0942574   SB466.G7

  ISBN 0–85967–724–9 PBK

Typeset in Baskerville 11 on 12pt by
System 4 Associates Ltd, Gerrards Cross, Buckinghamshire
Printed and bound by Redwood Burn Ltd, Trowbridge, Wiltshire

Contents

Illustrations

Colour plates

Acknowledgments

Most of all I should like to thank Mrs Ruth Duthie for her great help and encouragement. I should also like to thank Mrs Audrey Blackman, Mrs Catherine Cole, Dame Sylvia Crowe, Dr Sylvia Landsberg, the late Dr Mary Lunt, Lady Mander, Mrs Herta Simon, Miss Rachel Trickett, Mr Ken Burras, Sir Norman Chester, Dr Howard Colvin, Dr Barrie Juniper, Mr McDermott, Mr C. L. Olive, Mr Edward Quinn, Mr John Simmons, Mr Michael Turner, the staff of the Bodleian Library, Christ Church Library and the Oxford City Library; and the University Surveyor, Mr Jack Lankester.

Detailed acknowledgement of illustrations subject to outside copyright, or otherwise lent or given, is made at the end of the book.

M.B.

And that sweet city with her dreaming spires,
She needs not June for beauty's heightening,
Lovely at all times she lies, lovely tonight!

Matthew Arnold (Professor of Poetry
at Oxford for ten years), *Thyrsis.*

Yet, O ye spires of Oxford! Domes and towers!
Gardens and groves! Your presence overpowers
The soberness of reason...

William Wordsworth, *The River Duddon.*

Introduction

A visitor to Oxford who climbs the tower of St Mary's or the cupola of the Sheldonian is rewarded by the sight of a unique collegiate layout of ancient buildings set in green quadrangles, gardens and groves. Oxford and Cambridge are distinguished from European universities by the dominance of the colleges, each individually founded and with its own statutes, buildings and gardens.

The gardens, quadrangles and meadow walks were an important and necessary part of collegiate life. Each college appointed its own garden master or equivalent from among its fellows. At first the gardens were a haphazard arrangement of herb and vegetable plots, orchards and walks, but the Renaissance brought new ideas in garden design, as well as in learning, which were first seen in Oxford in the gardens laid out for the humanist Warden of All Souls.

Oxford became the royalist capital of England in the Civil War and the college gardens were given over to the royal family and the courtiers, the quadrangles turned into parade grounds and the meadow walks made part of the fortifications. When building and garden-making resumed in Oxford after the Restoration, elements of baroque garden design appeared from Europe in the form of parterres, fountains, statues and even a miniature Versailles courtyard at New College with an elegant grille looking onto the garden. Full scale baroque space design with interacting vistas of college buildings as envisaged in the Hawksmoor plan was, however, rejected. Later in the century fashionable landscaping was also resisted by Magdalen and Christ Church whose riverside settings might have allowed such improvement to take place; the old alleyed walks round the water meadows and the secluded gardens were preferred as being more in keeping with ancient foundations. Even a sumptuous Red Book with before and after improvement scenes did not tempt the Fellows of Magdalen to avail themselves of the services of Humphry Repton.

Oxford made its own contribution to the history of gardening, both in the ideas that influenced the peculiarly English landscaped garden and in the actual cultivation of plants. Much has been said of the influence of poets and painters on the natural landscaped garden but coming to terms with Nature was largely due to the natural philosophers who 'reasoned freely' on the works of Nature in Oxford. Their 'interrogation of Nature' ranged over a wide field and included interest in the natural growth of vegetation denied in the formal gardens of the time. When at Magdalen Addison had a fondness for walking through the water walks, which are now named after him, and enjoying the rural prospect across the Cherwell meadows. He criticized formal gardens, garish parterres, water works, topiary and other 'deviations from Nature' such as could then be seen in the clipped evergreen gardens of Trinity College. His was the first voice raised in favour of natural. gardening which was to become an eighteenth century obsession.

The Oxford Physic Garden, renamed the Botanic Garden in 1840, was founded by Henry Danvers, Earl of Danby, in 1621 and is the oldest physic garden after Pisa and Leyden. It was intended for 'the advancement of the faculty of medicine' but, from the first, botany, medicine and practical gardening were linked in systematic study. It became a centre for the cultivation of plants introduced from abroad and through seed exchange contributed much to the modern development of horticulture. In the era of Brown and Repton, when trees and shrubs were treated as elements in a landscape composition, the interest in plants was kept alive by naturalists and botanical illustrators. New and wonderful worlds were opened up to plant collectors in the nineteenth century and the material they brought back by way of seed and herbarium specimens transformed the English garden. Oxford's finest contribution to plant collecting and botanical illustration was Professor Sibthorp's monumental *Flora Graeca* and many of the plants he brought back were grown in the Botanic Garden.

Oxford was not, however, planned as a university town. In the Middle Ages the colleges had to fit into the back streets and waste land of an existing market town. Although the High Street now presents a predominantly academic scene, this appearance is a fairly recent development. All Souls was the only college able to build on the town's coveted High Street in the fifteenth century and then only on a narrow frontage. The Queen's College did not obtain a High Street front until the eighteenth century, Brasenose College until the nineteenth century and Oriel College only in the present century. The citizens' shops and houses, such as were then knocked down to make way for the colleges' High Street fronts, are now acknowledged to make a vital contribution to the street scene and are strictly protected. In 1980 St Edmund Hall received an Oxford Preservation Trust environmental award for making its belated appearance on High Street by building above the shops at 48-52 and 55 High Street and leaving the street scene relatively unchanged.

The gardens of the colleges within the town walls were of necessity limited in size, and when further building was needed even these small gardens had to be sacrificed, as at Oriel and All Souls. The colleges which were built on monastic land outside the walls, Worcester, Christ Church, St John's, Trinity and Magdalen (the latter on land which had belonged to the Hospital of St John the Baptist), had much more scope for making gardens. There was still a monastic feel about the Oxford colleges and their gardens when Paul Hentzner visited the city in 1598 and recorded that 'the students lead a life almost monastic; for as the monks had nothing in the world to do, but when they had said their prayers at stated hours, to employ themselves in instructive studies, no more have these . . . as soon as grace is said after each meal, every one is at liberty either to retire to his own chambers, or to walk in the college garden, there being none that had not a delightful one.'

Oxford can present its own history of garden design with some rare and historic features, such as the New College cloister garden and the garden mount, the Merton terrace, Addison's Walk and St John's rock garden. The Queen's College herb garden, All Souls' knot garden, and the Trinity Dutch garden have vanished, but there are still baroque quadrangles, the landscaped lake at Worcester and much of the Jekyll-style garden at St Hugh's. Unlike historic buildings, which usually need a total restoration to be effective, old gardens can often be evoked by small touches. It would be delightful to see a Chaucerian 'yarde' with a camomile lawn, a turf seat and sparsely planted flower beds behind the grille of the Nun's Garden on High Street or a little physic garden in the cloister of Christ Church cathedral. It would also be pleasing to be able to recognize the New College mount for what it is.

The student of Oxford's garden history is fortunate in having well-preserved college accounts and plans, the Agas map of 1578, the detailed engravings in Loggan's *Oxonia Illustrata* of 1675, Williams's *Oxonia Depicta* of 1733, and the illustrations for the Oxford Almanacks, which often portrayed college gardens in the eighteenth and nineteenth centuries. There were great men and great events in Oxford from the earliest times, and visitors frequently commented on their impressions, some of which, like those of the German Zacharias von Uffenbach, were not always favourable.

Oxford has had many famous sons, and many poets have written about its buildings and gardens. They have also been painted by artists including Malchair, Le Keux and Turner. Delamotte produced a handsome book of *Original Views of Oxford its Colleges, Chapels and Gardens* in 1843 and there were numerous engravings made of college gardens. Oxfordshire is fortunate in having Dr Plot's seventeenth-century natural history which gives much information about gardens and gardening in Oxford. Oxford was not without its antiquaries, and of these the gossipy seventeenth-century writer Anthony Wood, who recorded day-to-day events in the city and slated town and gown alike, is undoubtedly the best source of information on almost any matter concerning life in Oxford. The goings-on in the Physic Garden, the sly drinking habits of the Puritan fellows, the making of the New College parterre, the Merton summerhouse from which the Warden's wife spied on the College, are all duly noted in Wood's diaries. Dr Gunther, the botanist, wrote on Oxford gardens in 1912 and recorded the girth of college trees and gave a detailed account of the Botanic Garden. In 1932 Eleanour Sinclair Rohde, who had been an undergraduate at St Hilda's, published her book on *Oxford's College Gardens*, which gives excellent descriptions of the gardens as they were then, and is particularly valuable for the account of gardens such as St Hugh's, which had only recently been laid out.

Architecture, in Pugin's words, represents 'the history of the world'. Gardening can go even deeper and reflect the Spirit of the Age, not only because more people can actually participate in the art of gardening than in building, but because it involves man's attitudes to the natural world. From early times Oxford had believed that botany was fundamental for the study of life as a whole, and in the days of Boyle, Wilkins, Evelyn and Wren gardening was seen to be an important part of natural philosophy. The Oxford Physic Garden played a major role in the promotion of gardening as a science and in the nurturing of the plants which were essential to the art of gardening. Oxford college gardens can be seen to reflect monastic and Renaissance ideas, Puritan good husbandry, the exuberance of the Restoration and a taste for grandeur, Addison's classical philosophy, the ideals of the Pre-Raphaelites, the Aesthetic Movement and Arts and Crafts principles.

Designing a college or a garden for a collegiate body, instead of for one wealthy landlord, has special difficulties, as Nicholas Hawksmoor and Humphry Repton found in Oxford. Corporate decisions are difficult to come by and patience has usually run out before agreement is arrived at. Many Oxford colleges have in their archives rejected plans made by the very best designers, and even when schemes were actually in progress radical changes have sometimes been made as new suggestions or benefactions appeared. Many members of the governing bodies became amateur architects or garden designers and had the advantage of being backed by college masons and gardeners. The much-admired landscaped garden at Worcester College was laid out by the Bursar, as was the rock garden at St John's. Fellows were widely travelled and brought back plants and ideas for gardens from abroad. There was always a forester, a chemist, botanist, ecologist or plant physiologist on hand to give advice when needed.

Although Oxford is no longer in the 'rural keeping' of the days when Duns Scotus walked its streets it still has a girdle of water meadows to the South and the East and a medieval atmosphere lingers on in its cobbled lanes and cloisters. William Morris and Edward Burne-Jones revelled in the grey walls, pinnacles and green settings, in the sound of bells and in the flowers of the meadows. The visual experience of Oxford has made a lasting impression on generations of undergraduates. For Arnold Toynbee a college garden was a place where 'one walks at night and listens to the wind in the trees, and weaves the stars into the web of one's thoughts.' Any Oxford Romantic worthy of the name still dreams his dreams under the shadow of pinnacles and buttresses in 'gardens spreading to the moonlight.'

1

Medieval Oxford

Oxford was a flourishing town long before the University came and gave it its special character and claim to fame. The settlement, which had grown up round the priory of St Frideswide, was first mentioned as Oxnaforda in the *Anglo-Saxon Chronicle* of 911. It had been created as a stronghold against the Danes and marked the division between Mercia and Wessex. At the heart of England, situated at the confluence of the Thames and the Cherwell, it has always been an important meeting place and crossing, not only for the oxen at the nearby ford.

After the Conquest King William assigned Oxford to one of his barons, Robert D'Oilly, who strengthened the town's walls and defences and built a castle to guard the river crossing. His son founded the great Abbey of Oseney in 1129 and Oxford was highly favoured by the Norman kings, ranking as ninth in importance in the kingdom. The royal palace of Beaumont, where Richard Coeur de Lion was to be born, was built by Henry I outside the North Gate (later called Beaumont Street) with a hunting lodge at Woodstock. Oxford also flourished commercially. There was a cloth and weaving industry and a Jewish settlement and in 1155 Henry II confirmed the town's 'gild-merchant' and 'all other customs and liberties and laws of their own which they have in common with my citizens of London.' Oxford has one of the earliest seals, given in 1191, when a charter enabled the prosperous merchants to take control of the markets. The development and growth of the medieval borough, with its craft and trade guilds, was thereafter to be restricted by the rise of the University.

It is not known when Chaucer's 'clerk of Oxenford' first began to change the character of the thriving town. Henry I was said to have enjoyed conversation with the clerks, and European scholars are known to have visited Oxford in the early part of the twelfth century. Oxford had, by the end of the century, a Studium Generale, a gathering of masters and students, centred on St Mary's church and, alongside the traders, book binders, parchmenters and illuminators set up in business to meet the new demands of scholarship. The requirements of this guild of teachers were small, a meeting place at St Mary's, a library and a school for teaching where they could sanction others to teach by licence. Chaucer's clerk of Oxenford was of this modest community and 'gladly wolde he lerne, and gladly teche.'

> For hym was levere have at his beddes heed
>   Twenty bookes, clad in blak or reed,
> Of Aristotle and his philosophie,
>   Than robes riche, or fithele, or gay sautrie.
> But al be that he was a philosophre,
>   Yet hadde he but litel gold in cofre;
> But al that he myghte of his freendes hente,
>   On bookes and on lernynge he it spent,
> And bisily gan for the soules preye
> Of hem that yaf hym wherwith to scoleye.[1]

Chaucer's Miller also paints a picture of a 'poore scoler' at Oxenford in his bawdy tale. This student had a room at Oseney and his landlord was a carpenter working for the abbey. His room, besides its bookshelf, had some calculating devices, sweet-smelling herbs and the musical instrument spurned by the more sober teaching clerk. We know of this Nicholas that,

> A chambre hadde he in that hostelrye
> Allone, with-outen any companye,
> Ful fetisly y-dight with herbes swote;
> And he him-self as swete as is the rote

Of licorys, or any cetewale.
His Almageste and bokes grete and smale,
His astrelabie, longinge for his art,
His augrim-stones layen faire a-part
On shelves couched at his beddes heed:
His presse y-covered with a falding reed.
And al above ther lay a gay sautyre,
On which he made a nightes melodye
So swetely, that al the chambre rong;
And Angelus ad virginem he song;
And after that he song the kinges note;
Ful often blessed was his mery throte.
And thus this swete clerk his tyme spente
After his freendes finding and his rente.[2]

By the early fifteenth century such poor scholars as Nicholas would have been under better supervision in a hall or college in the centre of Oxford. It was the need to provide proper accommodation on a permanent basis for the students who came to Oxford as a seat of learning that gave rise to the college system.

The students were required to contract with a master of a Hall for teaching and residence, as the colleges were at first only for senior students. As early as 1249 William of Durham bequeathed a sum of money to the University for the maintenance of ten Masters of Arts. This became the first corporate body or 'collegium' and in 1280 became University College. In 1255 John Balliol, condemned to do penance for misconduct, took steps to found a small community of scholars in Oxford, which was first mentioned in 1266. Walter de Merton at the same time set about building a college better endowed and planned than anything else yet attempted. The religious houses which had been sending students to Oxford from earliest days also realized the advantages of bringing their students together under one roof instead of allowing them to scatter in lodgings throughout the town. In 1283 the great Benedictine Abbey at Gloucester founded a house at Oxford as a place of study for thirteen of their monks. This was called Gloucester College until it was suppressed and refounded as Worcester College in 1714. The cottages on the south side of the Quadrangle are of the original foundation and the pre-Dissolution college's name is perpetuated by

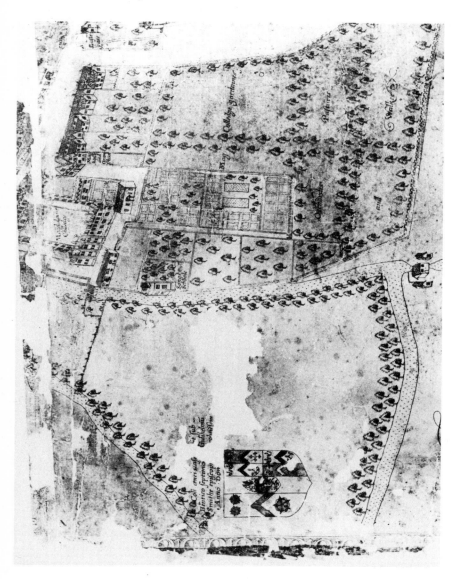

1.1   Magdalen's medieval gardens and orchards

The colleges built outside the city walls found more space for gardens.
From the Agas map of 1578 (see also Figure 2.2).

Gloucester Green opposite Worcester College. Other monastic houses built for scholars were Durham College founded in 1286 for the Benedictine Monks of Durham, later to become Trinity College; Canterbury College founded for the monks of Canterbury in 1363, later to become part of Wolsey's Christ Church; St Mary's Hall for the Augustinian monks in 1435; the Cistercian St Bernard's College in 1437 later to become St John's College.

The colleges and the collegiate system took firm root in Oxford and became increasingly important. After the town and gown riots of St Scolastica's Day in 1355 the townspeople's control over the market and inns was taken away from them and given to the University in a new charter. Oxford had begun to assume its role as an University town. The town had suffered severely in the economic depression and depopulation by the Black Death at the end of the fourteenth century and there were many empty spaces within the walls. New College in 1369 and All Souls in 1438 were able to acquire land for development in the heart of the town. Magdalen was built outside the walls in 1458 on extensive grounds once those of the Hospital of St John the Baptist. The fashion of founding colleges continued throughout the fifteenth century and the unique shape of a University town with dozens of separate collegiate entities, varied as their statutes and their benefactors decreed, emerged. It was quite unlike any European university town.

All that is now left of the castle built by Robert d'Oilly in 1071 is the motte or mound, 250 feet in diameter and 64 feet high, and St George's Tower. There may have been a garden compressed within the castle walls, but it seems that the atmosphere was sufficiently relaxed for the ladies of the castle to walk beyond their confined pleasaunce. According to the chronicles Robert d'Oilly's wife used to walk out from Oxford Castle with her maidens and wander by the streams to the west of the castle; but it was said that the chattering of the magpies in the elms disturbed her so that she consulted her confessor, who told her that they were souls in purgatory, crying out to her to found an abbey for their sakes. She persuaded her husband to give the southern half of Oseney, where an island is formed by the two branches of the river

Thames, for the foundation of a house of Canons Regular, which was to become one of the greatest monasteries in England. Beaumont Palace was chosen as a site for a royal retreat 'for the great pleasure of the seat and the sweetness and delectableness of the air', according to Anthony Wood. This royal palace and its gardens were subsequently given to the Carmelite Friars by Edward II, but there is nothing to be seen today save a few pieces of the ruins erected in nearby gardens.

Norman castles and monasteries are the first places where gardening is recorded in England. Many of the present college gardens are on the sites of the old monastic foundations with inherited gardens, but the only one that has the feeling of monastic days is Worcester College (see plate 10) where an arch of the old Gloucester College has been restored by what is now a landscaped lake and may once have been fishponds. The Friars, in spite of the mendicant nature of their orders, owned a considerable amount of property in Oxford and some flourishing gardens. They came to the town with the blessing of Robert Grosseteste, the first Chancellor of the University. The Dominicans or Blackfriars in 1221, the Franciscans or Greyfriars in 1224, the Austin Friars who came in 1252 and moved to where Wadham College now stands, the Trinitarians in 1286 and other short-lived sects such as the Friars of the Sack and the Crutched Friars followed in their wake. There were many famous scholars in their numbers, including Duns Scotus, William of Ockham and the remarkable Roger Bacon.

The garden of the Greyfriars is perpetuated still by name in Oxford. They had settled in the swampy land between the ancient St Ebbes and the river Thames, and it is recorded that 'Agnes the wife of Guy gave them most part of that ground which was afterwards called Paradise.' It was referred to as the 'Graye Fryars Paradise' still in the seventeenth century and serves to remind us of the origin of a 'paradise.' The word comes from the Persian *pairidaeza*, meaning an enclosure and was usually applied to a hunting park. It occurs in the Old Testament as *pardes* to indicate a garden or park and then came to be seen as the Garden of Eden, a celestial paradise. For the Grey Friars it would have been an earthly rather than a spiritual garden and used for growing vegetables and herbs for cooking and medicine. The gardens were taken over as pleasure gardens after the departure of the friars and later became market gardens. Paradise Square is now swallowed up by the Westgate development. We can see nothing of what the shape of a merchant's garden of the period would have been. It is possible that some space was spared for vegetables and flowers in the storage space of the burgage plots in High Street. From the High Street by the Queen's College, and now part of it, a little garden known as 'Nun's Garden,' (probably by reason of the owner's name rather than any monastic origin) can be glimpsed through an iron gateway and passage.

Gardens were specifically mentioned in the Aularian Statutes drawn up by the University at the end of the fifteenth century to give internal regulations to the seventy or more halls then existing. Fines were instituted for disordering rushes and straw with which the floors were strewn, spilling liquor on the table clothes, defacing walls, doors or windows. All these offences were punishable by a fine of a farthing, but the fine for running over grass or breaking down plants was one halfpenny. The halls were not endowed by private munificence as were the colleges and everybody had to help in running the hostel to keep down costs. On the day or days appointed by the Principal all members of a Hall were to be ready to help 'put the garden in order and to work usefully in it for the benefit and honour of the Hall.' Failure to do so was punishable by a fine of 2d.[3]

It is clear, also, that provisions for gardens were made when the colleges were built and they are mentioned in the earliest Bursars' rolls. These gardens were utilitarian in purpose to provide fruit and vegetables, herbs for cooking and medicine and flowers for chapel altars. By Balliol's statutes a small plot of ground was allotted to each chamber for the growing of herbs and vegetables. This is reminiscent of the arrangements of a Carthusian monastery where every monk had his own garden plot attached to his cell, but at Balliol the individual gardens were the result of the numbers of small plots attached to the various tenements that were incorporated into the college.

Each college had an 'ortulanus' or 'gardinarius' and some
of them would undoubtedly have picked up some gardening
knowledge from the monastic gardens. Before the days of
printed books instruction was passed down by word of
mouth and a good gardener accumulated knowledge as he
worked the earth. A treatise on gardening written about 1440
tries to record reasoned instructions for growing fruit, herbs
and flowers, which might in the first place have come from a
monk:

> Thre ynchys depe they most sette be
> And this seyde mayster John Gardener to me.[4]

In addition to their ortulanus, who in 1358 was named as
John Godspede, the Queen's College employed casual workers, mostly female, and their surplus produce of herbs,
beans, onions and garlic was sold to the townspeople. In
1415–1416 as well as payment for onions, leeks and garlic an
item 'xvd.ob.qr. de croco' is recorded.[5] This was for 'safer-
owne', the *Crocus sativus*, which was very important in medieval times for flavouring, drugs and its yellow dye. It was
probably the Romans who introduced the saffron crocus to
Britain, but as with many other of their introductions it died
out after the fall of the Roman Empire and was reintroduced
about the fourteenth century.[6] Crocus comes from the
Greek word meaning thread because of its thread-like stigma
and it is only the dried stigmas of the flower which are used
to produce saffron. The illuminators who had set up business
in the St Mary's Church area probably bought their saffron
for dyes from the nearby Queen's College garden.

Clearly most of the Queen's College garden was a kitchen
garden, but a chapel garden, which was probably a cemetery,
was also mentioned in 1420. A disportus or sportus is mentioned at The Queen's College, also at University College, and
elsewhere there is reference to gardens for cooks and bache-
lors, as though some part of the garden ground was set aside
for relaxation of the fellows. These may just have been
sitting places in the orchards and herb gardens such as the
Lincoln record of a payment 'for mendying the seat under
the bay-tree' suggests. Although Warden Woodward at New
College declared, when the formal garden was made in the

seventeenth century, that the ground there had been 'ancy-ently not for pleasure and walking, but for Profitt,' the college, sheltered by the city walls, had from the earliest times grown vines, and the walls must have provided an attractive background to the garden. When in 1379 New College received the royal licence to develop the waste land

1.2 New College walls

When New College was allowed to develop waste land for its garden in the 14th century it was decreed that the college should for all time keep the town walls in good repair. The college has always done so and the walls provide an attractive background for the garden.

behind the walls, it was decreed that the college should for all time keep the walls in good repair and that the Mayor and burgesses should inspect it to see that the college was carrying out its obligations. Still today the City Fathers inspect the New College walls to enforce the regulation, although the City has long since knocked down all traces of the rest of Oxford's defensive walls. In the old moat outside the walls there were fishponds, and records show that the right to fish there cost a citizen a halfpenny a year. Many labourers were employed in constructing the mount in 1529, perhaps originally as a means of clearing rubble from the area, rather than with the intention of making a garden feature.[7] It became part of the formal garden later, but if, as Warden Woodward claimed, there were only kitchen gardens originally at New College, an ascent of the mound would allow an enterprising fellow to look abroad over the walls to the fishponds, the groves of Magdalen and the Cherwell Meadows.

When Corpus Christi College was founded by Bishop Foxe in 1517 he saw his college allegorically as a bee garden:

> We . . have founded . . a certain bee garden, which we have named the College of Corpus Christi, wherin scholars, like ingenious bees, are by day and night to make wax to the honour of God, and honey dropping sweetness to the profit of themselves and of all Christians.

The bees became a reality and according to Anthony Wood loyally followed the fortunes of the college:

> Ludovicus Vives when he took up his abode at Corpus, was welcomed thither by a swarm of bees, which to signifie the incomparable sweetness of his eloquence settled themselves over his head under the leads of his study where they continued about 130 year. In the year 1630 the leads of Vives his study being pluckt up their stall was taken and with it an incredible mass of honey; but the Bees as presaging their intended and imminent destruction (whereas they were never known to have swarmed before) did that spring send down a fair swarm into the President's garden, which in the year 1653 yielded two swarms; one whereof pitched in the garden for the President, the other they sent up as a new colony to preserve the memory of the mellifluous doctor.

2

Collegiate Oxford

A collegium was, like a monastery, a community living under a rule, but its way of life was more secular and more in the style of a manor house. The buildings are more like medieval manor houses than those of a monastery, although the scattered disposition of the collegiate buildings has an institutional look, and many people who now come to Oxford colleges for summer schools are taken aback to find how far separated geographically the various necessities turn out to be. However, all the colleges made provisions not only for devotions, studies and domestic comforts, but also for the exercise and amusements of their members. Members dined communally in hall but slept in chambers instead of in a monastic dormitory, and they could walk abroad and divert themselves in bowling greens and ball courts. Hand tennis is mentioned as a college sport as early as 1487. A sphaeristerium or ball court is mentioned in sixteenth-century accounts at Queen's, and in 1566 Lincoln was putting up 'railes for the tennys-court.' Exeter with the Divinity School and University Library abutting its garden was especially cautioned in 1581 not to 'make any bowling allee or tennis court which may be noisome to students or any hogsty or dunghill or any other filthy savour.'

Architecturally it is the quadrangle which gives the college its special character, but it was not part of any original plan. In fact, there was no plan for the earliest colleges. They were

built and endowed by private munificence, each with its code
of statutes, and the form of the buildings was dictated by
adapting the growing needs of the community of scholars.
The loose arrangement of the hall, master's lodgings, chapel,
muniment room and library, each being separate and needing
its own light, almost inevitably evolved into a courtyard plan.
Merton's famous Mob Quad, the first collegiate quadrangle,
assumed its form only gradually. The hall was built by 1277,
the chapel by 1294, the treasury and the lodgings on the east
and north sides by about 1304, and finally when the library
was added in 1373 an Oxford quadrangle had come into
being and thereafter became a college tradition.

2.1 The New College cloister garden
In 1379 William of Wykeham planned a 'new college' of quadrangular
form, which became a model for subsequent college planning, and also
introduced the cloister into collegiate architecture.

William of Wykeham made plans for a purpose-built quadrangular college in 1379, and his New College became the
accepted model for all later college planning.[1] Wykeham also
introduced the cloister into collegiate architecture, bringing
the association with the idea of the monastic cloister garth.

The New College cloister garden was intended for the cemetery and, as at the Abbey of St Gall, may have combined an orchard and graveyard.[2] The New College cloister was only for perambulation and there were no rooms around it. The blackened wall along the north side of New College Lane is in fact the back of the cloister and is a good example of how collegiate architecture forms, even indirectly, the shape and character of Oxford's lanes. All Souls later copied the idea of cloister walks for sheltered contemplation, looking onto a garden space planted with trees. It was ideal for the daily exercise of the confined scholars and cloister walks were later to be extended into wooden gallery walks, as in France.

Magdalen College, in 1474, was to fuse the two ideas of cloister and quadrangle with a covered perambulation looking onto a green space but having rooms built above the cloister. In 1508 allegorical figures were set up to adorn the buttresses of three sides of the cloister, representing arts, divinity, law, and medicine, and heraldic emblems.[3] Magdalen's fellows undoubtedly had the privilege of walking in the finest setting in Oxford. Not only had they their dry cloister walk but garden, orchards and walks more extensive than those of any other college. The college had been built outside the city wall adjoining the Cherwell meadows and open countryside and had apparently had a menagerie even in its earliest days, as it is recorded that in 1509 it was presented with a she-bear by Henry VII. There was also a swannery from the earliest days. The college had to build its own walls around its extensive gardens in 1466. These decoratively embattled stone walls along Longwall Street are often mistakenly thought to be part of the city walls. The college accounts record that hedges were being repaired as early as 1513 and make reference to a tower 'in virgulto' (a grove or shrubbery) in 1531. The rural walks, which were later called the 'green natural cloister of our Academe', have always been one of the delights of residence at Magdalen. The Founder had not chosen the site because of these rural delights, however, but with a view to the possibility of later building extensions. Waynflete was aware that it might be thought that his college offered the possibility of real country pursuits and in his statutes sought to curb any hunting or hawking aspirations of the scholars. In the interests of quiet and privacy he ruled that no member of the college should keep 'a Harrier, or other Hound of any kind or Ferrets, or a Sparrow-hawk, or any other Fowling Bird, or a Mavis or any other Song Bird.' In spite of these regulations, however, a Visitation report by the Bishop of Winchester's commissary records in 1507 that 'Smyth keeps a ferret in College, Lenard a sparrow-hawk, Parkyns a weasel, while Morcott, Heycock and Smyth stole and killed a calf in the garden of one master Court.' Dr Routh, President from 1791 to 1854, called his dog a cat in order to comply with the Founder's statutes.

2.2 The Agas map of 1578

The map shows the increasing ascendancy of the colleges at the expense of the existing market town. University College and All Souls have achieved High Street frontages but the Queen's College with its gardens and orchards is still fitted in behind the shops and houses of the citizens.

The Agas map gives a picture of post-Reformation Oxford showing the ascendancy of the colleges at the expense of the town. The large gardens and orchards and empty plots show the decline of pressure for living space in the market town, following the population and economic decline at the beginning of the century. The results of the Dissolution are clearly visible in the new layout. The Oxford colleges which depended on Gloucester, Durham and Canterbury fell with their mother houses and the property of the friars had been seized. Trinity College and St John's had been built on their lands. The Welsh college of Jesus had been founded just before Ralph Agas made his survey of Oxford. The Grey Friars' Paradise garden of five acres appears as a pleasaunce by the river to the South of the castle and may already have become a riverside pleasure garden for the University, as described by the German visitor von Uffenbach in 1710.

> Next we went on to a garden which they called Paradise Garden. This is hard by an end of the town, near a tavern, which is in connection with it, and at the back of which, on the water, are countless little boxes, partitioned by hedges, where the fellows drink in summer. There are beautiful fruit trees and many yew-trees.[4]

In the sixteenth century the colleges assumed control of most of the halls — the old hostels rented by graduates to keep students as lodgers and to teach them on the premises. The halls had been in decline even before the Reformation as more colleges came to be founded. In 1450 there had been about seventy halls but by 1550 there were only eight remaining.[5] Beam Hall in Merton Street is a good example of what one of these hostels or 'hospicia' looked like. The scale of the building fits in with the medieval townscape, whereas the dominating collegiate buildings drawn on the Agas map show that Oxford had already assumed the architectural layout for which it was to become famous. Beam Hall was not incorporated into the precincts of a college, as was the case of St Mary's Hall and Oriel College, although it was bought by Corpus Christi after the Dissolution of St Frideswide's Priory to whom it had belonged. St Edmund Hall is the only one of the medieval halls to survive. The 'Aula Sancti Edmundi' is mentioned on a rent-roll of Oseney Abbey in 1317 but after the suppression of the monastery it was acquired by the Queen's College. It led its own separate existence, and eventually gained complete independence in 1957.

The biggest change in the appearance of sixteenth century Oxford was that brought about by the building aspirations of Cardinal Wolsey, who had set his heart on founding a college which would outshine even those built by Wykeham and Waynflete. Wolsey, who was almost as rich as Henry VIII himself, was a prodigious builder and if his Cardinal College had been finished as he had planned it might well have 'excelled not only all the colleges of students, but also palaces of princes.'[6] Wolsey, who was already falling from favour in 1525, did not make himself popular by outdoing royal works; even presenting newly-built Hampton Court to his master did not save his final fall. When he was stripped of office as Lord Chancellor, however, and all his possessions were forfeited to the Crown, the great prelate-statesman made an impassioned plea for the completion of his 'poore College of Oxford.'

The work on Cardinal College ceased abruptly in 1529 with the great chapel on the north side of the quadrangle, which was to rival that of King's College, Cambridge, only a few feet off the ground and the gatehouse towerless, as it remained until Wren completed it a century and a half later. The Great Hall and kitchens were finished, however, and the members of Wolsey's new college were able to eat Christmas dinner in the finest perpendicular hall in Europe with its shining gilded bosses, one of which bears the ominous date of 1529, the year of glory for Cardinal College and of doom for its founder.

Wolsey had been fellow and bursar of Magdalen College until 1500 and it was Waynflete's Magdalen he strove to emulate and surpass. He had watched the great bell tower being built and envisaged a similar collegiate symbol for his Cardinal College to dominate the entrance to Oxford from the South across the River Thames as Magdalen's tower dominated the eastern approach to the town across the Cherwell. This was not carried out and the Agas map shows only a truncated tower East of the hall, which was later levelled to the height of the hall, and only given the consequence the Cardinal had intended by the Victorian architect Bodley. Cloisters round the great quadrangle in the Magdalen tradition had also been planned but these, designed by Henry Redman, the King's master mason and Wolsey's chief architect at Oxford, Hampton Court and his Whitehall Palace, would have been more magnificent. The shafts on the walls from which the projected stone vaults would have sprung suggest that Redman had intended fan-vaulting similar to his work in the cloister of the royal college of St Stephen at Westminster.

Cardinal College was indeed intended to be an Oxford palace. A huge team of masons had been employed to get the building up as far as it was in the four years before Wolsey's fall. The large-scale demolition of tenements it had necessitated had antagonised Oxford. An undergraduate, who foresaw something sinister in the speed of the Cardinal's operations, chalked on a wall of the college; 'Non stabit illa domus, aliis fundata rapinis; Aut ruet, aut alter rapto habebit eam.' Shakespeare's epitaph on the founder of Cardinal College was more generous:

> . . . though unfinish'd, yet so famous,
> So excellent in art and still so rising,
> That Christendom shall ever speak his virtue.[7]

After 1529 Wolsey's college was only to be called Cardinal College by Hardy in *Jude the Obscure*. It was to become Aedes Christi, Christ Church, a unique foundation of cathedral and college. In 1532 Henry VIII had refounded it as 'King's College' to be an ecclesiastical, rather than an educational, college but, shortly before his death in 1546, he combined the college with a new cathedral see, which at first had been planned to be sited at the dissolved Oseney Abbey. Some of the buildings of the St Frideswide Priory on the site of Christ Church, which had been dissolved along with twenty other houses by Wolsey, were incorporated into the college. No new building was undertaken at Christ Church in the sixteenth century, and the Cardinal's devices, his hat and pillars set saltire-wise, were left ornamenting the walls of the college, and its arms remain those of Cardinal Wolsey. The Great Quadrangle was left open on the North side with piles of stone in front of the unfinished chapel, and dogs had to be kept by the porter 'to dryve oute cattell and hogges out of the House.'[8] According to tradition the Broad Walk was raised by the earth and rubbish removed in the building of the college and Agas's map shows trees planted along the walk. What he refers to as the 'Christes Church medowes and walkes' must always have been a great asset to the citizens. Lady Elizabeth Montacute gave the land which is now Christ Church Meadow to maintain a Chantry in the Lady Chapel of the Priory of St Frideswide; with the other possessions of the Priory, the Meadow became part of the endowment of Cardinal College.

Cardinal Wolsey having fallen before the completion of Christ Church and King Henry VIII having died a few months after its refounding, the college had no encumbering statutes. No founder had forbidden the students of Christ Church to sing or leap in the hall as Wykeham had done at New College; nor, as Waynflete had laid upon Magdalen, were there any restrictions on hawking in the Meadows, and from time to time birds of prey have been kept in Christ Church Meadows. Dogs may also be called dogs at Christ Church.

In some colleges gardens were kept locked and specially reserved for senior members. At St John's the Grove was reserved for the upper ten and the others had to make do with the small garden on the site of the present Canterbury Quad. A decree of 1584 ruled that:

> it was condescended . . . to binde all the students of the College, not excepted, that no person whatsoever, Master, Bacheler, scholler, chaplayne, commoner, servant or poor scholler, shall from this day forwarde come or entre into the garden (or bring a stranger) here called the tenn Seniors garden in the Grove, except he be one of the simpliciter tenne seniors, under the payne of every man that shall make default for every tyme to forfeyte tenne shillings. The like penaltie is agreed to fall uppon those that shall eyther make any keye to the said garden dore, or use any other man's keye, or use any keye that he shall finde except he be the scholler or servant of one of the tenn simpliciter seniors, sent by his Master to doe some service there.[9]

3

Renaissance Oxford

Intellectual movements penetrate all aspects of life, including garden design, and the humanistic Renaissance was the most profound and far-reaching of all such movements. Humanism, which began in fifteenth-century Florence, opened up new worlds for the Middle Ages, giving man a feeling of self-esteem and a desire to enter into the whole life around him. The new worlds of the Renaissance were discovered by unlocking old stores of classical wisdom which had been obscured in the mysticism and superstition of scholasticism.

Renaissance ideas had important effects on garden design and the plants grown within the garden. Medieval gardens had been the ladies' pleasaunce, the 'bowers of bliss' of romance which were the setting for courtly love, mirth and indolence. With the coming of the Renaissance, gardens were designed to cultivate the open air life of the philosophers and scholars of antiquity, who like Epicurus taught in a garden. An Oxford college was an ideal place to emulate the scholarly habits of the ancients, especially as there were no family encumbrances. As in More's Utopia, the fellows entertained one another in discourse in garden retreats and enjoyed the company of visiting humanists. The Dutch humanist Erasmus, who visited Oxford in 1498, advocated that when pursuing study there was 'entertainment of the sight, the smell and refreshment of the very mind' if the library overlooked a garden.

There were many in Oxford who found it hard to turn from the precepts of Christian scholasticism to pagan classical studies, but Erasmus pointed to John Claymond of Magdalen College whose character, he said would do much 'to win over those who are apt to assert that the new studies corrupt men, and are unfavourable to Christian piety.' In 1483 John Claymond had written his *Notes and Observations on the Natural History of Pliny* and the rural walks and environs of Magdalen must have helped him to appreciate Pliny's love of nature. It was Pliny the Younger's description of the gardens surrounding his villas which influenced Renaissance thinking on gardens. As Erasmus had indicated, care had been taken to place each individual room in relation to the garden features and for use in different seasons of the year. There were porticos and courtyards and a cryptoporticus, a covered gallery connection, shaded for summer and perfumed with the scent of violets in the spring; and a little garden pavilion standing on its own.[1] The covered gallery was a popular feature in Oxford college gardens and the tower in the grove mentioned in the Magdalen records in 1513 may have been a Pliny type pavilion for looking abroad into the neighbouring countryside.

Pliny's descriptions were well known, but the most influential book on garden design, which had the advantage of woodcut illustrations, was the *Hypnerotomachia Poliphili*, published in Venice in 1499 by the monk Francesco Colonna and translated into English in 1592. The Dream of Poliphilus is largely fantasy but the Renaissance garden features are real enough, arbours, knots and topiary work. Box shapes and the 'tonsile evergreens' mentioned by Pliny were reintroduced into Renaissance gardens in England. The word 'topiarus' was used as an ornamental gardener in general terms in Ciceronian Latin but came to be used in England specifically for the art of clipping evergreens into various shapes. John Leland, the Tudor antiquary who was also Rector of Haseley, records that at Little Haseley, near Oxford there were 'marvellous fair walkes, topiarii operis, and orchards and pooles.'

We are fortunate in having for an Oxford college the most detailed plan of a Renaissance garden, complete with covered galleries, arbours, cut hedges and marvellously intricate knot gardens. This was made for the humanist Robert Hovenden who became Warden of All Souls in 1571, at the age of 27, where he presided for forty-two years. Hovenden was the first married Warden and it may well be that his wife, Katherine Powys of Abingdon, had taken an interest in the laying out of the garden. Certainly, in post-Reformation days, lodgings were enlarged to accommodate wives and families. The first married Rector of Lincoln decided that the original plot of land bought from Abingdon Abbey and situated on the opposite side of the road facing the gateway was inconvenient for his lady's garden and had a new one made within the precincts of the college. In the reign of Queen Elizabeth Katherine Hovenden was safe from persecution as a lady at All Souls. The first Reformation Katherine had been a victim of changing religions. She was Katherine Martyr, the wife of a Canon of Christ Church, Peter Martyr, who had come to England at Cranmer's invitation, only to be driven out of the country on the accession of Queen Mary. Katherine had died at Christ Church in 1552 and was buried in the cathedral near the shrine of St Frideswide, which had been desecrated in 1538. The Roman Catholic Commissioners dug poor Katherine up and she was buried in a dung heap in the Dean's stableyard until she was honourably restored to the cathedral in Queen Elizabeth's reign. It was resolved this time to reinstate St Frideswide, and the Saint and the bones of the first lady of Christ Church were buried together 'permixta et confusa' in one common grave with due ceremony.[2] A relic of the trials of Peter Martyr and his wife can be seen on the Loggan engraving in the form of a building two stories high in the southernmost garden behind the cathedral, erected to find peace away from the jeers and bricks thrown by Roman Catholics opposed to clerical matrimony.

The beautiful map of All Souls commissioned by Warden Hovenden is one of eighty-five maps of College properties based on surveys by Thomas Langdon and Thomas Clerke between 1586 and 1605. The Typus Collegii, being an aerial perspective, gives an excellent view of the gardens. The Warden's Lodgings are to the East of the central gable on the High Street and the garden behind them was acquired by Robert Hovenden in 1573, shortly after he became Warden.

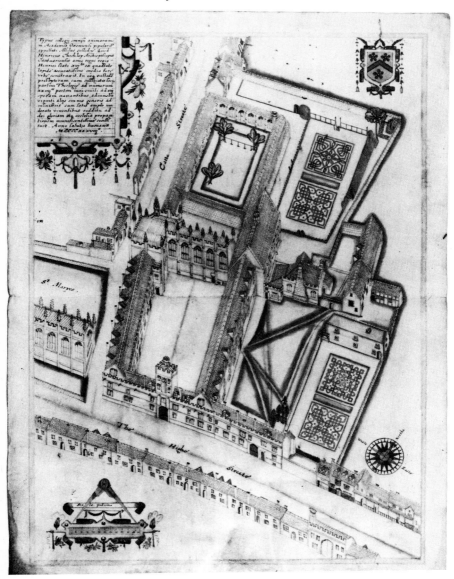

3.1 Hovenden's map of All Souls, c. 1585

Warden Hovenden's map, known as the Typus Collegii, shows covered galleries, arbours, cut hedges and marvellously interlaced knot gardens.

In his own words:

> The Warden's garden was some time the Rose Inn, and being
> purchased by Sir W. Petre and given ye coll. it lay waste till 1573
> when Master R. Hovenden desired the Compy. to grant it him and
> he would enclose it and remove the well, which was called the
> Roswell standing in it (whereof it was said merrily the fellows
> wash'd every day in Rose water) upon his own charges. The week
> before Easter 1574 he began to level ye ground, and the whole
> charge came to £14 2s 10d and ye well with ye pump 40s.[3]

The cloister garden and possibly the garden to the East of it
were already in existence before the garden laid out on the
site of the old Rose Inn.

The cloister and its garden, demolished in the Hawksmoor
era, was clearly monastic in concept. It was part of the original plan for the College of All Souls of the Faithful Departed
founded by Henry VI in 1438. The co-founder was Bishop
Chichele, who had been a Fellow of New College. The cloister was not built until 1490 but follows the monastic pattern
of that of New College. Archbishop Chichele's first Oxford
college was St Bernard's, for the Cistercians, which was
suppressed in 1539 and later became part of St John's College.
All Souls had a special ecclesiastical connection wherein in
addition to its studies it was required to pray for the souls of
Henry V and Henry VI and all Englishmen who had died in
the wars with France. The chantry element had disappeared
by the time Warden Hovenden and his wife came on the
scene, but the monastic cloister garth remained. The Elizabethan plan shows the cloister planted with trees and a
simple line of railed posts across. These may have served the
purpose of leaning posts for Renaissance fellows in discourse
in the open air. The ladies' pleasaunces had been provided
with turf seats in medieval gardens, and in illustrations the
lady always seems to be playing with 'wanton toys' and wait-
ing for the lover's appearance through the garden door. Turf
seats would clearly not have suited the contemplative purpose of the All Souls' cloister garden.

Elsewhere in the adjacent garden there is every evidence of
a garden to delight the senses, particularly the visual. The
tunnel arbour of the *Hypnerotomachia Poliphili* 'decked
with pleasant and odiferous flowers commixt' leads to a

summer house on a mount. Thomas Hill, in his *The Gardeners Labyrinth*, 1577, describes the purpose of these covered walks.

> The commodities of these Alleis and walkes serve to good pur-
> poses, the one is that the owner may diligently view the prosperi-
> ties of his herbes and flowers, the other for the delight and
> comfort of his wearied mind, which he may by himself or fellow-
> ship of his friends conceyve in the delectable sightes and fragrant
> smelles of the flowers, by walking up and downe, and about the
> Garden in them, which for the pleasant sights and refreshing of
> the dull spirites, with the sharpening of the memorie, many
> shadowed over with vawting or herbes, having windowes properly
> made towards the Garden, whereby they might the more fully
> view and have delight in the whole beautie of the Garden.

Thomas Hill wrote the first English gardening book, his *Most Briefe and Pleasant Treatyse*, in 1563, showing in the vignette on the title page the type of arbour of carpenter's work which became so popular in college gardens. He explains how these 'herbars' should be framed with ashen poles or willow and covered with branches of vine or melon for shade. He adds the practical note that 'if they be made with juniper wode, you nede not to repyre nothyng therof in ten years after: but if they be made with willow poles, then you must new repayre them in three years after.' The hedges around the All Souls knot garden are cut into battlements and arches echoing the buildings on the High and also the type of embattled walls and palisades seen in *Romance of Alexander*, where a King and Queen are seated playing chess in a garden. If All Souls was using Hill as the text book then they would have been well advised to take his advice about making the walks dry by sifting them over with 'river or sea sand, to the end that showers of raine falling, may not offend the walkers in them, by the earth cleaving or clagging to tneir feete.'

The design for the knots must certainly have come from Hill's *Labyrinth*. It is not known where Hill got the patterns from but he offers them as 'Proper Knottes to be sette with Hysope or Tyme' as though specifically designed for gardens. Patterns for Renaissance linear designs were normally used for carving, embroidery, book binding, frets and adapted for garden knots. *A Book of Sundry Draughts*, published by W. Gedde in 1615, commends his designs as 'principally serving

 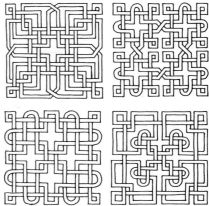

'A proper knotte to be cast in the quarter
of a Garden...'

'PROPER KNOTTES to be set with Isope
or Tyme.'

Pages from Thomas Hill's *The Gardener's Labyrinth* (1577). Note that the pattern at top right closely resembles the upper knot visible in the All Souls High Street garden in Figure 3.1.

One of the four All Souls Knots, and (on right) its possible derivation as a variation of Thomas Hill's knot shown at upper left.

Lines common to All Souls knot and *Gardener's Labyrinth* knot.

Lines added to *Gardener's Labyrinth* knot to produce All Souls knot.

3.2 Knot garden patterns and the All Souls design

glaziers and not impertinent for plasterers and gardeners.'
The knots were originally patterned shapes to contain flowers
but the design became an end in itself, particularly after the
influence of the strapwork devices brought from Flanders in
the 1560s. A greater emphasis was placed on the strap
effect and the spaces between were taken up by coloured
earth, sand, coal, dust, broken bricks or powdered tiles
which sharpened the design, especially if heraldic devices
were used. Hill could have got his patterns from the layouts
shown by Androuet du Cerceau in his *Les Plus Excellents
Bastiments de France* (1576), particularly those for Gaillon,
Blois and Verneuil. It is the interlacing of the patterns in the
Labyrinth which makes them so striking when seen demonstrated in the All Souls garden.

The All Souls cartographer has given the knot patterns
much more clearly than those shown by Du Cerceau in the
gardens of the French castles. One of the knots looks as
though it had been taken direct from the Hill page of patterns, but the three others may have been derived by manipu-
lating the very fanciful knot that Hill uses as a key knot. It
has been ingeniously suggested[4] that this was not intended to
be copied (indeed it would be impossible to carry it through
as a garden knot) but was a master key or pattern generator,
so that when different interlacings were linked an original
design could be arrived at. There were no garden designers to
call on in an Oxford college. In royal palaces the gardens
were under the surveyors in the Office of Works who would
produce plats or drawings for the gardeners to carry out. The
All Souls college gardener could not presumably have been
responsible for drawing out the intricate knot patterns within
the 40ft squares and it is intriguing to imagine Warden
Hovenden and the Fellows trying out designs from Hill's
fantasy knots. Another interesting question is whether the
garden was laid out in preparation for Queen Elizabeth's
visit to Oxford in 1592. It is not shown on the Agas map of
1578, but is in good shape on the Hovenden map of the 1590s.
We read of buildings going up in a matter of weeks for reception of the Queen on her royal progresses but a little notice
would be needed to get a new garden ready to delight the
sovereign. (The Carews of Beddington were expecting a

visit in August 1599 and wanted to give the Queen a dish of her favourite cherries. They covered up a cherry tree with a great tent which they removed only when her arrival was confirmed and earned her gratitude for an out-of-season treat.[5])

The plants which formed the design of the All Souls knots could have been put in at any time. One of the features which delighted the owner of a knot garden was that it was 'green all the winter,' the plants being low-growing thyme, hyssop, cotton lavender or box. The last was not so popular as it had a sour smell and the clippings of the sweet-smelling herbs could be used for strewing floors inside the building. In 1575, Lincoln College records a payment of 6d 'for herbs to sett our knotts.'[6]

When Queen Elizabeth came to Oxford in the thirty-fourth year of her reign in 1592, the University spent £7560 on her entertainment, with the colleges making contributions according to their wealth. Christ Church paid most, £2000, Magdalen £1200, New College £1000, All Souls £500, down to newly-founded Jesus College which got away with £70. The Queen attended plays and disputations and herself made a much admired Latin oration in St Mary's Church. As she left Oxford, all along the High the walls of All Souls, University and Magdalen colleges were hung with verses and emblematical expressions of poetry in her honour. When she was taken away up Shotover Hill she looked wistfully back and said in Latin: 'Farewell, farewell, dear Oxford, God bless thee and increase thy sons in number, holiness and virtue.'

It was in scientific thinking that Queen Elizabeth's 'dear, dear scholars' were going to progress as the full impact of the Renaissance was absorbed and it was not only as an art that gardening was to be influenced but it was to assume a new role as a science. In the University botany and medicine had been associated from the earliest days and gardening was a by-product of the art of simpling. The study of physick had a place in the 1325 statutes and there was 'a great Hall in the Street of Cats in the Parish of St Mary for the better training of physicians.' Anthony Wood thought that this Physick School was previously known as Herberowe Hall when it had belonged to St John's Hospital in the thirteenth century. The

Apothecaries had settled nearby on the South side of the High Street and many of their pharmacy pots have been dug up over the years.

It was the great Oxford thinkers of the thirteenth and fourteenth centuries who had paved the way to a conception of experimental science and natural philosophy. One is reminded by a plaque on the Westgate car park that close to where one's mini is parked Roger Bacon 'known as the wonderful doctor, who by the experimental method extended marvellously the realm of science' died in 1292. Bacon, who had been a pupil of Grosseteste, is said to have had a laboratory over the gateway on Folly Bridge, and there through his prodigious studies in all fields he hoped to lay bare the secrets of nature. His dictum 'Sine experienta nihil sufficienta sciri potest' is to be seen over the entrance to the Daubeny Building in the Botanic Garden. His reputation increased in the Renaissance but in his own time this remarkable man, who foresaw gunpowder and flying machines, was regarded as a magician. 'Doubtless though people were possest that our Frier conversed with the Devil,' said Anthony Wood, 'yet certainly what he did was purely by his learning.'

Theology then reigned supreme but it was challenged in Oxford by such men as the logician William of Ockham, who is remembered by 'Ockham's razor,' the method by which the simplest explanation is sought, and study advocated of things as they are. Although Merton College's statutes were designed to promote the secular priesthood and specifically forbade the study of medicine for this reason, a group of physicians and medical men flourished there. One of their number, John Gaddesden, was mentioned by Chaucer as one of the learned physicians alongside 'Esculapius and Deiscorides, and eek Rufus, Old Ypocras, Haly, and Galien' whom the doctor in the Canterbury Tales had studied. In 1309 Gaddesden wrote *Rosa Medicinae*, of which he said he had 'so called it on account of five appendages which belong to the rose, as it were five fingers holding it, . . . and as the rose overtops all flowers, so this book overtops all treatises on the practice of medicine.' It seems a quaint medieval proof of excellence, erring on the boastful. Gaddesden was physician to Edward II and bequeathed his books to his College at his death, but according to Wood they were thrown out in the time of Edward VI. The study of physic was part of wider scholastic studies and it was not until the Renaissance that an outstanding Oxford humanist, Thomas Linacre of All Souls, devoted his studies primarily to medicine. He accompanied an embassy sent by Henry VII to the court of Rome. He studied Greek and is said to have been the first Englishman to read Galen in the original. When he translated Galen's *Methodus Medendii*, Erasmus rejoiced that scholars read 'now Galen by the help of Linacre, speaking better Latin than they ever before spoke Greek.' He became guardian of Henry VIII's health and in 1518 founded the Royal College of Physicians which extended the privilege of licensing medical practitioners from the two universities to London. Linacre also studied the *Materia medica* of Dioscorides, the great compendium of medicinal uses of plants which had been lost to Europe in the dark ages and rediscovered in the Renaissance.

The study of plants as a science was part of the general Renaissance concept of acquiring knowledge through direct observation. Plants have always played a great part in man's life and imagination because of their organic nature. In medieval times they were therefore seen as prototypes of the Divine and in representation were depicted symbolically and as moral allegory. The intensity of the feeling and unity with the spiritual world of the living plants is unmistakeable in the St Frideswide shrine in Christ Church cathedral. The face of the little Saxon saint looks out from garlands of leaves of oak, ivy, vine, sycamore and bryony. In medieval illuminations allegory and personification are one; the lily is for purity and the madonna becomes a lily. The garden itself is a special symbol for it becomes, as in the Romance of the Rose by Guillame de Lorris, a complete allegory of man's life. The 'Hortus conclusus' was a special enclosed Mary garden with mystic symbols and based on the verse in the Canticles, 'a garden enclosed is my sister, my spouse.'

This feeling that everything in the external world was symbolic of the true reality of the spiritual world also found expression in the 'Doctrine of the Signatures.' It was thought that any plant which resembled a human organ must be helpful in treating any malfunction of that organ. Paracelsus, who lived between 1493 and 1541, believed in the relationships between biblical doctrines and natural philosophy and medicine and wrote:

> I have oftime declared how by the outward shapes and qualities of things, we may know their inward virtues, which God hath put in them for the use of Man. So in St John's wort we may take notice of the leaves, the veins. 1. The porosity or holes in the leaves signifies to us that this herb helps inward or outward holes or cuts in the skin. 2. The flowers of St John's wort, when they are purified, they are like blood, which teaches us that this herb is good for wounds, to close them and fill them up.

The mandrake, because of the humanoid shape of its root system, could, according to the Abbess Hildegard, 'cure every infirmity except death.' Being a narcotic and an emetic it did presumably have its medical uses, but a dog was used for digging it out of the earth as it was still believed, even in Shakespeare's day, that if the roots shrieked when being torn up 'living mortals hearing them run mad.'

The Doctrine of Signatures and astrological botany existed side by side with the new learning and scientific method of observation and seeing how things worked. Renaissance minds, however, which forsook Signature and symbolism and studied plants scientifically began to realise that the living nature of the plant world was a lead in to the study of life itself. Not only were more reliable classical texts available to scholars but the introduction of printing in the fifteenth century revolutionised the dissemination of knowledge. Travel to the Continent was easier and contact with botanists abroad brought with it the exchange of knowledge and of plants, especially after the establishment of the first botanical garden at Padua in 1545. At that time there was no authoritative work on the English names of plants which would relate to the continental herbals and in 1548 William Turner, known as 'the father of English botany,' published *'The names of Herbs in Greek, Latin, English. Dutch and French, with the common names that herbaries and apothecaries use.'* William Turner aspired to be Provost of Oriel or President of Magdalen but his unorthodox religious beliefs were against him, and when he visited Oxford in 1540 he was put in goal for preaching without a licence. He was a true child of the Reformation, with an unprejudiced mind and ability for objective study. His *Herbal* of 1568 was to be updated by John Gerard's *Herball* of 1597, which took account of the plants that had been brought back to England by the Elizabethan travellers to strange new lands.

In the sixteenth century plant husbandry had passed from the monasteries to the country houses of the nobility and it was as gardener to Lord Burleigh that Gerard had compiled his *Herball*. There was still no permanent place where the new plants could be nurtured and studied and Gerard recommended to his employer that he should establish a physic garden at Cambridge with himself as its head, 'to encourage the faculty of simpling.'[8] It was, however, at Oxford that such a garden was to be founded, but not until 1621. Here botany, medicine and practical gardening were linked for the first time in systematic study, as they have been ever since.

The Oxford Physic Garden was founded by Henry Danvers, Earl of Danby, who, being 'minded to become a benefactor to the University, determined to begin and finish a place whereby learning, especially the faculty of medicine might be improved.' It was primarily founded for 'a Nursery of Simples and that a Professor of Botanicey should read there, and shew the use and virtue of them to his Auditors,' according to Anthony Wood. The Chair of Physic had been endowed by James I who linked the Professorship with wardenship of the Ewelme almshouses, a retreat which remains one of the delights of the Regius Professor of Medicine today. The first Professor, Thomas Clayton, who signed himself His Majesty's Professor of Physicke, Oxon, wrote in commending Parkinson's *Theatrum Botanicum* that 'Oxford and England are happy in the foundation of a spacious illustrious physicke garden, completely beautifully walled and gated, now in levelling and planting with the charges and expences of thousands by the many wayes Honourable Earle of Danby, the furnishing and enriching whereof and of many a glorious Tempe, with all usefull and delightfull plants, will be expedited by your painefull happy satisfying Worke.' A new note was to be found in Parkinson's book, for he was as concerned with the ornamental delights of the plants as with their medicinal value. The word 'curious' was often used in connection with plants, especially for the introductions brought in by the plant explorers. John Tradescant, described by Parkinson as 'a painful industrious searcher and lover of all nature's varieties' was the first true plant explorer. He travelled in Russia and Algeria to buy 'rootes, flowers, seedes, trees and plants' for his employer Lord Salisbury at Hatfield and later made his own expedition to Virginia to stock his public garden at Lambeth. His introductions, among which are lilac, phloxes, lupins, stocks, Michaelmas daisies and the tulip tree, transformed the English garden.

There is little doubt that Henry Danvers intended his Oxford physic garden to be a repository for 'curious' plants as well as to grow the herbs necessary for the medical faculty. His brother Sir John Danvers had a garden at Chelsea which was highly praised by John Aubrey who said of him: 'He had well travelled France and Italy, and made good observations. He had in a fair body an harmonicall mind. He had a very fine fancy, which lay chiefly for gardens and architecture.'

Henry Danvers appointed John Tradescant, who had been promoted to Royal gardener and displayed at his Lambeth garden 'all nature's varieties,' as the first keeper of the Oxford Physic Garden, but Tradescant was already in failing health and was unable to take up the post.[9] It is thought, however, that his son may have sent some of his rare plants to Oxford.

Lord Danby leased from Magdalen College five acres of meadow land outside the city walls, which until 1290 had been the cemetery of the Jews in Oxford. It was low lying and four thousand loads of 'mucke and dunge' was used to raise the land above the Cherwell flood plain and prepare the ground to receive the plants. The foundation ceremony took place on 25 July 1621 with Dr Clayton, the new Regius Professor of Physic giving the oration. The walls, which were to be as 'well fair and sufficient as All Soules Colledge walls, Magdalen Colledge Tower, or any of the fairest buildings in Oxford both for truth and beauty,' were not finished until 1633. The gateways to the Oxford Physic Garden were as fine as those in the finest country house in England. They were built by Inigo Jones's master mason Nicholas Stone and executed in 1632-3. They are in the mannerist style of St Mary's porch which he was to build in 1637 and are reminiscent of Serlio's portals. The pedimented archways terminating the walks are similar to those built by Nicholas Stone at Kirby Hall in Northamptonshire for Inigo Jones.

The haphazard medieval arrangement of buildings with gardens fitted in had given way to a design conceived as a whole and architecturally related to the whole. The Renaissance architect Leone Battista Alberti had laid it down in his *De Re Aedificatoria* (1458) that the main lines of the design should be in strict proportion and regularity so that the pleasing harmony of the whole should not be lost in the attraction of individual parts. Such ideas developed in England only under Inigo Jones at the Court of James I. Jones had begun his career as designer for Court Masques and in August 1605 was employed on entertainments for the King at Oxford. His architectural career began as Surveyor of the King's Works in 1615 and his Queen's House at Greenwich and the Whitehall Banqueting House introduced new ideas of symmetry and proportion into English architecture of the 1620s. The first Oxford college to show a feeling for Renaissance symmetry and balance was Wadham, built 1610-13. The Schools Quadrangle of the Bodleian (1613) has axially aligned doorways from North to South giving a through vista. The Renaissance feel for linear design which had begun with the Elizabethan love of matching conceits and symmetry in frets and knots had extended to the alignment of courtyards, garden doors, terrace steps and the forthright or path. Canterbury Quadrangle at St John's College, built by the munificence of Archbishop Laud, with Renaissance arcades and archways aligned to the Front Quadrangle, brought Oxford into the height of architectural fashion. Charles I and Queen Henrietta Maria were taken to see it by Laud when it was completed in 1636, while they were on a three-day royal visit to Oxford, which included a play at Christ Church with scenery by Inigo Jones. Time was running out, however, for Laudian Oxford, King Charles and court architecture.

4

Commonwealth Oxford

Oxford became a garrison town in the Civil War, its medieval walls were strengthened for a different kind of attack and the whole pattern of life changed for the University and colleges. For four years from 1642 until 1646 it was Charles I's capital and the centre of the Royalist cause. The King took up residence at Christ Church, the royal foundation. Royalist parliaments met in the hall and ambassadors were received with the kind of ceremony that the setting of Wolsey's would-be 'palace of princes' could provide. The colleges were each to be used for specific purposes. The Privy Council met in Exeter Hall. Queen Henrietta Maria's court was set up at Merton College, the college silver was melted down for use by the Mint set up in New Inn Hall. New College cloisters became a magazine, troops drilled in the quadrangles and in Christ Church Meadows and the artillery was accommodated in Magdalen Grove. The Schools were used as granaries for the garrison and for the making of uniforms.

University life did continue, however; lectures were given and degree ceremonies were held. Dugdale pursued his antiquarian researches in the Bodleian unmoved by the coming and goings of the troops to the ammunition repository in the Bodleian Tower. The courtiers moved into college rooms and the colleges had to lay in stores of food for them and for the remaining undergraduates for the event of a siege. Lincoln

College seems to have found time to put its ornamental knot and rose garden in order even when Cromwell's troops surrounded the city and a cannon ball fired from Marston had hit Christ Church hall. In their accounts for 1645 is recorded: '5s.0d for cutting the box-knot, the rose trees and hedges.'[1] The gardens were of course much frequented by the courtiers and their ladies and an entry in the *Brief Lives* of John Aubrey, who was at Trinity College, suggests that their behaviour shocked some of the clerical dons.

> Our grove was the Daphne for the ladies and their gallants to walke in, and many times my lady Isabella Thynne would make her entry with a theorbo or lute played before her. I have heard her play on it in the grove myself, which she did rarely; for which Mr Edmund Waller hath in his Poems for ever made her famous. . . She was most beautifull, most humble, charitable, etc. but she could not subdue one thing. I remember one time this lady and fine Mris. Fenshawe (her great and intimate friend, who lay at our college — she was wont, and my lady Thynne, to come to our Chapell, mornings, halfe dressd, like angels), would have a frolick to make a visitt to the President. The old Dr quickly perceived that they came to abuse him; he addresses his discourse to Mris. Fenshawe, saying, 'Madam, your husband and father I bred up here, and I knew your grandfather; I know you to be a gentlewoman, I will not say you are a whore; but gett you gonne for a very woman.'

Some of the Oxford college gardens still have traces of Civil War fortifications which were later used as garden features, such as the embankment on the east side of the Warden's garden at Wadham. The water defences provided by the Thames and the Cherwell were the most important feature and these were designed by one Richard Rallingson of Queen's, for which he received an M.A. degree. In April 1643, 'the Cutt of grounde toward the further end of East bridge by St Clement's was made for the lettinge in of Charwell river the better to overflowe Christchurch mede and Cowley landes about Millham bridge, by the meetinge of Charwell and Thames together, for the defence of the cittie.'[2] Earthworks were erected on the line of the Broad Walk and the remains of a bastion is still to be seen. The Magdalen walks were extended to a bastion commanding the Cherwell, called Dover Pier after its commander, the Earl of Dover.

4.1　A Civil War earthwork
Now made into a garden terrace at Rhodes House.

The appearance of Addison's Walk banked above the water ditches is the best example of a war earthwork being used to advantage as a garden feature. The door in the wall between Corpus and the cathedral garden through which Queen Henrietta Maria was given access from Merton to the King at Christ Church is now planted with roses and lilies as a record that it was made for the 'Rose and Lily Queen.'

Market gardens were in demand for the increased population and one notable nursery run by Thomas Wrench was set up in the old Paradise Gardens of the Franciscan friars.[3] The Physic Garden flourished under Jacob Bobart, a retired soldier of the German wars who was also a very capable gardener. When Danby had been unable to get John Tradescant as Horti Praefectus, he finally discovered in 1642 when he was staying at the Greyhound Inn opposite Magdalen College that the tenant would be ideal as the keeper of the Physic Garden. What was needed was clearly a good practical gardener to take care of the exotic plants that had been arriving, and Bobart could continue to live in his premises just across the road. Jacob Bobart worked painstakingly during the Civil War, undeterred by what was going on around him. He trained fruit trees along the new stone walls, sorted out the plants into beds and made a special clay-bottomed trench for preserving boggy plants. He was both diligent in obtaining rarities and skilful in cultivating them, and in 1648 he produced a catalogue of plants growing in the Physic Garden, listing about 1,600 different species and varieties.[4]

Bobart's garden had a great part to play in the new Garden of Eden, the scientific Utopia of the Puritan world of the Commonwealth.[5] When Charles I was defeated and the gay ladies, portrait painters and pastry cooks had left Oxford, University life picked up again. Cromwell was given a degree and Puritans were intruded as heads of colleges. For some academics there was a cultural revolution brought about by a widespread belief in the Millenium. Paradise Lost, the Garden of Eden, Adam the Gardener became the current imagery. In Eden Adam had been commanded by God to 'dress and keep his garden' and he had worked willingly and found the work pleasant, and could control the world about him until the Fall. The New Eden on earth would redress the balance; man should toil and the earth would bring forth fruit. Profits and Pleasures was stamped on the title page of Ralph Austen's *The Spirituall Use of an Orchard or Garden of Fruit Trees*, published in Oxford in 1653.[6] The first part of the book gave clear instructions for planting based on experimental methods and the second part of the book was aimed at promoting Puritanism. Austen had his own nursery in Oxford and academics started their own orchards. So great was his trade that he estimated that he could sell 20,000 plants a year from his seedlings and grafts.[7] Bobart was always available in the Physic Garden to give advice on grafting to the Adam gardeners who believed that by tilling the soil and encouraging fruit to grow they were hastening the advent of the Millennium.

Ralph Austen's *Treatise of Fruit Trees* which showed 'divers Similitudes between Naturall and Spirituall Fruit Trees: according to Scripture and Experience,' had a frontispiece showing a walled orchard bearing the inscription that many of the medieval Mary gardens bore: 'A Garden inclosed is my sister my spouse,' and adds: 'Thy Plants are an Orchard of Pomegranates, with pleasant fruits.' The seventeenth-century Puritan biblical inspiration was very different from that of the medieval church. For the medieval man the good things of the earth were but symbolic of Heaven which was the true goal, whereas the Puritan ideal was to hasten the Millennium of Christ's kingdom on earth by making the earth bear fruit. The garden was not symbolic but fundamental to righteous living.

William Coles of New College published in 1657 *Adam in Eden*, in which he tried to bring together all that was known in the art of physic gardening and at the same time revive the Doctrine of Signatures in the search for scriptural bounty. The full title of his book was: 'A history of Plants, Fruits, Herbs and Flowers with their several names, whether Greek, Latin or English, the places they grow, their descriptions and kinds, their times of flourishing and decreasing, and also their special signatures, anatomical appropriations and particular physical virtues.' Walnuts were to be used for brain disorders, and as a hair restorative quinces, moss and maidenhair were suggested. 'The down of Quinces doth in some sort resemble the hair of the head, the decoction whereof is very effectual for the restoring of hair that is falling off by the French Pox, and being made up with wax and laid on as a plaster, it bringeth hair to them that are bald and keepeth it from falling if it be ready to shed. A decoction of the long Moss that lays upon trees in a manner like hair is very profitable to be used in the falling of the hair and this it doth by signature. All these being capillary herbs do cure all the diseases of the hair by signature.' William Coles called on all academics to garden wholeheartedly, 'if a man be wearied with over-much study (for study is a weariness to the Flesh as Solomon by experience can tell) there is no better place in the world to re-create himself than a Garden, there being no sense but may be delighted therein. . . By this time I hope you will thinke it no dishonour to follow the steps of our Grandsire Adam, who is commonly pictured with a Spade in his hand, to march through the Quarters of your Gardens with the like

Instrument, and there to rectifie all the disorders thereof. . .
So that this Art, with the rest, being improved may bring
forth much glory to God, much Honour to the Nation and
much Pleasure and Profit to those that delight in it.'

The real Honour to the Nation and the advancement of
human knowledge was not brought about by the new Adam
in Eden gardeners, however, but by a brilliant group of
natural scientists who made Oxford a centre for their enquiries and demonstrations in the Commonwealth, and became
the foundation of the future Royal Society. Experimental
science flourished again in Oxford, making it as important a
centre of scientific learning as it had been in the days of
Roger Bacon. Orthodoxy and scholasticism had always
impeded scientific progress in Oxford. For centuries Oxford
scholars had discoursed on natural philosophy founded on
Aristotle rather than observation of Nature. In Commonwealth Oxford men of the calibre of Wren and Boyle began
to reason freely upon 'the works of Nature' and one by one
the preconceived notions that had been handed down un-
critically from age to age were brought out into the light
and examined. Wren, the 'miracle of a youth,' set up an
observatory in the Bodleian Schools tower, once stored
with royalist ammunition, and Boyle, the most diligent of
all the 'enquirers into the works of Nature,' established a
laboratory in the High Street opposite the Queen's College.
Here he worked on an air pump which led to the discovery
of his law relating to the pressure and volume of gases, and
his assistant Robert Hooke of Christ Church made through a
microscope the first identification of the cell on which life
is based. To these great natural scientists Nature was a concep-
tual whole, the law by which the Universe proceeded, and
their enquiries ranged over a wide field.

Thomas Sprat, who was one of this illustrious company, in
writing later his *History of the Royal Society* looked back
with great feeling on these days in Oxford when reason and
sanity were made to prevail in extraordinarily difficult circumstances:

It was . . . some space after the end of the Civil Wars in Oxford,
in Dr Wilkins his Lodgings, in Wadham College, which was then

the place of Resort for Vertuous, and Learned Men, that the first
meetings were made, which laid the foundations of all this that
follow'd. The University had, at that time, many Members of
its own, who had begun a free way of reasoning; and was also
frequented by some Gentleman, of Philosophical Minds, whom
the misfortunes of the Kingdom, and the security and ease of
retirement amongst Gown-men had drawn thither. Their first
purpose was no more, than only the satisfaction of breathing a
freer air, and of conversing in quiet with one another, without
being ingag'd in the passions, and madness of that dismal Age.
And from the Institution of that Assembly, it had been enough,
if no other advantage had come but this: That by this Means
there was a race of young Men provided, against the next Age,
whose minds receiving from them, their first Impressions of sober
and generous knowledge were invincibly arm'd against all the
inchantments of Enthusiasm. But what is more, I may venture
to affirm, that it was in good measure, by the influence, which
these Gentlemen had over the rest, that the University itself,
or at least, any part of its Discipline, and Order, was sav'd from
ruine.

Oxford had indeed been spared by civilised moderation on
both sides. It was Dr Wilkins who had been made Warden of
Wadham by Cromwell (whose sister he married), who refused
religious disputes in the college. He did not wish to separate
science and religion but sought to demonstrate that there
were errors on both, and, above all, encouraged those studies
of natural science which were common ground for all beliefs.
He inspired the confidence of the young Christopher Wren,
royalist and High Church, whose uncle Bishop Wren was
imprisoned in the Tower. Retribution on the University for
having espoused the King's cause had been amazingly light.
Fairfax, who had summoned the garrison city to surrender,
had said, 'I verie much desire the preservation of that place
(so famous for learning) from ruine,' and had placed a guard
on the Bodleian Library. Only minor reforms were made but
discipline was tightened within the University. Selden, one of
the most influential men on the side of Parliament, had
warned that too much interference would 'destroy rather
than reform one of ye most famous and learned companyes
of men that ever was visible in ye Christian world.'

There was little need for the Corpus bees to leave at the
Parliament Visitation out of loyalty, as Robert Plot reported;[8]

it seems likely that they too could have come to a working arrangement. When John Evelyn visited his old University in 1654 he found that ceremonies were not wholly abolished even though Dr Owen was now 'Cromwell's Vice-Chancellor,' and he left 'satisfied with the civilities of Oxford.' True, he hadn't much liked the sermon at St Mary's (Mary's as the committed Puritans preferred to call it) but he had enjoyed being conducted round the Physic Garden by Jacob Bobart and had admired the sensitive plant. Poor Bobart was suffering from arrears of payment after the endowment lands of Lord Danby had been sequestered, but he seems to have carried on until things were put right.

On all sides scientists were taking an interest in practical aspects of their experiments, whether in grafting good fruit trees or in testing for good fertilisers. Boyle was of the opinion that 'ther is scarce any mold comparable for flowers to the earth which is digged from under old stacks of wood, or other places where rotten wood has been lain,' and Bobart found that dung from New College's 'house of office' when rotten was 'an excellent soil to fill up deep holes to plant young vines.' Boyle was the pivot for empiricist thinking in Oxford. Experiment and sound deduction were the basis of his work in *The Sceptical Chemist*, in which he tried to sweep away Paracelsian ideas on the composition of matter and to disentangle chemistry from alchemy. 'Does it work or is it a myth?' was the yardstick to be applied. Many books based on real observation of plants were published in Oxford. *The history of the propagation and improvement of vegetables by the concurrence of art and nature* by Robert Sharrock in 1660 was dedicated to the great master of vegetative philosophy, Robert Boyle.

Ralph Austen also dedicated his *A Treatise of Fruit Trees* to Robert Boyle, who had encouraged him in the planting of fruit and forest trees, approving of the experimental method and the simple and clear instructions for planting. Austen had made experiments with the fermentation of apples with Robert Boyle and promoted cider as soothing to the mind. In 1676 Isaac Newton applied for some of Austen's best cider-apple grafts for Cambridge academics but the request came too late because Austen had died.[9] The colleges largely preferred ale and many had their own brewhouses. Wood maintained that home brewing was popular when the Fellows were not able to frequent taverns and so tippled in their rooms. Certainly the Parliamentary Visitors reported on 31st December 1651 'some Fellowes of Newe Colledge abusing themselves by excessive drinking.' The Fellows professed innocence. Experiments with grafting vines in the Botanic Garden produced a 'white Frontiniac grafted upon the Parsly Vine' which also proved popular, give or take the Puritans.[10]

Various improvements were made in Oxford gardens although there was nothing but essential building in Commonwealth days. New College garden flourished under Dr Pinck whose obituary notice called him 'the pride of Wykeham's garden, cropt to be made a flower in paradise.' When Oxford was besieged the Warden had supervised the drilling of the volunteers in the Great Quadrangle from the windows of his lodgings and Anthony Wood, who was then a chorister at New College, said that it was such an enthralling spectacle that the boys could never be brought to their books again. The Warden, an ally of Laud, was sentenced to imprisonment by Parliament, but was released on bail and allowed to return to Oxford. William Coles, the author of *Adam in Eden*, considered him to be 'a very learned Man, and well versed in Physick, and truly he would rise very betimes in the morning even in his later dayes, when he was almost four-score years old, and going into his Garden, he would take a Mattock or Spade, digging there an houre or two, which he found very advantageous to his health.'

New College was defiantly loyalist and on 20th May 1647 the college, including Wood and the choir boys, celebrated Prince Charles's birthday with a bonfire on the Mount. Shortly afterwards in 1648 the sixteenth-century mount was, in Warden Woodward's words, 'perfected with stepps of stone and setts of ye hedges about the walks.' It seems likely that the mound recorded in the Bursar's Rolls for 1529-1530, when five hundred wagon-loads of rubbish were tipped there, was largely a means of disposing of accumulated rubble from demolished buildings, and that there was no easy access to the top such as Leland described in the 1530s for mounts he had seen in his *Itinerary*: 'writhen about with degrees like turnings of cockilshilles, to come to the top without payn.' The Fellows' precarious ascent for the celebration bonfire was perhaps not 'without payn' or they may have decided in 1648 to 'shut out the madness of a dismal age' by going in for some stylish gardening. There is no actual date for the making of the parterre to the west of the Mount, first described by Anthony Wood in 1658, but the wish to ascend the Mount would suggest that there was a formal garden beneath, which was best seen from above. Parterre was a new word brought to England from France and although, like the knot garden of Elizabethan days, it was designed to be seen from above ground level, it was much more elaborate in design. It was often arabesque and curved within the rectangle and resembled embroidery, rather than simple geometrical patterns or the strap shapes seen in the Hovenden knot at All Souls. The parterre was usually laid out in box, this being a plant more manageable than the hyssop, rosemary and lavender used for knot edging. There was a centre gravelled walk with compartments on either side and these balanced one another. It was the Mollets, the French royal gardeners, who had introduced the *parterres de broderie* to England. Henrietta Maria had brought over André Mollet, who had been her father's gardener at Fontainebleau, to redesign Wimbledon in the new fashion. New College was the first Oxford college to follow the French style of parterre gardening in balanced quarters, all to be viewed from an elegant mount. There was a column and a sundial on the top of the mount and a living sundial in one of the compartments of the parterre.

Wadham's garden was first laid out in 1651 in a manner to please the distinguished set of natural scientists who made the college their home at Dr Wilkins's invitation. Hitherto it had been left as an orchard, as instructed by Dorothy Wadham. John Evelyn visited it shortly after it had been made. Evelyn, who had been at Balliol College in 1637 but had left before the outbreak of the Civil War, was at heart one of the Wadham set. He considered that gardening and natural philosophy were closely related and that the study of gardening was part of the scientific movement. His great classic on

D. Loggan delin. et Sculp. cum Privil. S.R.M.

gardens, the *Elysium Britannicum*, which contains all his ideas on garden design and 'stupendous and wonderful plants,' is still in manuscript form.[11] He had gardened assiduously at his Surrey home during the Commonwealth after his return from the Continent, and at the Restoration he was instrumental in obtaining the charter for the Royal Society and wrote extensively for it. His great arboricultural work *Sylva*, published by the Society in 1664, was to prove most influential in the replanting of woodlands after the depletion of timber caused by the Civil War. The Oxford set was absorbed into the Royal Society, whose first chairman was Dr Wilkins, and there Evelyn met up with the old Wadham fellowship, Robert Boyle, Christopher Wren, Jonathan Goddard, once physician in Cromwell's army and later Warden of Merton, Hooke and William Petty the statistician, Vice-Principal of Brasenose. The 'universally curious' Dr Wilkins had entertained Evelyn on his visit to Oxford on 13 July 1654, when Evelyn recorded the content of the new Wadham garden in his diary:

> We all din'd, at that most obliging and universaly Curious Dr Wilkins's, at Waddum, who was the first who shew'd me the Transparent Apiaries, which he had built like Castles and Palaces and so ordered them one upon another, as to take the Hony without destroying the Bees. These were adorn'd in variety of Dials, little Statues, Vanes etc; very ornamental, and he was abundantly civill, as finding me pleased with them, to present me one of these Hives, which he had empty, and which I afterwards had in my Garden at Says-Court, many Yeares after; and which his Majestie came on purpose to see and contemplate with much satisfaction. He also contrived an hollow Statue which gave a Voice and utter'd Words, by a long concealed pipe which went to its mouth, whilst one spake thro' it, at a good distance and which was at first very surprising.

Dr Wilkins' speaking statue in the Wadham garden speaks volumes for the ideas and attitudes of this brilliant latitudin-

---

4.2 The garden of Wadham College

As depicted by Loggan in *Oxonia Illustrata* (1675). The college that was the centre for experimental science during the Commonwealth extended its scientific enquiries to the garden. There were transparent beehives designed by Wren, a speaking statue and artificial rainbows.

arian and experimental scientist. Joke fountains and automata of all kinds filled the early seventeenth century mannerist gardens designed for lavish outdoor entertainment, but the Wadham speaking statue was not just to trick and amuse: it was a serious experiment by the 'universally curious' Warden. It was a part of the Wadham philosophy, later to become a Royal Society attitude described by Sprat as the desire 'to assist familiarly in all occasions of human life.' Sprat was a pupil of Dr Wilkins and learned from him the necessity for 'a close, naked, natural, way of speaking; positive expressions; clear senses; a native easiness' which was to be exacted from members of the Royal Society.[12] Wilkins was preoccupied with language and communication. He tried to invent a universal language and worked on speech pathology by which he hoped to teach deaf mutes. The speaking statue with pipes into his study was set up for this purpose. Dr Plot was full of admiration for another of the Warden's contrivances, 'whereby, of but few galons of water forced through a narrow Fissure, he could raise a Mist in his Garden, wherein a Person placed at a due distance between the Sun and the Mist, might see an exquisite Rainbow in all its proper Colours.'[13]

Another genius was to hand to assist in the making of Wilkins's experiments and it was he, the future builder of St Paul's, who had delighted in making the dials and vanes on top of the transparent beehives.[14] Evelyn describes some of the ingenious devices that the Warden and his protegé had gathered at Wadham:

> He had above in his lodgings and gallery a variety of shadows, dyals, perspectives, and many other artificial, mathematical and magical curiosities, a way-wiser, a thermometer, a monstrous magnet, conic and other sections, a ballance of a demi-circle, most of them his owne and that prodigious young scholar, Mr Chr. Wren, who presented me with a piece of white marble, which he had stain'd with a lively red very deepe, as beautiful as if it had been natural.

From the age of seventeen until he was thirty-three, Christopher Wren was engaged entirely in scientific pursuits and it was as mathematician, astronomer and natural philosopher that he won fame in Oxford. Hooke, himself an architect, spoke of the perfect combination of 'such a mechanical hand and so philosophic a mind' which was to lead Wren on later to his great architectural achievements. He was an inventor from an early age and Dr Wilkins gave him every encouragement to go further with his experiments with telescope, meterological instruments and his diplographic pen for writing in relief for the blind. During the Civil War, Wren's father held a living at Bletchington, a few miles north of Oxford, and it was here from 1646—1649 that Wren became interested in astronomy and constructed dials and vanes.

He went up to Wadham under Dr Wilkins in 1649 and took his degree in 1651. He was a Fellow of All Souls from 1653-7 and during those years he continued his experimentation and astronomical studies. He discovered a graphic method of computing solar and lunar eclipses and designed a huge sundial for All Souls. This was originally in the Front Quadrangle but was later removed to the wall of the Codrington Library, where it adds distinction to the baroque quadrangle. Dials, models of the moon, contrivances for planting corn or measuring rainfall, all were grist to the mill for the true Renaissance mind of Dr Christopher Wren. His first models were probably those of the brain made on paste-board for the anatomy scholars.[15] Physiology and anatomy had also been rapidly advanced by the experimentation of the Oxford Commonwealth set. William Harvey, discoverer of the circulation of the blood, had come to Oxford to attend Charles I after the Battle of Edgehill and used his time in the besieged city more profitably than did the courtiers. According to Aubrey, he used to visit George Bathurst at Trinity, 'who had a hen to hatch eggs in his chamber, which they dayly opened to discerne the progress and way of generation.' Some of his empirical exercises in early embryology were published in his *Exercises on the Generation of Animals* in 1651. Of particular interest to Wren was the work of Thomas Willis, whose book on the anatomy of the brain he illustrated. Christopher Wren was the very epitome of the young man whom Sprat, the historian of the Royal Society, said had 'provided against the next Age' by having devoted himself in fanatical times to the disinterested search for truth in the Oxford of Dr Wilkins.

5

Restoration Oxford

There is no doubt that the end of Puritanism came as a relief to academic Oxford, although as Edward Hyde, Earl of Clarendon and the first Vice-Chancellor of Restoration Oxford acknowledged in his *History of the Great Rebellion*, the Interregnum had 'yielded a harvest of extraordinary good and sound knowledge in all parts of learning' and 'when it pleased God to bring the King back to his throne, he found that University abounding in excellent learning, and devoted to duty and obedience, little inferior to what it was before its desolation.'

There was a clamour for maypoles to be set up in the streets on Restoration Day, May 29th 1660, the jollity continued all through the night, and, according to Wood, the Puritans 'tack'd about to participate of the universal joy.' The King's Head was able to display its sign again and the dons could drink openly. On the first visit of Charles II to the City, the Carfax Conduit flowed with claret for the citizens. New College added the King's Arms to its parterre to balance the College Coat of Arms. Magdalen chopped down the trees that had been planted in 'fanatick times'[1] and presumably the loyal Corpus bees returned to the college leads.

Archbishop Sheldon, who was Warden of All Souls, felt that the University required a building which would provide an appropriate setting for its ceremonies, other than in St Mary's church, and provided the money for it. A baroque sense of the occasion was wanted and he persuaded Christopher Wren who had just returned to Oxford as Savilian Professor of Astronomy, after four years away at Gresham College, to undertake it. Wren decided on a Roman theatre and produced a model of the trussed roof for the Royal Society in 1663. The ability for making models of the moon and of the brain, the ingenuity he had shown in all his experimentation and, above all, the mathematics which had been fundamental to the clarity of thought of the Wadham set, almost imperceptibly coalesced into a genuis for architecture. The lessons of the Civil War had given the country a new national unity and creative energy which was gloriously reflected in Wren's architecture. It was fitting that his first building was for Oxford, which had been the starting point of his brilliant career.[2]

Wren's Sheldonian Theatre was inaugurated on 9 July 1669 and John Evelyn records that it had been resolved to celebrate its dedication 'with the greatest splendour and formalitie that might be' and to draw 'a world of strangers and other Companie to the University from all parts of the Nation;' there were panegyric speeches, triumphal organ music and an oration 'in praise of Academical Learning;' all this lasted from 11.00 am until 7.00 pm and concluded with 'bells ringing, and universal joy and feasting.' Evelyn stayed on for a few days and was disgusted to find that before he left people had already begun to scratch their names on the Arundel marbles which he had persuaded Lord Howard to give the University and which Wren had built into niches on the walls beside the theatre. John Evelyn, always the practical gardener, advised the Vice-Chancellor to plant holly in front of them. Before leaving he was given one of the first honorary degrees in Wren's new ceremonial theatre.

Oxonia Illustrata, published in 1675 by David Loggan, gives a complete picture of Restoration Oxford with the Sheldonian in its proud place. Loggan, who lived in Holywell, was appointed engraver to the University in 1669. He took many years over *Oxonia Illustrata*, which he probably began in 1663. In the preface to *Cantabrigia Illustrata*, which he undertook after his completion of the Oxford survey, he explains his technique of submitting

> everything to the closest examination of the mind, as well as of the eye; to observe the limitations imposed by optics as well as by Geometry, to examine from some distant point the roofs of all the buildings which came within my field of vision, all the objects which the subtle and varied art of architecture brought under my notice in the different materials which it employs; to draw them first on paper, then to engrave them on copper, and lastly, to print them properly.

He surveyed Oxford with conscientious accuracy down to the last woodpile or ladder on the roof. Every detail of the buildings and gardens can be seen in the individual engravings of the colleges and in the overall plans of the city. *Oxonia Illustrata* appears to have been intended to some extent as a companion to Wood's *History and Antiquities of the University*, published the year before, in 1674. The Table of Contents gives opposite to each plate a reference to the page of Anthony Wood's work where a description of the building represented is to be found. It is amusing to fit Wood's gossip in his diaries into Loggan's engravings. At Merton in *Oxonia Illustrata* the open knot garden and old-fashioned carpenter's work arbour can be seen and above it a stylish summerhouse with sixteen steps leading up to it. As a viewing point for Merton Field and Christ Church meadows it appears superfluous as there is a good lookout from the terrace formed in the city wall. All is made clear by Anthony Wood's description for this feature and for the rest of the alterations made for the Warden's wife, Lady Clayton:

> new trees planted, arbours made, rootes of choice flowers bought etc; All which tho unnecessary, yet the poore college must pay for them and all this to please a woman. Not content with these matters, there must be a new summer-house built at the south end of the warden's garden, wherin her ladyship and her gossips may take their pleasure, and any eaves-dropper of the family may harken what any of the fellows should accidentally talk of in the passage to their owne garden. And this the warden told the society that it would not cost the college above £20 yet when it was finished there was £100 paid for it by the bursar, wanting some few shillings. This work was thought unnecessary by many persons, because it joyned almost to the long gallery, the large

bay window whereof at its south end affords a better prospect than that of the summerhouse.

Anthony Wood lived opposite Merton College and would himself be in a good position to observe Lady Clayton spying on the Fellows from her new summerhouse.

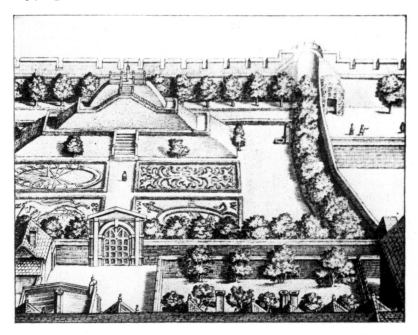

5.1 New College after the Restoration

Detail from *Oxonia Illustrata* (Loggan, 1675). At the Restoration New College added the King's arms to its parterre, which had been mentioned by Wood as early as 1658. There was a living sundial in one of the compartments of the parterre and a sundial on top of the mount.

Loggan shows donnish games in progress on tennis and five courts at Merton and in a bowling alley at Pembroke. Most of the college gardens have neat knots and edged grass plots. Only New College has the real fashionable embroidered look about the beds, although it seems as though Exeter had sported a Coat of Arms in box as well. Elsewhere the knots are open as the Merton layout, the better to enjoy the flowers. The box scrolls and heraldry were only to be admired from the gravel path at New College, but at Wadham one clearly walked inside the pattern to get to the centre, the beehives and the different plots. Loggan shows the mound at Wadham with the figure of Atlas 'holding a world curiously gilded' on top. Apart from these few additions the gardens of the 1670s in Oxford had changed little since the beginning of the century. The old-fashioned wooden galleries and raised beds are everywhere to be seen; even above Pembroke's new floral sundial the old herber which might have come from *The Dream of Poliphilus* still persists. Balliol with its small pleasaunce entered through a herber, its narrow beds and trained fruit trees on the wall could scarcely have changed since the time when the author of *Elysium Britannicum* was there in pre-Civil War days.

One garden in Loggan is, however, shown as formal in layout, and that is the Hortus Botanicus. Bobart had presumably laid out his physic garden of the 1640s based on some rough system of botanical classification or for medicinal uses and had decided which part of the garden was best suited to the exotic plants which were brought to him from all over the world. But it is unlikely that the old soldier from Brunswick had any hand in the formal design of the garden as illustrated by Loggan. This was the work of an eminent botanist, physician and gardener who was, in every sense of the word, a true man of the Restoration. Robert Morison, who was appointed by Charles II as first Professor of Botany in Oxford in 1669, had served the Stuart cause with passionate devotion. He graduated at Aberdeen University in Latin, Greek and philosophy and turned his attention to natural history with the idea of studying medicine. He was badly wounded fighting on the Royalist side in the Civil War and fled to France, where he resumed his medical studies. He took his degree in medicine and devoted himself to the study of botany under Vespasian Robin, the King's Botanist. Robin recommended him to Gaston, Duke of Orléans, the brother of Louis XIII, who gave him the appointment of physician to his household and superintendent of his famous garden at Blois. Morison searched for rare plants for the Blois garden and began a treatise on the classification of plants, which the Duke of Orléans intended to publish, but the Duke died in 1660 before it was finished.

Queen Henrietta Maria was the sister of the Duke of Orléans and visited Blois with her son, the future Charles II, during their exile in France, where they met Robert Morison. All the royal parks and gardens had to be remade when Charles II returned triumphantly to England, and the King invited Morison — although Fouquet wished him to stay in France — to be superintendent of his royal gardens while acting as his personal physician. Morison dedicated his *Blois Hortus* to Charles II. The appointment of a Professor who had studied the medicinal properties of plants as well as their ornamental uses in royal gardens was to add a new dimension to the work of the Oxford Physic Garden. Not only had the new Professor grown accustomed to the formal gardens of the great Renaissance chateau of Blois, but he had also spent some time at Fontainebleau, the royal garden laid out by André Mollet for Henrietta Maria's parents Henry IV and Marie de Medici. He set about designing the sophisticated partitioned plots, some with circular centres as he had been used to for setting off his rare plants at Blois.

The German gardener, who had hitherto managed the Physic Garden without the supervision of a Professor, was full of admiration for his plans. John Ward,[3] who was a friend of Bobart's, wrote: 'Jacob Bobart spake with Dr Modesay and says of him ye whole world yields not ye like man, hee never heard a man talk att ye gallant rate in his life. Hee shewed you all his deigns in ye new Garden; There are to bee walkes in itt of 30ft wide as hee saes. . . ' Morison was often referred to as Dr Modesy in Oxford, but it is not clear whether that was a pointed corruption or whether it was left over from Anglo-French days. The Scots professor was by all accounts fluent, if sometimes unintelligible. Anthony Wood could not resist a gibe at him for apparently when the King visited Oxford in 1683 and called on his former physician and Superintendent of the royal gardens the incorrigible antiquary recorded, 'At the Physick Garden where Dr Robert Morison, the botanick professor, speaking an English speech also, was often out and made them laugh. This person, though a master in speaking and writing the

Latin tongue, yet hath no command of the English, as being much spoyld by his Scottish tone.'

The Professor took small groups of students into the Physic Garden to study 'the nature and distinction of herbs and other plants,' and for five-week sessions he gave lectures three times a week, reading from a table in the middle of the garden. These were always well attended and distinguished visitors such as John Evelyn went to hear him. Morison continued to work on his evolutionary plant classification, which John Ray was also developing after preliminary correspondence with Dr Wilkins, but Morison commented tartly that Ray, in Cambridge without a Physic Garden, 'studied Plants more in his Closet than in Gardens and Fields.' Bobart learned the Professor's system and, in general greatly profited by his association with Morison. On his side, the Professor was greatly assisted by having such a well-grounded and down-to-earth physic gardener. Bobart had himself studied the mechanism of the sensitive plant, the *Mimosa pudica*, admired by Evelyn in 1654, and it was his watchful eye that spotted the hybrid Plane which was later to become so popular in the streets and squares of London. *Platanus acerifolia* is a hybrid of the oriental and American planes and was raised and described by Bobart about 1670. An original specimen leaf is still preserved in Bobart's herbarium[4] and one of the finest specimens in Britain, a direct propagation from the original tree, can be seen in the grounds of Magdalen College.

The Professor of Botany, aided and abetted by his observant gardener, introduced striped plants into our gardens. The Striped Bittersweet was one of the first variegated plants to be introduced into cultivation and this had been observed by Morison when superintendent of the Blois gardens. In his *The Natural History of Oxfordshire*, Dr Plot recorded that 'the Learned Dr Morison informs us he observed it in Dulcamara creeping through Lime and other Rubbish of Buildings, at the Duke of Orleans his House at Blois, whence not only ours, but most other Gardens of Europe have since been supplyed with the white striped Dulcamara.'[5]

The Professor found a striped sycamore growing in Magdalen Grove and brought it across the road for Bobart to grow in the Physic Garden. Plot voiced the accepted view that 'such Stripings are nothing but Disease, appears plainly in that most, if not all striped Plants, are somewhat deformed and imperfect in their Leaves . . . and such Stripings to be only Discolorations, and no Ornaments of Perfection, though Ornaments of our Gardens.' Morison's 'striped' plants are still preserved in the present collection of variegated chimaeras in the Botanic Garden, which has always made a specialised study of the nature of variegation.[6] It is now known that the patterns may be quite natural in variegated plants and not necessarily the result of mutation, nutrient deficiencies or infection. In an experiment on over 400 different variegated plants undertaken at the Oxford Botanic Garden only twelve showed symptoms identifiable with infectious organisms. Flower arrangers and gardeners are all indebted to this interest in chimeral variegation, initiated by the Professor of Botany in Oxford, particularly in grasses and hostas striped or out-lined with white tissue.[7]

The example of the striped sycamore cultivated in the Physic Garden shows well the link between academic interest in botany and practical enrichments to gardening established from the earliest days by Danby's benefaction. The Physic Garden, 'beautifully walled and gated' as Parkinson described it, has always been a source of inspiration to gardeners. The beautiful Nicholas Stone gateway received the addition of the figures of Charles I and Charles II in the two niches of the arch in 1693. These were paid for by a fine imposed on Anthony Wood for libelling Lord Clarendon. The offending pages of his book were burned and the Vice-Chancellor, Dean Aldrich the amateur architect and arbiter of Oxford's taste, put the fine of £40 to good use by commissioning the statues.

Bobart was always remembered in Oxford as a remarkable eccentric. He is shown in all his portraits with an enormous beard which on rejoicing days he used to have tagged with silver.[8] Anthony Wood adds to the beard legend with his anecdote of 'Mark Colman, a melancholy distracted man, sometime a singing man at Christ Church, walking in the physic garden, catcht fast hold of his beard crying "Help! Help!"; upon which people coming and and enquiring of the

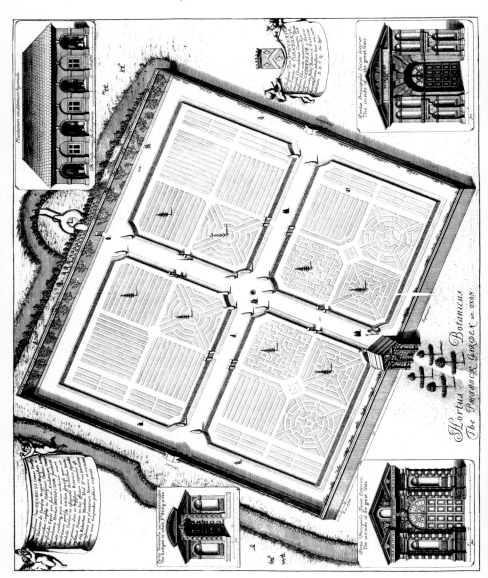

5.2 The Oxford Physic Garden

Plan in Loggan, *Oxonia Illustrata*, 1675, showing in top right corner
the early greenhouse. The plots were laid out in a formal design under
the direction of Professor Morison who had been Superintendent of
the gardens of the Duke of Orléans at Blois.

outcrie, Colman made reply that, "Bobart hath eaten his horse and his tayle hung out of his mouth".'

To add to Bobart's strange appearance visitors usually found him accompanied by a goat. This did not detract from his undoubted skill in his profession. Dr Plot described him as 'an excellent gardener and botanist' and clearly the old soldier was a very versatile man. He had no stipend during the Civil War and sold his fruit at Carfax and helped in college gardens to eke out a living. In the Magdalen accounts he appears as Jacobo Bobart hortulano. He may have received the odd tip from distinguished visitors such as John Evelyn calling in for 'hortulan refreshment.' His contract with the Founder of the Physic Garden for 'dressing, manuring and planting the sayed garden' he carried out assiduously. He was on good terms with both dons and undergraduates. The Rev. John Ward, who in later years became a botanist of some standing himself, wrote with enthusiasm of what he had learned from Bobart in the days before a Professor of Botany was appointed. He noted how he spread white sand under his plants so that he could see when the seeds needed for propagation and distribution fell. He had the gift of diffusing knowledge as well as having a love of plants. His topiary yew giants, which he had formed himself, stood at the entrance to the garden and were greatly admired. Poems were written in their honour and they were illustrated by Loggan in his view of the Hortus Botanicus.

Bobart became extraordinarily proficient in fruit-growing. He took pride in presenting his figs to the Vice-Chancellor and one year counted 500 balusters on his double pomegranate tree which had grown as high as the walls. Not every gardener could claim the personal interest of the great Boyle, who was a near neighbour until 1668. The eminent Dutch Professor of Botany and Medicine, Hermann Boerhaave, said of Boyle that 'to him we owe the secrets of fire, air, water, animals, vegetables, fossils; so that from his works may be deduced the whole system of natural knowledge.' Both Boyle and John Evelyn were interested in the conservation of plants in special greenhouses, and it is not surprising that Oxford had one of the first greenhouses in the country. The earliest one was situated on the High Street, as shown in

Loggan, and was 60 feet long. It had an arcaded front and solid roof in the manner of an orangery. It was heated in severe weather by hauling around the pathways a grated iron wagon filled with burning charcoal. It was not until 1691 that Evelyn, after discussion with Wren and Hooke, published a design for an internally heated green house. This means of housing tender greens became a true Royal Society interest. The founding of the Royal Society in 1662, which consolidated the work done in Oxford during the Interregnum, was a great Restoration boost for natural philosophy and Boyle had been one of its projectors.

Bobart died in 1679 and was buried in the churchyard of St Peter's-in-the-East. His memorial is inscribed: 'To the Pious Memory of Jacob Bobart, a native German. A man of great integrity, chosen by the founder to be the keeper of the Physic Garden. He dyed Feb 4. 1679 in the 81st year of his age.' Professor Morison was killed in a coach accident in London in 1683. Bobart's son, also Jacob, took over both posts. His second son Tilleman worked under him before setting up as a professional gardener and working at Blenheim, Wroxton, Hampton Court and Canons. Both advised on Oxford college gardens as their father had done, but it is not clear which of the brothers was consulted about the New College gardens, as reference is merely to 'Mr Bobart.' The younger Jacob Bobart was, like his father, a man of many parts. He had enterprisingly sold not only the fruits of the garden at Carfax but also his seeds in London. He circulated a seed list for exchange among botanic gardens,[9] which proved to be the beginning of an important world-wide service. He obviously enjoyed teasing academics as well as profiting from their knowledge and it was said that once when he found a dead rat in the Physic Garden he made it look like the 'common pictures of dragons, by altering its head and tail, and thrusting in taper sharp sticks, which distended the skin on either side till it mimicked wings . . . The learned immediately pronounced it a dragon.' Later Bobart admitted the deception but the object was looked upon as a work of art and deposited in the Museum. It has been suggested that the Oxford Almanack illustration of 1719 celebrated this story.[10] As a boy Bobart the younger would have met

Boyle, Hooke and Evelyn in his father's garden and would have been impressed by their powerful enquiring minds and empirical attitudes. He also learned from his father to look and learn and it was from such observations that he drew the inference of sexual reproductions in plants. After Robert Morison's death he completed Part 3 of his unfinished *Planatarum historiae universalis Oxoniensis* in which Hearne said he was greatly assisted by Mr Dale of the Queen's College who 'put it into proper Latin for him.'

The Physic Garden continued in its well established role of Use and Ornament and was praised by John Ayliffe of New College in his *Antient and Present State of the University of Oxford* in 1714 for the pleasure it gave as a means of relaxation and as a storehouse of vegetative philosophy. 'It was,' he said,

> for the Use and Honour of the University; serving not only for Ornament and Delight and the pleasant Walking and Diversion of Academical Students and of all Strangers and Travellers; and of great use, as is easily found, among all persons willing to improve their Botanical inclinations and studies and for the pleasant Contemplation and Experience of Vegetative Philosophy, for which is here supposed to be as good Convenience as in any Place of Europe (if not the best) and also for the service of all Medicinal Practitioners, supplying the Physicians, Apothecaries, and who else shall have occasion for things of that nature with what is right and true, fresh and good for the service of Health and Life.

When the German Zacharias Von Uffenbach visited Oxford in 1710 he thought that the number of items did not approach the interest of either Leyden or Amsterdam and was critical of the classification used. He was rather taken aback by the appearance of the Professor-cum-Gardener, although he admitted that his work in the garden was praiseworthy:

> We entered the Hortus Medicus and Professor Bobart was waiting for us. I was greatly shocked by the hideous features and generally villainous appearance of this good and honest man. His wife, a filthy old hag, was with him, and although she may be the ugliest of her sex he is certainly the more repulsive of the two. An Unusually pointed and very long nose, little eyes set deep in the head, a twisted mouth almost without upper lip, a great deep scar in one cheek and the whole face and hands as black and coarse as those of the poorest gardener or farm-labourer. His clothing and

especially his hat were also very bad. Such is the aspect of the Professor, who might most naturally be taken for the gardener. In point of fact he does nothing but work continually in the garden, and in the science of botany he is the careful gardener rather than the learned expert. Yet the industry of the man in publishing the works of his predecessor Morison, who far excelled him in learning, is as praiseworthy as his work in the garden.[11]

Bobart told his learned and critical visitors that two years previously he had lost a great deal in the cold weather whereupon he was informed that the cold winter had indeed robbed the botanical world not only of many plants but 'of three of the most famous Botanici who have ever lived, namely Tournefort of Paris, Hotton of Leyden, and Triumfetti of Rome.' Bobart then told the Europeans a fascinating story of a hi-jacked plant:

> As Dr Bobart was showing us *Amygdalus Nana Aegyptica flore pleno*, he told us how when he first got it Dr Hermann of Leyden was staying with him here in Oxford, and on seeing this plant, he had cried out with tears in his eyes: "That is my plant." This was actually true, for when he was bringing the plant home together with many others which he had been eleven years collecting in India amid great hardships, the ship was taken by a French privateer and the good man lost everything. Afterwards some of these plants were sent to Mr Bobart, and when he heard that they belonged to Dr Hermann he returned them to him.

Oxford took in its stride the aspect of the Professor of Botany, who according to the disdainful German savant might 'naturally be taken for the gardener.' Oxford valued the Bobarts' truly empirical gardening and their skill in the propagation and cultivation of plants. Plot referred to them in his *The Natural History of Oxfordshire* as 'those excellent Gardeners and Botanists, the two Bobarts,' and Dr Plot was not a man to make unchecked statements. Robert Plot took the degree of M.A. in 1664 and proceeded to Doctor of Law. He had been acquainted with the Wadham set and their empirical enquiries and it became his ambition to write a history of Nature in the county from enquiries sent out to its most ingenious men. His questionnaire[12] asked about everything concerning the heavens, waters, stones, metals, plants, husbandry, animals, arts, and antiquities in the county. It was the most comprehensive survey anyone of the day could

have thought up and his gardening enquiries included observations on 'what manure is most proper for this or that
natural earth, or what Earths are best mixt together, and for
what Plants most agreeable . . . what Insects are peculiar to
plants, and whether the same Plants have not sometimes different Insects, especially in dry and wet years . . . Has there
any body hereabout observed the diseases of Plants, or knows
ways of prevention or cure, especially of the blebs or blisters
we find on the leaves of many shrubs and trees? thinks he
them infected from the Air without, or by the juices within,
or by both?' Within the buildings of Oxford every possible
echo was investigated and measured in a way which would
have delighted Wilkins and Wren. The cloisters of New College
could 'return a Stamp or Voice, seven, eight, or nine times;'
on the East a dissyllable and on the West only a Mono-
syllable. Magdalen with a flat roof to the cloister could
produce nothing at all, but in the cloister of All Souls 'in the
North and West sides, where no Doors hinder, there is much
such another, which to the Stamp of ones Foot, or Clap with
the Hands, answers Four or Five times, with a Noise not
unlike the shaking of a Door.' The investigations were completed and published in 1677, dedicated to Charles II. Staffordshire was tackled next with the same enquiries sent
round and analysed and published in 1683. The Staffordshire
squires who received the enquiries used to boast that they
had "humbugged old Plot" when they filled them in. Oxford
academics seemed to take it all seriously enough and went to
work making echoes in their cloisters and gardens, and
landowners like James Tyrrell at Shotover, the friend of
Boyle, were only too pleased to make observations on
blights on their trees and stones 'curiously wrought by
nature.' Plot took part in many of the investigations himself
and his observations of an incident at Deddington suggests
that away from Oxford and its empirical traditions he was
aware that plots might be hatched against the ingenious
doctor:

> A Salt-spring there is also at Clifton near Deddington, within a
> Quoits-cast of the River side; but its saline Particles are so subti-
> lized in the Water, that they can scarcely at all be perceived by
> the Palate, and yet it lays them down plentifully enough on the

Stones and Earth over which it passes. What sort of Salt this is I care not to determine, because it will be difficult not to mistake; for upon Evaporation of about a Galon, it yielded a Salt of a Urinous Taste; which at first I must confess was so surprising to me, that I could not but think, that during my absence, some waggish Fellow had either put a Trick on me, or else that I might have used some unfit Vessel; whereupon I caused a new Earthen Pot to be bought, well glazed, and then repeated the Experiment very carefully, but found in the end all had been honest about me, for I had a Salt of the very same Taste.[13]

It was surprising that the learned doctor should have had time for anything else besides his sorting and sifting experimentation but he was Secretary to the Royal Society and published their transactions for 1683 and 1684. In 1683 he became the first Keeper of the Ashmolean Museum and the University lecturer in Chemistry.

The Ashmolean Museum in Broad Street was a scientific institution rather than a Museum, with a library, a chemical laboratory fitted with furnaces, and a dissection room. It began as a repository for 'John Tredeskin's rarity' and was first opened during a royal visit on 21st May 1683 as the first public museum in Britain. Tradescant the elder who had been unable to take up his appointment as Horti Praefectus of Danby's Physic Garden could not have known when he died in 1638 that his name was after all to be linked with Oxford. During his plant hunting exploits he had looked around with a gardener's delight in all Nature's rarities and had collected all manner of curiosities including shells, fauna and precious stones and on his return displayed them in the Ark or Cabinet of Rarities at his Lambeth House. His son added to it and was helped in the compiling of a catalogue by Elias Ashmole who inherited the collection at the death of Tradescant the younger and presented it to his University in 1682.[14] The rarities which had been for the London Public in the nature of baubles in the Lambeth Museum cum Garden Centre became the basis of scientific study in Oxford. Ashmole, who was a founder fellow of the Royal Society, saw that a study of anthropology was a way to understand Man and Nature and that Tradescant's collection was best placed in the care of the painstakingly, empirically-minded Dr Plot, whose natural history survey had proved his undoubted abilities. The rarities were sent down by barge from Lambeth and on March 20th 1683 Anthony Wood described the arrival of the collection for the new musum: 'Twelve Cartloads of Tredeskyns rarities Came from Mr Ashmole at London at his new Elaboratory at Oxon.' The cases, which included the remains of the last Dodo, were enthusiastically unpacked by Robert Plot. 'Many that are delighted with the new philosophy are taken with them,' commented Wood, 'but some of the old look upon them as baubles. Christ Church men not there.' Perhaps the clerics had some premonition that the study of such anthropological matter would lead to ideas about evolution. The Museum, built by a local mason, Thomas Wood, delighted everybody and the undergraduates called it Plot's 'knickknackatory.'

The 'vegetable rarities' that came in the Tradescant collection have long since disappeared, although at the beginning of this century R.T. Gunther discovered a botanical rarity which had been part of the collections, in the shape of a bamboo cane 60ft long. The Hortus Siccus made by the Tradescants is now in the Bodleian Library. When the new University Museum was built in 1860 most of the Tradescant collection, including the remains of the Dodo, was transferred there, but now in the new Ashmolean Museum in Beaumont Street a Tradescant Room has been made to celebrate the tercentenary of the founding of the original museum. The name of the gardener founder is thus honoured in its own right and plants cultivated and introduced by the Tradescants to England, such as the *Tradescantia virginiana*, will grow in the windows. The rarities they collected on their travels are displayed in an Ark-like atmosphere. They include the deerskin mantle attributed to Powhatan, a Russian abacus, and an African drum.

6

The Grand Manner in Oxford

New college building after the Restoration took longer to complete than garden designs. The college most in need of further work was Wolsey's Christ Church, which was still uncompleted. No new building in the main quandrangle had been undertaken since its sixteenth-century foundation and in the 1630s a member complained that it looked more like a ruin than a college.[1] Piles of stone had been left on the north side of the quadrangle in front of the unfinished chapel, the entrance to the hall was still an unworthy make-shift one, and cattle, which wandered in from the open north side, were often to be seen grazing in what the Cardinal had planned to be the grandest show place in Oxford.

The impetus to complete Christ Church had first come in the time of Dean Duppa, whose building aspirations were largely inspired by the Treasurer Samuel Fell, who was to become Dean in 1638. In 1634, when so many chapels were being upgraded in the Laudian Revival, improvements were made in the cathedral to make it more suitable for college services and, as Wolsey's idea for a separate chapel was then finally abandoned, the site could be cleared and plans be made to finish the Great Quadrangle. The first needs were to cover the hall staircase, to build a north bastion on the west front of the college to correspond with the one built by Wolsey on the south and to build lodgings on the north side of the quadrangle to house the canons and keep the cattle out. Only the beautiful fan-vaulted staircase, executed with real Gothic flair as the Founder had intended, was completed, however, before once again work on Christ Church was halted. This time the interruption was caused by the Civil War and by Charles I taking possession of the royal foundation.

Nothing was done during the Interregnum and the parliamentarians actually removed the timber intended to roof the buildings begun on the north side of the quadrangle. Dean Fell had been evicted from the Deanery but Mrs Fell defiantly refused to leave her home even when the Roundheads moved in and smoked and used foul language over her. In the end she and her children had to be carried out into the quadrangle on planks 'going like so many Pyes to the Oven,' as Anthony Wood observed, but not before it was rumoured she had concealed some precious items in the Deanery garden.

John Fell, their son, enthusiastically applied himself to the task of finishing his father's building when he became Dean at the Restoration. Subscriptions poured in from old members[2] as a thank-offering but, although Dean Fell strove to carry out Wolsey's wish to build a college to compete with the palace of princes, it was the spirit rather than the letter of the Cardinal's wishes that he chose to follow. His father had intended to erect Redman's projected cloisters, for which the great fan-vaulted staircase already built was to have provided the climax. In the 1660s, more in keeping with the spirit of the age, the low walls which had been intended for the cloisters were covered up and the shafts from which the fan-vaults would have sprung were smoothed back to form the blind arcades seen in the Loggan engraving. The rhythm of the arcades was continued on the walls of the new canonries built on the north side of the quadrangle. The east tower was levelled to make the east side of the quadrangle regular and a classical balustrade on the roof substituted for Wolsey's intended battling. The Great Quadrangle now assumed a uniform Renaissance appearance. The central space was used to enhance the buildings and, in order to increase the impressive effect, the quadrangle was lowered leaving a broad gravelled terrace in front of the arcaded walls. Stately steps were built down to the sunken quadrangle and a basin and

6.1 Christ Church after the Restoration

The great quadrangle completed, buildings levelled, balustrade and blind arcades added to give uniformity. Baroque steps, gravel terraces, globe and serpent fountain made it the grandest quad in Oxford. Tom Tower by Wren was to complete the spectacle in 1682. (Loggan, 1675).

jet d'eau placed in the middle, which served as a reservoir. A Chapter order of 22 July, 1670 records the act and names the donor:[3]

> Whereas Richard Gardiner, Doctor in Divinity, and Senior Prebend of this Church, hath at his own cost and charges in the Great Quadrangle belonging to this Church made one large bason 40ft in the diameter of stone work and lead well soldered, and in the midst thereof a rock of stone with a large globe covered with lead and gilt, and a fountain of water conveyed through the centre of the said rock and globe by a pipe running through the mouth of the serpent into the said bason, expending in the same work the sum of £250 and upwards, to the great beautifying and adorning of the said Quadrangle; in consideration whereof it is this day ordered by the said Dean and Chapter, and they do for themselves and their successors promise and grant that the said bason, rock, globe and fountain shall from time to time be ever hereafter repaired, maintained and kept by the said Dean and Chapter and their successors.

Twenty-five years later Canon Anthony Radcliffe, himself a member of the said Chapter, presented the college with a statue of Mercury, the body of lead, the head and neck of bronze, to replace Dr Gardiner's globe and serpent, the work of William Bird.

Loggan shows the new Christ Church of the 1670s with the grand uniform quadrangle, the baroque steps, globe and serpent fountain and the formal gravel walks. There was nothing to compare with such grandeur in Oxford; the Queen's College had a grassed quadrangle, All Souls quad was paved; and Brasenose had a fenced knot garden in the centre of the front quadrangle. The sunken quadrangle space at Christ Church gave additional height and consequence to the buildings, but this arrangement would not have been possible if Wolsey's college had been completed, as had been intended in the 1630s, with cloisters. The dominating feature of Christ Church, Tom Tower, is missing in Loggan and the gatehouse is shown uncompleted.

Only one man was fitted for the challenging task of building on to the work of Henry Redman, the great medieval master-mason — Christopher Wren, Savilian Professor of Astronomy and architect of St Paul's. It was twenty years since he had put up his first building, the Sheldonian Theatre, in Oxford, but he had maintained close contacts. Whatever his brief from Dean John Fell had been, when sending his proposed plan for the tower to cover the gatehouse, Wren informed the Dean in a letter dated May 26th, 1681:

> I am resolved it ought to be Gothick to agree with the Founder's worke, yet I have not continued soe busy as he began. It is not a picture I send you or an imperfect Essay but a design well studied as to all its bearing.[4]

Not only had Wren to complete the medieval gateway as seen from the street with all its Gothic 'business' but also, on the inner side, to complete Fell's elegant Italianate quadrangle with the emphasized rhythm of the blind arcades and its now classical elegance. Tom Tower was a wonderful architectural solution uniting the medieval and the new enlightenment of thought in which Wren had played so great a part. 1681 had been another occasion when the eyes of the nation had been turned on Oxford. Charles II had chosen Oxford as the stage to play out his struggle with his Parliament, summoning it to meet there as his father had done, feeling that he could count on its loyalty. The schemes of Monmouth and Shaftesbury were defeated and it seemed as though the Whigs were ruined. The Epilogue written by Dryden for a play performed before the King at the time of the Oxford Parliament commends Oxford and all it stands for as the place to learn reconciliation of old and new thinking:

> This Place the seat of Peace, the quiet Cell
> Where Arts remov'd from noisy business dwell,
> Shou'd calm your Wills, unite the jarring parts,
> And with a kind Contagion seize your hearts:
> Oh, may its Genius, like Soft Musick move,
> And tune you all to Concord and to Love.
> Our Ark that has in Tempests long been tost,
> Cou'd never land on so secure a Coast.
> From hence you may look back on Civil Rage,
> And view the ruines of the former Age.
> Here a New World its glories may unfold,
> And here be sav'd the remnants of the Old.

Wren, the royalist, had learned the art of conciliation and open-mindedness from Cromwell's brother-in-law Dr Wilkins in his Wadham days. Tom Tower is an architectural reflection of the idea of continuity between the 'glories' of a

New World and respect for the 'remnants of the Old.' It was the year Wren became President of the Royal Society. The two events are eulogized in the Oxford Almanack for 1683, in which the illustration shows a group of mathematicians in the foreground paying tribute to Wren and the Royal Society with a backdrop of the Oxford skyline newly graced by Tom Tower.[5]

The publication of the Almanacks had been instigated by John Fell in 1673 and it was Henry Aldrich who was responsible for most of the designs. Aldrich of Christ Church, like Wren a man of wide interests and accomplishments who came to architecture through mathematics, showed his admiration for the architect of Tom Tower in his Almanack illustration, the first to identify an Oxford building specifically in an allegorical scene. Henry Aldrich played a great role at Christ Church, being Dean from 1689-1710. He went up in 1662 and remained there for the rest of his life. He wrote a treatise on geometry, was skilled in chemistry, heraldry and logic, and was a highly trained and gifted musician. He wrote many anthems, but is chiefly remembered for his round 'Hark the bonny Christ Church bells.' His mathematical mind and sense of harmony equipped him for his career as a gifted Oxford amateur architect. All Saints Church in the High Street has been attributed to him and he may have been involved with Trinity College Chapel, the Fellows' Building at Corpus, and the Queen's College library. Unfortunately, all his personal papers were destroyed at his death, in accordance with his will, so that there is no record of his activities. Undeniably his work, however, includes Peckwater Quadrangle at his own college, as the foundation stone of 1705 described Aldrich as the architect. Anthony Radcliffe, the donor of Mercury to the Great Quadrangle basin, was the benefactor for the Dean's new building.

Peckwater Quadrangle with its Palladian uniformity was an innovation, not only in Oxford but in the whole country. Many of the young men who occupied the Peckwater staircases would in later years live in the Palladian country houses which were to spring up all over Georgian England, but in 1710 when von Uffenbach saw Aldrich's new building and described it as 'well and sumptuous like a royal castle with a corps de logis and two wings, one of which is not yet finished,' this was new indeed. It was rare praise from von Uffenbach. He who had turned his nose up at the Physic Garden had also disliked collegiate Oxford. Merton had only 'ugly old buildings' and Magdalen was 'badly built.' As for the rest of Christ Church he found the Perpendicular Hall 'fearfully large and high but otherwise poor and ugly in appearance; it also reeks so strongly of bread and meat that one cannot remain in it.'

Dean Aldrich's Palladianism was the result of an academic classicism rather than that of a dilettante cult. The Dilettanti Society, formed for those who had travelled in Italy and devoted to the patronage of the fine arts, only came into being in 1732. The Grand Tour only became routine for the aristocracy after the Peace of Utrecht in 1713, which made European travel possible, and it was the returning Whig aristocrats, who had seen at first hand the Palladian buildings copied by Inigo Jones in the early seventeenth century, who were responsible for the Palladian Revival in England. Peckwater was, however, being lived in before Coke of Holkham and Lord Burlington set out on their Grand Tours, and fourteen years before William Kent had returned from Italy to play his part in Burlington's Palladianism. It was also before two influential publications, the first volume of Colen Campbell's *Vitruvius Britannicus*, and Leoni's English translation of Palladio's *Four Books of Architecture*, appeared, in 1715. Although Aldrich travelled as a young man his enthusiasm for architecture was aroused by contact with Wren and by the study of original books on architecture in the Oxford libraries. Aldrich was an outstanding collector of books and engravings long before such collections became fashionable with the Burlingtonians. Many of his Italian and French engravings were of architectural subjects and his three thousand books of classical authors included the architectural works of Alberti, Palladio, Scamozzi and Serlio. He studied his collections deeply and his studies bore fruit in his own drawings and architectural works. His own book on architecture, containing many quotations from Vitruvius and Palladio, was published after his death as *Elementa Architecturae Civilis* (1789).

When Dean Aldrich died in 1710 his place as Oxford's virtuoso and man of taste was taken by his friend Dr Clarke, Fellow of All Souls. George Clarke had been away from Oxford and had engaged in public affairs, unlike Dean Aldrich, and would have known the London set of cultivated men. He departed from politics after the death of Queen Anne in 1714 and retired permanently to Oxford, to scholarship and architecture.[7] He was the promoter and patron of Hawksmoor, who was responsible for most of Oxford's baroque-style university and college buildings, particularly at All Souls and including the Clarendon Building. Hawksmoor was a pastmaster of baroque grandiloquence, having been co-creator with Vanbrugh of the great houses of Castle Howard and Blenheim. The nearness of Blenheim to Oxford brought contact with architects, craftsmen and designers of great distinction who had all been called in to work on the great palace given to the Duke of Marlborough by the grateful nation. It also called on the abilities of the Oxford college masons in the execution of the designs. One man in particular, William Townesend,[6] the Christ Church mason, who worked with all the leading architects and garden designers at Blenheim, greatly profited by his experience and later worked independently not only in Oxford but on houses and gardens of neighbouring country estates. Townesend came of a well-known family of masons who owned most of the quarries near Oxford and were greatly experienced in building in stone. Townesend had not travelled but he knew every pinnacle, niche and arch in Oxford, whether designed by Redman or Wren, and the amateur architects Dean Aldrich and Dr Clarke relied greatly on the practical skill of the ingenious mason in carrying out their designs. Dean Aldrich died before the library planned for the South side of Peckwater quadrangle was built and the designs for it were made by George Clarke and executed by Townesend. Their building matches up to the Blenheim concept of grandeur, and with its giant Corinthian columns and broad bays is in startling contrast to the restraint of the rest of the quadrangle. Elsewhere in England the Palladian was to oust the Baroque but at Christ Church, because Aldrich had anticipated the Palladian Revival, his Peckwater buildings were put up before the library was begun in 1717 in the mood of Blenheim.

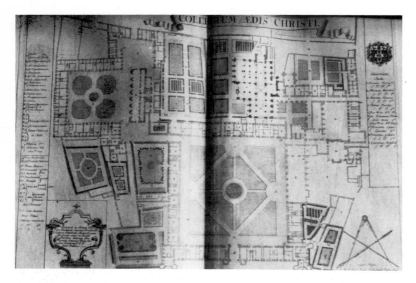

6.2 Christ Church: the plan of 1733
The plan of Christ Church, from *Oxonia Depicta* of 1733 by William
Williams.

The interrelationship of the buildings and the spaces
between them in Peckwater allow an exciting baroque
progress. At Blenheim the progress to the baroque palace
was, in the Vanbrugh-Hawksmoor pre-landscape era, through
an avenue over a mile long, planted in the formation of the
Battle of Blenheim by Tilleman Bobart of the Physic Garden
family, with the Column of Victory to Marlborough inset,
and continuing over Vanbrugh's bridge until finally the
carriage brings one face to face with the monumentality of
the building. The build-up of sensation is achieved through
changes of levels along the ride to give the impression of an
approach to a distant citadel. Landscape could not be pressed
into service in this way in the limited space of Oxford quadrangles, which had to be negotiated on foot. The baroque
sensation had to be achieved through Space and Movement.

The Peckwater progress is now suitably begun through a
triumphal arch at Canterbury Gate but this was only added
by Wyatt in 1773. One is confronted by the impressive end
of Clarke's massive library, but instead of walking by the
main facade the visitor should then proceed to walk round
the eastern side of Aldrich's buildings to a central point. The

6.3 Peckwater Quad: the plan achieved

Baroque shapes of grass and paths, taken from the unexecuted designs in *Oxonia Depicta*, were laid down in 1978. They tie up the Palladian symmetry of the three sides of the quad with the baroque library and lead the eye through to Wren's Tom Tower.

centre of the quadrangle has baroque grass shapes which serve to unite the Palladian symmetry of the three sides of the quadrangle with the sculptural baroque effects of the giant columns of the two-coloured stone library building. The sweeping curves of the contrasting gravel coloured paths lead the eye through the gap between the library and the west side of Peckwater to the supreme visual satisfaction of Wren's tower. The walk continues round the western end of the library when suddenly, in a more confined space, the cathedral spire bursts on the eye. An additional visual surprise is provided by the reflecting panes of the windows on the main facade: these are alternating convex and concave in the bays so that in one there is an intriguing reflection of Peckwater with the spire of Aldrich's All Saints above, followed by the reverse view with the spire, chimney pots and pediments upside down. Dr Clarke had intended the library, Renaissance fashion, to be on the first floor with an open piazza underneath, but a later benefaction of pictures necessitated the conversion of the arcade into a room to house the bequest and these windows were inserted.

The layout of the new Peckwater Quadrangle is shown clearly in *Oxonia Depicta* of 1733 by William Williams. The baroque shapes shown in the centre were probably never laid down but in 1978 when the quadrangle had to be levelled and resurfaced it was decided to carry out what the eighteenth-century eye had intended to complement the buildings of Aldrich and Clarke. It was only when the shapes had been formed using the small guide in *Oxonia Depicta* that it was realised how effective the eighteenth-century eye was in the treatment of the surroundings of its buildings. Whereas Loggan accurately illustrated what he saw from his chosen vantage points of the Oxford of the 1670s, Williams includes in his depictions unexecuted designs he learned of in the course of his survey work and discussions.

Oxonia Illustrata and *Oxonia Depicta* are sixty years apart and a comparison between the two shows how much Oxford colleges had changed in terms both of growth and fashion. The garden layouts have become noticeably more sophisticated and even the canons of Christ Church are shown as having baroque volute-shaped edgings to their garden plots.

6.4 New College Mount seen through the garden gate
The Mount, described by Celia Fiennes as having 'a round of green
paths, defended by greens cutt low' is now overgrown. The wrought
iron screen linking the North and South ranges of the new buildings was
erected in 1711 by Thomas Robinson.

The poor scholar of Oxenford sharing his sleeping accommodation had largely been replaced by the gentleman commoner
who wanted his own room or set of rooms. New ranges were
put up in most colleges in the first decades of the century.
Magdalen's new building was free-standing and when the deer
were put in the grove around it in 1740 it looked like a
Petworth. Other colleges extended on the existing buildings,
often to give quadrangles opening onto the gardens. The
Garden Quadrangle at New College developed most successfully in two stages. It was originally envisaged as a conven-
tional closed quadrangle but there were obvious advantages in
leaving one side open to the garden. Wren had already in
1668 advocated the abandonment of the quadrangle in the
Trinity scheme and, knowing the conservatism of Oxford,
added that if benefactors insisted on having one, then 'let
them have a quadrangle, though a lame one, somewhat like a
three-legged table.'[9] The second stage of the New College

development was largely the work of William Townesend, and his buildings, stepped back from those already built by William Bird in 1682, gave the appearance of a perspective stage set from an Italian engraving. The entrance front of Versailles had clearly influenced Wren and others in designing garden courts. At New College the stepping back of the later buildings was almost inevitable to the design when fellows did not wish their views of the garden to be obstructed. In 1714 John Ayliffe described the completed quadrangle as 'erected according to the model of the Royal Palace of Versailles, saving that it is not built with pillars; or to come nearer home, 'tis of the like plan with the Queen's House at Winchester, with its several projections and fallings back in a uniform and elegant manner.' The finishing touch to the Versailles appearance was the linking of the north and south ranges of the new buildings by a handsome wrought iron screen with gates to the garden. The screen was erected in 1711 by Thomas Robinson, who had worked for the emigré Tijou, and the money had been provided by the Duke of Chandos of Canons fame. The Michael Burghers engraving of *The Ichonography of New College* of 1708 shows two gardeners measuring the ground where the screen was to be laid.

Dr Clarke was instrumental in giving a new look to Brasenose front quad which in Loggan is seen planted with an old-fashioned railed knot garden. In 1727 he presented his old college with a statue group of Cain and Abel, a leaden replica after Giovanni de Bologna's 'Samson killing the Philistine,' which had been presented to Charles I on his visit to Spain as Prince of Wales in 1623 and given to the Duke of Buckingham. It was referred to by John Pointer as a 'fine, yet shocking, Statue of Cain and Abel' in *Oxoniensis Academia* (1749) and at the time of its erection, Thomas Hearne, the Oxford antiquary, commented sourly:

> Last week they cut down the fine pleasant garden in Brasenose College Quadrangle, which was not only a great Ornament to it, and was agreeable to the quadrangles of our old monasteries, but was a delightful pleasant Shade in Summer Time, and made the rooms, in hot seasons, much cooler than otherwise they would have been. This is done, by the direction of the Principal and

some others purely to turn it into a grass Plot and erect some silly
statue there.[10]

The Victorians sold the 'silly statue' for scrap in 1881.

The biggest and grandest face-lift that Oxford might have
been given was, as most people would now agree, mercifully
abandoned. This was the baroque town-planning scheme put
forward in 1712 by Hawksmoor, at the same time as he
produced a plan for 'the town of Cambridge as it now ought
to be reformed,' which was also rejected.[11] Wren had begun
to dramatize the academic scene with the building of the
Sheldonian theatre but Hawksmoor planned a great academic
complex, uniting university and town visually with the lining
up of objects and vistas as in the Rome of Sixtus V. The
Sistine plan was, however, for a sixteenth-century Rome
much shrunken within its ancient layout and vistas were to
be opened on to distant classical buildings. There was little
opportunity in Oxford for intersecting vistas on an heroic
scale and (as ideas have changed) pleasure is now derived
from unexpected views of spires and domes from medieval
lanes. Although Hawksmoor's total design, which would
have included a Forum Civitatis at Carfax with colonnaded
buildings and a central Trajan's column, was rejected, the
baroque concept of Radcliffe Square as a University Forum
was master-minded by Hawksmoor.[12] The Radcliffe Camera,
built by James Gibbs in 1748, the Bodleian complex, St
Mary's and Hawksmoor's All Souls give a unique sequence of
architectural experiences in space and movement, which now
seem better enhanced by the approach through the narrow
lanes leading to the Square than opened up to the focal
column at Carfax as Hawksmoor had intended. A much-
altered Brasenose College would have had a new quadrangle
opening on to the High, a new university church would have
been built where Hertford College now stands and New College lane was to have been widened and straightened on the
axis of the Bodleian and an underground road, a 'Pausilyp,'
was planned under the New College mount.

Visitors today find the dark medieval windings of New
College lane one of the delights of an Oxford tour. New
College was founded at a time when the St Scholastica's
Day town and gown riots of 1354, when the streets ran with

blood, were still remembered and the college was built away from the main thoroughfares with a strong gatehouse and warden's rooms above to keep a watchful eye on all who came and went. A sense of history played no part in baroque planning, however, and the conservation view held today that the smaller town houses act as both foil and complement to the grand architecture would have astounded a Hawksmoor. Oxford had seen great changes in the first decades of the eighteenth century under Aldrich, Clarke, Hawksmoor and William Townesend, the right-hand man of the Oxford amateurs. The Warden of All Souls, Sir Nathaniel Lloyd, preached a sermon in 1721 observing that 'the Buildings in Oxford were so strangely altered and encreased that if our old Founders and Benefactors were to rise from the Dead, they would not know Oxford even in Oxford.'[13] The Warden, who himself was a benefactor, was clearly of the opinion that enough was enough. To do Nicholas Hawksmoor justice, he felt as his master Wren had done at Christ Church, that pious respect must be shown to the Founder's architecture and in the *Explanation of Designs for All Souls*,[14] February 1715 he made the statement that is now often quoted on title pages of books on the conservation of historic buildings; 'What ever is good in its kinde ought to be preserv'd in respect to antiquity, as well as our present advantage, for destruction can be profitable to none but Such as Live by it.' His assurance that in the old buildings he would not use 'ye founder Cruelly' may have been in response to the All Souls brief, as the proposed, but rejected, plan for Brasenose shows little respect for founders' intentions.[15] The new quadrangle with the Codrington library and the twin-towered range of buildings is Hawksmoor's true monument in Oxford; the design for the great south front on High Street was not carried out, nor was the cross portico leading across the old quadrangle to the Hall and Chapel. In 1734 the Warden took a firm stand; 'He Designs Grandly, for a College, I will not lead the College and myself into these Difficultys; into new plans, & new Worke. Wee shall not know where it will End.' Two years later when the architect and his patron Dr Clarke were dead and the indefatigable William Townesend was in his seventies, the Warden of All Souls wrote with evident relief: 'I reckon now, Hawksmooring and Townsending, is all Out for this Century.'

The new buildings at All Souls and elsewhere took away garden spaces and even the colleges built outside the city wall with room to expand had little scope for baroque vistas on the French scale, assuming they had wanted them. The grand formal landscape concepts belonged to the great houses of parade, and college gardens needed a more inward-looking treatment. The designs which influenced their layouts came from Holland rather than France. Dutch gardens were themselves a version of the French baroque but on a smaller scale, more detailed and intimate and less theatrical. There was also a strong connection with Holland after the Glorious Revolution which gave Dutch gardening a great boost in England.

7

The Glorious Revolution and Dutch gardening

Oxford had played a significant part in the Glorious Revolution of 1688 and the triumph of Whig ideas of constitutional liberty. The Stuarts exploited the traditional loyalty of Oxford to the Crown, and when Lord Shaftesbury's party was actively seeking to exclude James from succession Charles II dissolved Parliament at Westminster and ordered another one to meet in Oxford where he could count on the support of the University. As during the Civil War, the Court took up residence at Christ Church, where John Locke was a tutor. The Whig philosopher, who was friend and adviser of Lord Shaftesbury, retired to James Tyrrell's house for refuge. The Exclusionists were defeated at the end of the Oxford Parliament and suffered a further setback when support rallied to the King after the discovery of the Rye House plot in 1683. Lord Russell and Algernon Sidney perished on the scaffold and Lord Shaftesbury died in exile in Holland. Oxford tutors were ordered to instruct their pupils in the doctrine of passive obedience and Whig books were burned in the Bodleian quadrangle at what was, in fact, to be the last public burning of books in England. Locke was expelled from Christ Church by order of Charles II and fled to Holland in search of liberty of thought.

It was not long, however, before the views of Locke and the Whigs on absolutism were vindicated. James II, like Charles

I, chose Oxford for a demonstration of divine right, but this time the royal hand was overplayed. In 1687 he expelled the Fellows of Magdalen, intending to turn their college into a Roman Catholic seminary, and followed his action by a declaration of indulgence admitting Roman Catholics to office. The loyalty of the University was to the Anglican church which provided livelihood and security to the colleges and this had hitherto been linked with loyalty to the Crown. Oxford had been instrumental in putting James on the throne and was up in arms at the expulsion of the Fellows. Orange colours were flown in the High Street, the doctrine of passive obedience was ended, and the Glorious Revolution soon followed. The resistance of the Magdalen dons is part of English history.

The arrival of William III from Holland as the constitutional monarch brought new gardening fashions to Oxford as else-where in his kingdom. Daniel Defoe recorded that 'It is since the Revolution that our English gentlemen began so univer-sally to adorn their gardens with those plants we call ever greens.'[1] The King was, Defoe continues, 'delighted with the decoration of ever greens, as the greatest addition to the beauty of a garden, preserving the figure in the place even in the roughest part of an inclement and tempestuous winter. With the particular judgement of the King all the gentlemen in England began to fall in; and in a few years fine gardens, and fine houses began to grow up in every corner; the King began with the gardens at Hampton Court and Kensington, and the gentlemen followed every where, with such a gust that the alteration is indeed wonderful throughout the whole kingdom.'

Walter Harris of New College was a great promoter of the King's Dutch gardening. He had come up as Founder's Kin in 1666 and had stayed on and practised medicine in the College. He became Physician to Charles II and later to Wil-liam III. He visited the King's palace of Het Loo and in 1699 wrote enthusiastically his detailed account of *The Gardens of Het Loo* in the hope that the 'reading might give some Diversion to the Curious, as the writing was pleasing to me. Also Persons of Quality, and Great Fortunes, may here find many things to Admire, and also to Imitate, if they please, when they are taking their Summer Diversions at their Country Seats.'

Dutch gardening had taken much from French ideas but the more restricted space of their gardens precluded grand vistas. Marot, the emigré pupil of Le Nôtre, had largely been responsible for adapting the French grand manner to the Dutch situation. The gardens were divided into compartments with more intricate boxwork, stunted trees and topiary work. Wrought iron gates and screens were popular through which the formal gardens could be surveyed to advantage. Daniel Marot worked on the King's broderie parterres at Hampton Court, where Tilleman Bobart of the Physic Garden family of Bobarts was also employed. The nurseries of Brompton Park, where the Kensington Museums now stand, flourished as all the garden-makers ordered more and more dwarf greens, moveable plants and exotics.

Fortunately a most lively and percipient young lady toured England 'on a Side Saddle in the time of William and Mary' and her comments on the journeys were later published.[2] The lady was Miss Celia Fiennes, granddaughter of the first Viscount Saye and Sele of Broughton Castle, near Banbury. She had an eye for the new building and gardening that were taking place in William's new reign. She admired the enfilade arrangement of house and garden, the 'through glides and vistos,' that she saw, and she gives details of the curiosities in cut hedges and trees everywhere to be seen in the new Dutch-style gardens. She dismisses the garden at Haddon Hall, which in spite of a fine grove of high trees and good gardens, could show 'nothing very curious as the mode now is.' She revels in the fashionable gardens with their gravel and grass walks, alleys of clipped trees, close arbours, topiary work, dwarf trees and 'grates to look through.'

Celia Fiennes took a particular pleasure in visiting Oxford in 1694. The Civil War had virtually been planned at Broughton Castle when Oxford was the Royalist capital and it was her grandfather 'Old Subtlety' who had occupied Oxford when Charles I withdrew. As 'Founder's Kin' he had been a Fellow of New College and his granddaughter inspected his college on her visit to Oxford and said with a patronising air:

New College which belongs to the Fiennes's, William of Wickham

the founder, so I look'd on my self as some way a little interested
in that; here I was handsomely entertained by Mr Cross which
was one of my Nephew Say and Seale's Tutors when at Oxford.

She thought the Fellows' apartments very well set up and
that they 'may live very neately and well if sober, and have
all their curiosityes.' The Fellows obviously enjoyed curiosities in their gardens and indulged in pot plants which were
set out upon the leads above in summer:

> They take much delight in greens of all sorts Myrtle Orange and
> Lemons and Lorrestine growing in pots of earth, and so moved
> about from place to place and into the aire sometymes; ther are
> severall New Lodgings added and beautifyed here, the Gardens
> also with gravell and grass walkes, shady, and a great mount in the
> middle which is ascended by degrees in a round of green paths
> defended by greens cutt low, and on the top is a Summer house,
> beyond these Gardens is a bowling-green, and round it a close
> shady walke, walled roung and a cutt hedge to the bowling-
> green.

Celia Fiennes's description 'walled round and a cutt hedge'
only comes to life when used in conjunction with the Williams engraving, where the full extent of the cutwork can be
appreciated. The beautiful stone town walls, which serve so
well as a background for the herbaceous border today, are
covered with cut yew panelling, as was the case in most of
the colleges. There are cut alcoves and doors in the hedges
and in front of the northern wall is a most complicated line
of stilted arched trees, rivalling anything that the New
College Fellow Walter Harris had seen and described in the
gardens of Het Loo. The gardens of Hartwell in Buckinghamshire, as seen in the well-known Nebot paintings, showed how
far the fashion for shaping trees architecturally could be
taken. The New College garden was covered with pyramids
and pillars cut in ornate shapes, and even the perambulating
dons in the Williams engraving might be topiary works.
William Gilpin, the picturesque traveller to be, described the
New College garden in 1742 with its cut greens still as shown
in Williams. He also describes the compartments of the
parterre made in Warden Pinck's day; a hundred years later it
has received some topiary additions: in one compartment
'you may discover His Majesty's arms cut out in box, in the
opposite one they have done as much for the Founder of

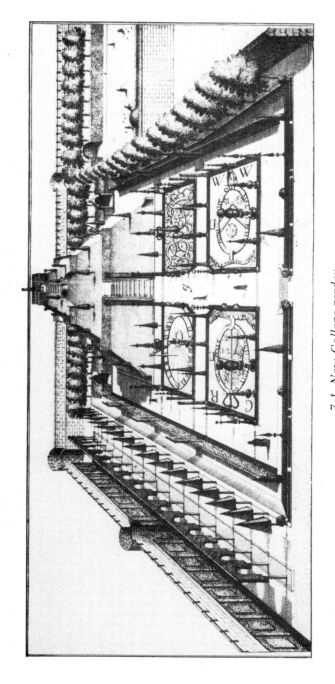

7.1 New College garden

From a print by William Williams (1732) dedicated to Lord Shaftesbury.
In front of the northern wall, a line of stilted arched trees.

their College, in the third you have a figure of a sundial cut out in the form of a Labyrinth.'[3] The difference between the Loggan and Williams depictions of the garden, apart from the additions of Celia Fiennes's well-loved 'curiosities' in evergreens, is the new appearance of grandeur given by the opening up of the courtyard. She did not see the beautiful Robinson wrought iron screen with gates to the garden which replaced the old visually restricting wall, but in her writings she always spoke approvingly of 'breast high walls' to gardens and 'grates to look through' which enabled a traveller on a side-saddle to 'discover the curiosities' within the gardens in the Dutch manner.

At St John's, Celia Fiennes had admired the 'fine grove of trees and walks all walled round.' When she saw the garden it was just being laid out in the manner shown in Williams and it was described more fully by Thomas Salmon in 1744. Of the two adjacent gardens, then separated by a stone wall, he says:

> In the first the walks are planted with Dutch elms, and the walls covered with evergreens: the inner garden has everything almost that can render such a place agreeable; as a terrace, a mount, a wilderness, and well-contrived arbours; but, notwithstanding, this is much more admired by strangers than the other, the outer garden is become the general rendezvous of gentlemen and ladies every Sunday evening in summer; here we have an opportunity of seeing the whole university together almost, as well as the better sort of townsmen and ladies, who seldome fail of making their appearance here at the same time unless the weather prevents them.[4]

It does seem a little strange, as Mr Salmon comments, that the outer garden with its stunted pollard Dutch elms should have been so popular. These palisades or pole-hedges were popular in Holland and were particularly decried by the next generations as 'green chests on poles.' In *La Théorie et la Pratique du Jardinage* (1709), D'Argenville describes designs of woodwork covering 'tall groves, close walks, quincunces, galleries and halls of verdure, green arbours, labyrinths.' It is difficult to know in which category the St John's outer garden fits. Perhaps it was a Verdant Hall with bowling greens or palisades with cabinets but, whatever it was, the citizens seemed to enjoy the whimsicalities that the Glorious

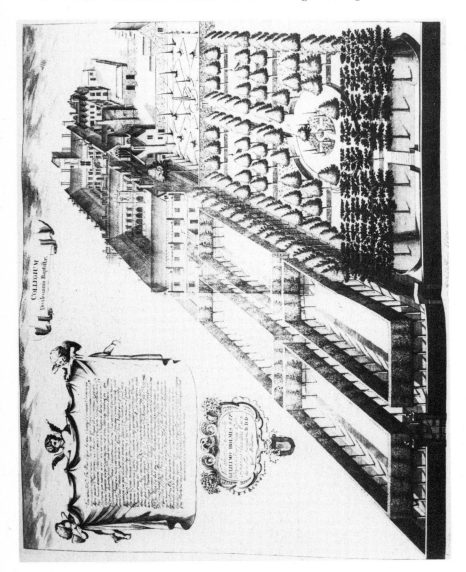

7.2 St John's College garden

Print by William Williams, 1732; showing the wilderness and garden of stilted elms.

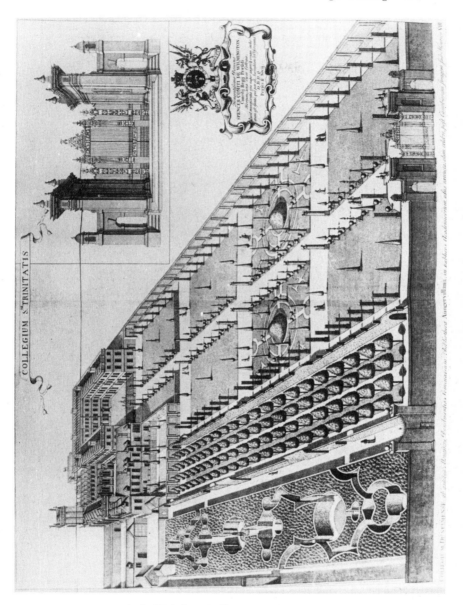

7.3 Trinity College garden, 1732
Such gardens were condemned by Addison as 'deviations from nature'.
Figures 7.1–7.3 from Williams, *Oxonia Depicta*, 1732.

Revolution had brought even to Oxford. Celia Fiennes had described similar stilted trees elsewhere as 'cut up smooth and about three or four yards up they lay frames of wood in manner of a penthouse, so plat the branches on it and cut it smooth.' The President's garden at St John's is entirely taken up with evergreen obelisks. Wadham went further in topiaried conceits and even sported topiary balustrades.

The formal evergreen craze was taken to an almost unbelievable extreme at Trinity College. It was first planted about 1706 and in the Loggan garden it is shown as quite unambitious and given over to domestic requirements, a farmyard, vegetable garden, pump and fruit trees trained along the walls. The President's lady walks her dog in a small garden consisting of a grass plot bordered by plants in pots. Beyond the walled garden the grove is laid out with pleasant gravel walks and naturally growing trees. What a transformation in the Williams depiction of the garden! The grove is regimented into pyramids and pillars of evergreens and the usual yew panelling adorns the stone walls. The most remarkable feature is the labyrinth cut out of block greens called by Salmon a 'wilderness adorned with fountains, close arbours, round stone tables, and other embellishments.' The beautiful grille set in urn-topped stone piers on Parks Road was erected in 1713. The wilderness was a formal arrangement of trees in a geometrical pattern, so often seen in the illustrations of gardens by Kip and Knyff in the first decade of the eighteenth century. The wilderness often included a bewildering maze as at Hampton Court or Trinity College.

The Oxford Almanacks also show some formal features of the college gardens. In 1743 a small topiary garden is shown at Lincoln and the 1726 illustration shows topiary shapes in the garden of Corpus Christi echoing that of the sundial in the front quadrangle. Bobart's Yew Men were flourishing when Joseph Addison was at Magdalen and were still guarding the entrance to the Physic Garden in *Oxonia Depicta*. Bobart tended his own topiary works in his Garden but many of the colleges would have bought well-formed specimens in containers from the local nurseries or may even have had them sent down from Brompton Park. Pots made out of hornbeam could also be obtained ready-shaped in which to grow standard trees.

The greens used in the formal college gardens would have been yew, Dutch box, juniper, phillyrea, the strawberry tree, bay, myrtle, laurestinus, oleander and pyracantha, most of which were mentioned by Celia Fiennes (quaintly spelt). Orange trees and the other tender greens would need stoves in the winter and, if a college went in for such delights, they would probably have been taken over to Bobart for him to take care of them. Practically all the cypresses in England had been killed in the severe winter of 1683–4.[5] A garden such as that of Trinity College would not be of unrelieved green colour. Variations were made by obelisks and globes of gold and silver hollies which would have stood out against the dark green of the yew panels and columns. Wrench, the nurseryman of Paradise garden, who supplied most of the college evergreens, specialized in variegations, an interest undoubtedly inspired by the work of Morison and Bobart at the Physic Garden. Wrench's brother kept a large nursery at Chelsea and the family gave rewards to encourage people to look out for accidental varieties from the common holly which would give ornamental effects such as saw-leaved and hedgehog varieties. One variegated holly still goes by the name of Wrench.[6]

8.1 Joseph Addison (1672—1719), MA,
Fellow of Magdalen College

'Great Patron of our Isis' groves
Whom Brunswick honours and Britannia loves'.

8

Addison, the prophet of natural gardening

The physicians, botanists, architects, craftsmen, nurserymen and just plain cooks who had determined the nature and design of the garden had their ranks joined in the eighteenth century by philosophers, poets and painters. The garden was seen to reflect the Spirit of the Age, and Enlightenment and the new national feelings of political liberty were felt to be unworthily represented both by the authoritarian French formality and the fussiness of Dutch taste. The garden, long-fettered by foreign ideas, was to develop a more representative native taste, natural and pleasing to the imagination and, as described by William Mason in *The English Garden*, shake off those ideas brought . . .

> Alike, when Charles, the abject tool of France,
> Came back to smile his subjects into slaves;
> Or Belgic William, with his warriour frown,
> Coldly declar'd them free; in fetters still
> The Goddess pin'd, by both alike opprest.[1]

The two critics of formal gardens whose writings led the way to landscape gardening were Addison and Pope.[2] Addison came first with his Spectator articles in 1712, and it was fitting that the spearhead attack on topiary and all its deviations from Nature should have come from a disciple of the Oxford natural scientists and a follower of John Locke. The

91

Oxford experiments and enquiries conducted by Plot and the natural historians had generated an interest in 'natural things', but this had not as yet influenced college gardens. On June 25, 1712 Joseph Addison of Magdalen College wrote in *The Spectator*:

> Our Trees rise in Cones, Globes, and Pyramids. We see the Marks of the Scissars upon every Plant and Bush. I do not know whether I am singular in my Opinion, but, for my own part, I would rather look upon a Tree in all its Luxuriancy and Diffusion of Boughs and Branches, than when it is thus cut trimmed into a Mathematical Figure; and cannot but fancy that an Orchard in Flower looks infinitely more delightful than all the little Labyrinths of the most finished parterre. But as our great Modellers of Gardeners have their Magazines of Plants to dispose of, it is very natural for them to tear up all the Beautiful Plantations of Fruit Trees, and contrive a Plan that may most turn to their own Profit, in taking off their Evergreens, and the like Moveable Plants, with which their Shops are plentifully stocked.

London and Wise and their Brompton nurseries must certainly have suffered in the wind of change when their grand customers turned to English gardening, but the colleges were always slow to change their gardening ideas and the Paradise gardens, stocked with evergreens for Oxford gardens, would have had plenty of time to adjust to accommodate ideas on natural gardening. Addison's call went largely unheeded in his University town since designs such as those of St John's and Trinity College would have taken years to grow to maturity and would not have been scrapped in their infancy. The century was well advanced before the colleges turned to landscape gardening and Trinity still had its formal gardens when Southey revisited Oxford in 1809.

Joseph Addison did have a considerable influence on the evolution of the English garden, however, particularly in the landscaping of the large estates, although he was not a notable gardener himself, nor a writer of a gardening treatise. His relaxed essays for the Spectator, written in the lucid prose advocated by Dr Wilkins, were said to have guided the manners and morals of the eighteenth century and to have exerted an influence stronger than that of the Bible. A few well-chosen paragraphs on estate management sparked off a gardening revolution. Addison's aim in writing the Spectator articles had been that he was 'ambitious to have it said of me, that I have brought Philosophy out of Closets and Libraries, Schools and Colleges to dwell in Clubs and Assemblies, at Tea-Tables and in Coffee-Houses.'[3] Addison had spent more than ten years in colleges, closets and libraries and during these years at Oxford he claimed that he had applied himself 'with so much Diligence to my Studies, that there are very few celebrated Books, either in the Learned or the Modern Tongues, which I am not acquainted with.'[4] He entered the Queen's College in 1687 at the age of 15 and was elected to a post-Revolution demyship at Magdalen two years later on the strength of his skill in Latin versification. After he had received his M.A. degree he was given a Fellowship which he held until 1711, although he ceased to reside or teach after 1699. In 1693 he gave an Encaenia oration on the merits of the new philosophy, which he claimed had effectively brought an end to metaphysics and scholastic philosophy. Locke's *Essay Concerning Human Understanding*, to which he was paying tribute, had been published three years previously.

Addison was a thorough-going empiricist and recognised, as Locke had done, that although it was the natural scientists who were advancing true knowledge, the same empirical principles could be directed to the understanding of the mental faculties. Addison was the first to suggest that the scientific enquiries and demonstrations on the laws of Nature would quicken 'a taste for the Creation' and give a new meaning to the 'works of Nature.' His statement in the Spectator that 'a beautiful prospect delights the Soul as much as a demonstration'[5] struck an entirely new note in 1712. The statement occurred in a series of essays called *The Pleasures of the Imagination*, most of which were written in his Oxford days and republished later for the Spectator.[6]

In *The Pleasures of the Imagination* Addison had sought to trace the source of aesthetic enjoyment in the same way as Locke had investigated our understanding. He considered the subject from many aspects, the pleasures to be derived from art, literature, architecture, the new philosophy and what would today be called the environment. The basis of his aesthetic theory was Locke's insistence that all knowledge was derived from sense perception and experience. As with sweetness, warmth, blueness and the like, Addison held that beauty was not a quality in the object but the result of form striking an internal sense through the organ of sight. This internal sense which could add the faculty of pleasure to perception he called the imagination, and he was at pains to emphasize that there was nothing in the imagination which had not been received by the organ of sight. This view was anathema to the later romantic imagination, which refused to accept that man was a mere looker-on in an external world.

Addison applied his theory of the direct psychological effect of form and colour on the beholder to architecture and gardening in a way which now seems oversimplified but was very convincing to the empirical mind. Largeness of scale was the source of great ideas, and for this reason bold classical outlines in buildings and wide prospects in landscapes extended the mind and pleased the imagination more than Gothic architectural detail or fussy gardens. The psychology of grand architectural concepts was then being applied by Hawksmoor in Oxford. The poet, James Thomson, took up the theme that 'what is great pleases the Imagination' and advocated a 'calm, wide survey' of landscape. 'There is something more bold and masterly in the rough careless Strokes of Nature, than in the nice Touches and Embellishments of Art,' wrote Addison in Spectator No. 414, his essay on the Pleasures of the Imagination relating to gardens. Although he offered philosophical reasons why the mind preferred natural, rural 'scenes to formal gardens, he was not advocating an actual system whereby gardens could be landscaped in a natural way.

> The Beauties of the most stately Garden or Palace lie in a narrow Compass, the Imagination immediately runs them over and requires something else to gratify her; but in the wide Fields of Nature, the Sight wanders up and down without Confinement, and is fed with an infinite variety of Images, without any stint or Number. For this reason we always find the Poet in love with a Country-Life, where Nature appears in the greatest Perfection, and furnishes out all those Scenes that are most apt to delight the Imagination.

Addison's ideas about what was pleasing to the mind were inseparably linked with the association of classical ideas,

particularly those aroused by Virgil's *Georgics*, which he
described as 'a Collection of the most delightful Landskips
that can be made out of Fields and Woods, Herds of Cattle,
and Swarms of Bees.' He had already published an *Essay on
the Georgics* in Dryden's translation of the Georgics (1697)
praising Virgil's poetry for addressing itself 'wholly to the
imagination. It is altogether conversant among the fields and
woods, and has the most delightful part of Nature for its
provinces. It raises in our minds a pleasing variety of scenes
and landscapes.'

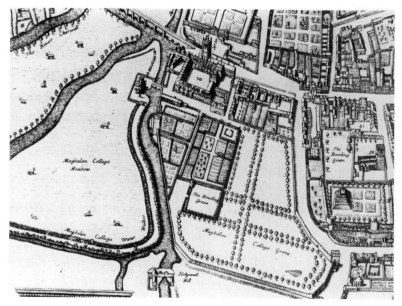

8.2 *The Magdalen walks*
From Loggan, *Oxonia Illustrata*, 1675.

While pondering his aesthetic philosophy and reading the
Georgics, Addison in his Magdalen setting had every opportunity to raise in his mind a 'pleasing variety of scenes and
landscapes,' which would have been denied to him if he had
been a Fellow of St John's College. He had rooms in the
north-east corner of the cloisters overlooking the Water
Walks, which were a constant source of delight to him, and in
the sight of fields and meadows. To the South and East

8.3 *The Cherwell walks*

Looking from the Christ Church side on to Magdalen. 'Philander used every morning to take a walk in a neighbouring wood, that stood on the borders of the Thames.'

Oxford was still in the rural keeping of the days of Duns Scotus with the Thames water meadows joining those of the Cherwell to make a green girdle round that part of the city. At Magdalen bridge the Cherwell branches into several streams and backwaters giving the college a large island meadow within its boundaries. The walks round it can clearly be seen on the Agas map of 1578 and extended on the Loggan map of 1675. Thanks to the provisions of William of Waynflete the meadows have become a nature reserve for botanists and naturalists over the centuries and Addision found there a due relish for the works of Nature and could take 'pains in forming his Imagination' in the way he counselled a Poet to do.

> He must love to hide himself in Woods and to Haunt the Springs and Meadows. His head must be full of the Humming of Bees, the Bleating of Flocks and the melody of Birds. The verdure of the Grass, Embroidery of the Flowers and the Glist'ning of the Dew must be painted strong in his Imagination.[7]

The Magdalen walks have frequently been compared to the classic haunts of the Muses. 'Go into the Water Walks,' urged Anthony Wood, 'and at some times of the year you will find them as delectable as the banks of Eurotas which were shaded with bay trees, and where Apollo himself was wont to walk and sing his lays.' William Collins delighted in them, as did Gerard Manley Hopkins and even Gibbon, who otherwise had not a good word to say for his college, fell under their spell when he had rooms in the New Building in the 1750s, and found the 'adjacent walks, had they been frequented by Plato's disciples, might have been compared to the Attic shades on the banks of Ilissus.' The New Building had not been erected in Addison's day and he walked out of his rooms over the small bridge into the Water Walks with gardens, orchards and groves on the western side and the grazed meadow to the East. For a longer walk he could continue on the Botanic Garden side of Magdalen bridge into the walks round Christ Church meadow leading to the Thames.

> Philander used every morning to take a walk in a neighbouring wood, that stood on the borders of the Thames. It was cut through by an abundance of beautiful allies, which terminating

on the water, looked like so many painted views in perspective. The banks of the river and the thickness of the shades drew unto them all the birds of the country, that at Sun-rising filled the wood with such a variety of notes, as made the prettiest confusion imaginable.[8]

It was these impressions of walks laid out through natural scenes that Philander recalled in the Spectator Essay no. 414 when the Imagination, he says, delights in 'a Prospect which is well laid out and diversified with Fields and Meadows, Woods and Rivers,' where a walker could also rejoice in the 'rough careless Strokes of Nature,' albeit from a gravel path. Here in these nature walks enjoyed in the Magdalen and Christ Church meadows the 'natural embroidery' of the meadows was greatly to be preferred to parterres of broderie as a pleasure of the Imagination. In these classic haunts Philander could slumber under the wafting trees and listen to the lowing of cattle with Virgil's 'Mugitusque boum, mollesque sub arbore somni' in his ears. 'The Poet,' Addison had written, must always be 'in Love with a Country-Life' and in pondering the question he had set himself the task of answering, 'What gives rise to the Pleasures of the Imagination?' he found that the philosopher and the poet were united in the high importance that must be given to rural scenes. What pleasure could the Imagination possibly derive from clipped rigid evergreens, abhorrent alike to man and birds, compared to 'Green Shadows of Trees, waving to and fro with the Wind' and woodland walks where the season's variations could be enjoyed accompanied by shade, movement and the melody of birds? There was already a strong poetic tradition of Albion's glades being the haunt of Wood-gods, of Orpheus with his lute making 'sweet Music's Power' in the trees and green thoughts in green shades. The time had come for the gardener to listen to the poets and philosophers.

Addison acquired his own estate at Bilton in Warwickshire when he lost office as Secretary of State after the fall of the Whigs in 1711, and it is as a new landowner, calling himself a 'Humourist in Gardening,' that he writes his Spectator essay no. 477, 6th September 1712. In it he points out that he was not one of the gardeners censured in Essay no. 414, who 'instead of humouring Nature, love to deviate from it as much as possible.' There were no clipped trees or 'artificial shows' at Bilton.

> Having lately read your Essay on the Pleasures of the Imagination, I was so taken with your thoughts on some of our English Gardens, that I cannot forbear troubling you with a letter upon that Subject. I am one, you must know, who am looked upon as a Humourist in Gardening. I have several acres about my house, which I call my Garden, and which a skilful Gardener would not know what to call. . . .
>   YOU must know, Sir, that I look upon the Pleasure which we take in a Garden, as one of the most innocent Delights in humane Life. A Garden was the Habitation of our first Parents before the Fall. It is naturally apt to fill the Mind with Calmness and Tranquillity, and to lay all its turbulent Passions at Rest. It gives us a great Insight into the Contrivance and Wisdom of Providence, and suggests innumerable Subjects for Meditation. I cannot but think the very Complacency and Satisfaction which a Man takes in these Works of Nature, to be a laudable, if not a virtuous Habit of Mind. For all which Reasons I hope you will pardon the Length of my present Letter.'

The 'Humourist' of Nature had become a practitioner of the tentative gardening theories put forward in his Spectator essays and, in 1713, was able to invite Alexander Pope, who held similar views, to Bilton telling him that he was 'wholly immersed in country business.' Atticus[9] — the satirical name given to Addison by Pope — was endeavouring to carry out the ideas of husbandry he admired in the *Georgics*. It was a time when landowners all over the country were in the throes of enclosure and agricultural improvement and Addison's remark in Spectator 414, the Gardens essay, 'But why may not a whole Estate be thrown into a kind of Garden by frequent Plantations, that may turn as much to the Profit as the Pleasure of the Owner?' had a powerful effect. This question has earned Addison a place in every book on garden history taken as it was with his condemnation of Dutch gardening. This section of the essay was added to his original treatise on *The Pleasures of the Imagination*, when this academic exercise was revised for publication in the Spectator. It was added some twenty years after Addison had left Oxford and had travelled in France and Italy,[10] joined the Kit Cat Club[11] and become a man of affairs and property.

He had not decried the great Le Nôtre gardens, as the land-

scapists were later to do, because they accorded with his
empirical philosophy that 'What is great pleases the Imagination' but he recognised that it was wrong to 'alienate so much
Ground from Pasturage, and the Plow.' Atticus's academic
delights in Virgil received an added stimulus when he trod on
'classic ground' in Italy,[12] and he returned home to call for a
new extensive form of estate gardening which would reconcile the satisfaction to the eye of Le Nôtre's unconfined
scenes with the Virgilian concept of Pleasure with Profit in
husbandry.

> Fields of Corn make a pleasant Prospect, and if the Walks were a
> little taken care of that lie between them, if the natural embroi-
> dery of the Meadows were helpt and improved by some small
> Additions of Art, and the Several Rows of Hedges set off by
> Trees and Flowers, that the soil was capable of receiving, a Man
> might make a pretty landskip of his own Possessions.

Addison said no more on the subject and retired to Bilton
but the cry 'in utile dolce!' was the slogan taken up by
Stephen Switzer in his *The Nobleman, Gentleman, and
Gardener's Recreation*, published in 1715 with proposals for
'Rural and Extensive Gardening,' which he also called a
'farm-like way of gardening.' Switzer acknowledged Joseph
Addison to be 'one of the greatest Genius's of this Age' and
quotes freely from his writings and through him from Locke
and Virgil; the contemplation of grand scenes rather than
'diminutive beauties,' raise an 'uncommon Pleasure in the
Imagination,' the Dutch taste is condemned and the wafting
of trees, warbling of Birds, the *mugitusque boum* and the
murmuring of streams become essential delights of the
garden. The confining walls of the garden should be thrown
down and the whole estate opened up so that the green
fields, meadows and rural scenes could be displayed to
delight and enlarge the mind of the beholder. It was an
auspicious moment for Switzer to encourage the peaceful
pursuit of gardening. The Marlborough Wars were over;
France was defeated; the Revolution Settlement ratified by
the Hanoverian Succession; England and Scotland were
united and the country set on a course of unprecedented
prosperity. No longer could a man be impeached or his
property seized on account of opposition to the State, and

8.4 The Holywell corn mill

The Holywell mill was on the circuit of Addison's walks. From Rowley Lascelles, *The University and City of Oxford*, 1821.

8.5 The polite imagination: entrance to Addison's Walk

Magdalen's New Building can be seen. From Rowley Lascelles, *The University and City of Oxford*, 1821.

the laying out of extensive grounds and the long term planting it entailed was a demonstration of faith in the Whig Constitution. James Tyrrell, the Oxford Whig historian and friend of Locke and Boyle, laid out his gardens at Shotover, near Oxford, in the 'natura-linear' way recommended by Switzer and followed Addison in demonstrating by direct appeal to the mind of the beholder the 'pleasures arising from the works of Nature.'[13] On his return from the Marlborough Wars his son, Colonel Tyrrell, threw himself into the task of completing his father's garden, for, as his tombstone records, he found himself urgently in need of an occupation to fill his unaccustomed leisure after an active war career.

Addison was undoubtedly the inspiration for the concept of the ferme ornée as popularised by Southcote at Wooburn Farm[14] and Bolingbroke at Dawley. In 1728 Robert Castell published *The Villas of the Ancients Illustrated*, giving plans of the villas at Tusculum and Laurentium from the well-known descriptions of Pliny the Younger. This gave form to the idea of estate gardening in the classical tradition as introduced by Addison, and in his Appendix to Volume III of his *Ichonographia Rustica*, Switzer gave his approval of the ferme ornée in strongest terms; 'I cannot, I say, but think that it is really the truest and best way of Gardening in the World, and such as the politest and best Genius of all Antiquity delighted in.' Addison visited his friend Lord Bathurst's ornamental farm at Riskins in Buckinghamshire at an early stage and inscribed admiring verses. When Riskins was sold in 1739 Lady Hartford described it 'as nearer to my idea of a scene in Arcadia than any place I ever saw.'[15]

Ornamental circuit walks round pastoral scenes, which was the basis of the ferme ornée, are in essence what Philander had delighted in when he took his daily walks round the grazed Magdalen meadow. Addison's route can be seen on the Loggan plan of 1675, the raised walk bordered with trees and shrubs, the streams running beside the walks with their banks of wild flowers, the groves and orchards, the natural meadow, the willow-covered marsh to the North, the Holywell corn mill and fields. In the original essay on the Pleasures of the Imagination written at Oxford, Addison mentions bells as an additional delight in a rural walk; sounds very familiar to Oxonians.

Addison was acclaimed in his lifetime by an Oxford admirer[16] as the

Great Patron of our Isis groves,
Whom Brunswick honours and Britannia loves.

and since the nineteenth century the water walks at Magdalen have been called Addison's Walk after the famous alumnus who frequented them. In recent times the wrought-iron gates from his house at Bilton, bearing his initials JA and those of his wife CW, have been placed in front of the stone seat on which he loved to sit in the wildest part of the water walks to muse on the 'Pleasures of the Imagination.'

9

The landscape movement

As the eighteenth century advanced, landscaped gardens increasingly reflected philosophical ideas, many of which had germinated from the seeds sown in Oxford. The Nature revered by Boyle, who could write from his house in the High Street, 'My laboratory is a kind of Elysium,' soon became a more romantic concept better appreciated in the Elysian Fields of the great landscaped gardens such as Stowe. Addison had foreseen that beautiful prospects of this kind could delight 'the Soul as much as a demonstration,' but the later full-blooded Romantic Movement, which sought Nature in untrodden places, poured scorn on the naturalised gardens which had, in fact, paved the way to a wider appreciation of Nature.

The early landscaped gardens, working on the general principles of 'humouring' Nature and consulting 'the Genius of the Place,' were individual essays by gifted amateurs such as Charles Hamilton at Painshill, Henry Hoare at Stourhead and John Aislabie at Studley Royal, or by Lord Burlington's protégé William Kent. Rousham, to the North of Oxford, where, in the words of Horace Walpole, Kent 'leapt the fence and saw that all Nature was a garden,' played a very influential part in the Landscape Movement. Most eighteenth-century visitors agreed with Walpole that Rousham was their favourite garden, surrounded as it was by the gentle integrated

Oxfordshire countryside, making 'the whole sweet.' There were no intruding boundary walls to act as a disillusionment, and the cattle were kept out of the garden by means of a ha-ha or sunken fence. Every 'rural circumstance' was brought into the concept of the garden with farm buildings picturesquely designed and sited by Kent, who went even further than Addison's suggestion that 'a Man might make a pretty landskip out of his own Possessions,' by seeking co-operation of landowners outside the boundaries of the estate. The lead statues look out over the Cherwell to meadows and fields not owned by Rousham. A distant eye-catcher, built on the glebe of Steeple Aston, takes the eye to rising ground beyond, and in the intervening scene the bridge over the public highway and a neighbouring mill are brought into the scheme by picturesque additions. In March 1727 Sir Clement Cottrell wrote approvingly that 'the Doctor Fellow of Merton has very civilly tipp'd down all the trees so that the view in front of the house is entirely open and beautiful.'

Rousham is the best surviving landscape garden by William Kent who, as the first professional in the field, has been called the Father of Landscape Gardening. As a painter he had a knowledge of painterly techniques and the garden he made within the circuit walks of the ferme ornée fused together poetry, painting and gardening into a new landscape art. He had studied the psychology of visual effects to carry out Alexander Pope's principles of 'variety, surprise and concealment of bounds,' the planning of lights and contrasting shades and the literary and emotional overtones of statues, ruins and temples. Rousham was the very place to 'enjoy a philosophic retirement,' the avowed purpose of the early landscaped gardens. Meditation in these Elysian retreats was usually guided by a thematic programme, such as Aeneas's walk to the Underworld at Stourhead. The Imagination, following Addison's tenets, was passive, and pleasure could be derived from the contemplation of scenes calculated to arouse polite ideas in the 'mind of the Beholder.' Addison's own Tatler Essay of 21st January 1710, an allegorical vision concerning the true nature of honour and virtue, is now thought, together with Whig overtones, to have been taken as the theme of Lord Cobham's landscape garden at Stowe. The

9.1 Rousham, Oxfordshire: view from the perimeter walk
The perimeter walk at Rousham was intended to show the house in a
picturesque light, with the grounds and animals presented as a ferme
orneé. Compare Figure 8.3, where Magdalen is picturesquely viewed
across the Cherwell meadows.

use of Gothic architecture for temples at Stowe and Shotover
was with political intent to guide the meditations of the
visitor.

The Shotover Gothic temple of c. 1718 has always been
cited as the first example of Gothic Revival, but it is not in
the mood of the later gothick garden buildings with their
rococo frivolity or feelings of romantic decay. For Locke's
friend, James Tyrrell, Gothic architecture was neither frivo-
lous nor gloomy but reflected the wisdom of the Middle
Ages. It was used to commemorate the Whig triumph of
civil rights over arbitrary government by the Oxford scholar
who had played a not insignificant part in the events leading
up to the Glorious Revolution, having helped to formulate
the Constitution through legal and historical arguments. He
contended that there was a divinely imposed natural law for
man as inviolable as the laws which governed the works of

nature, and in this he was encouraged by his friend Robert Boyle. These rights implied a limitation of power which Tyrrell maintained had been achieved in England by a form of social contract between the King and his subjects. Tyrrell worked assiduously through Saxon and medieval manuscripts in the Oxford libraries to find support for his theory that the Saxon Witan was the basis for English democracy, and that through the Coronation oath the social contract had been continuously honoured by monarchs from medieval times and had only been broken by the Stuarts.[1]

Shotover's temple was aggressively medieval and anti-Stuart. As an antiquarian Tyrrell wanted authentic work and for this he turned to Oxford, which not only had some of the finest medieval buildings in the country but also had college masons skilled in restoration work. The leading masons were the Townesends, one of whom had been college mason at Queen's, Tyrrell's own college.[2] It was almost certainly William Townesend, the Christ Church mason, who worked for Tyrrell at Shotover. He built many country houses near Oxford, many bearing similarities to the new buildings he was putting up for the Oxford colleges. To his traditional skills he added the experience gained from working with Hawksmoor and the Oxford amateurs, Dean Aldrich and Dr Clarke, who on their side profited by the practical skill of the ingenious mason. He also gained valuable experience through working at Blenheim with Vanbrugh, Bridgeman and Switzer in the siting of garden buildings in the landscape. In addition to building Vanbrugh's bridge and the monumental Column of Victory, Townesend constructed the canal which was obliterated in the landscaping of Blenheim later in the century. One of the Rousham temples designed by Kent has always been known as 'Townesend's building,' which suggests that the Oxford mason was involved in more than a minor way. He may have helped Allen Bathurst with his park buildings at Cirencester, and his anonymity in temple-building would have enabled the story to be put about that such garden temples were 'designed by his Lordship.'

The Shotover Gothic temple bears a strong resemblance to the end of the Codrington library which Townesend was building for All Souls in 1716 at the time that Shotover House was being built. The Fellows had decided that where Hawksmoor's library fronted Catte Street the facade should match the end of the 1438 chapel which had been built as a shrine to honour those who had returned victorious from France. Tyrrell would have seen Townesend working on it from the windows of the Bodleian opposite where he was engaged on his medieval researches and, with a soldier son home triumphant from more recent French Wars, a temple evocative of All Souls and the Middle Ages would have double meaning. Townesend knew every pinnacle and niche in Oxford and frequently restored the soft Oxford stone, much of which had come from the family quarries. Another Oxford man, this time an amateur, was also to take advantage of the opportunities to study Oxford Gothic (a member of the University and not an employee) for his own architectural work. This was Sanderson Miller of St Mary's Hall, whose work was not bread-and-butter collegiate Gothic, like Townesend's, but true pioneering rococo gothick.

Sanderson Miller, whose father was a successful Banbury merchant, came up to Oxford in 1734. He inherited the house at Radway acquired by his father in 1737, but remained up at Oxford until 1740, although he started on the Radway improvements during that time.[3] His friend Dean Swift wrote from Ireland in 1739 to wonder if his gardening preoccupations were interrupting his studies. Miller did not in fact take a degree but spent six relaxed years in literary and antiquarian pursuits, not entirely in libraries but revelling in the rich associations of Oxford's gothic architecture. Unlike the scholar James Tyrrell of Shotover or the Christ Church mason William Townesend, he saw turrets, buttresses and crockets with poetic feeling. He was essentially a romantic antiquarian. There was at the time a small circle of antiquarians with a centre at the Bodleian and in 1736 Sir Roger Newdigate, with whom Sanderson Miller was later to be closely linked at Arbury, founded the prize in English verse (which still exists) for a subject connected with the history of ancient architecture. Oxford influences can be detected in the buildings Sanderson Miller designed for his friends, the light, almost domestic Gothic, of the Divinity School

9.2 The Gothic temple at Shotover, c. 1718
Often cited as the first instance of the Gothic Revival. In fact it was not built in romantic mood but as a piece of Oxford collegiate Gothic.

opposite the back of the Sheldonian, the plaster fan-vaulting of Brasenose Chapel, a feature that he and his friend Newdigate used so successfully for interior decoration, the gothick glazing of windows evoking the traceried windows of his own St Mary Hall. Much of this Gothic work in Oxford was in any case seventeenth-century; the Brasenose fan-vault c. 1665, the Christ Church hall staircase c. 1640, the St Mary's windows c. 1639.

Miller's own particular contribution to the Spirit of the Age was his linking of landscape and local history. In this he was joined by his friend William Shenstone, whom he may already have known in Oxford when he was at Pembroke College. Shenstone had a taste for good company, literature and moderate drinking when he was at Oxford and enjoyed old ballads and anything which was considered through history or literature to show native taste. Both Miller and Shenstone introduced into their landscape gardening the feel for the picturesque past they had learned in Oxford. Shenstone inherited a small estate in Worcestershire, called the Leasowes, in the 1740s and, on a modest income of £300 a year, he created the most famous of all fermes ornées on a pleasure and profit basis. His gardening and pastoral poetry went hand in hand. The inscriptions from the Georgics in the garden would have delighted Addison and even Dr Johnson and Oliver Goldsmith, who were critical of landscape gardening, approved of the Leasowes with its winding walks, lake, lovers' walk, Priory ruins and cascade. Robert Dodsley said of his Virgil's Grove, 'None ever beheld this grove without a sense of satisfaction; and were one to chuse any one particular spot of this perfectly Arcadian farm, it would be this.'[4]

Shenstone's *Unconnected Thoughts on Gardening* was published by Dodsley in 1764 and in it he included the suggestion that 'wherever a park or garden happens to have been the scene of any event in history, one would surely avail one's self of that circumstance, to make it more interesting to the imagination. Mottoes should allude to it, columns etc. record it; verses moralize upon it.' His friend Sanderson Miller had been the first one to link natural scenes and historic associations. His links with the Oxford antiquarians, his

own architectural studies and friendship with the Warwickshire coterie of poets, Richard Jago, George Lyttelton,
Shenstone and his friend of Pembroke days, Richard Graves,
took expression in the building of Gothic ruins, now, since
the Romantic Movement, called follies. The earliest of
these was built in his own grounds in 1746 to cap Edgehill
at the spot where Charles I had set up his standard before the
battle in 1643. Radway Field, where the Miller house stood,
had been the scene of bitter fighting in the Civil War. In a
letter to Jago in 1754 Shenstone reported that Miller was
employing a surveyor at Radway in connection with proposed
enclosure but at the same time he was making plans of the
battlefield which 'he proposes to enrich with a number of
anecdotes, gleaned from his neighbourhood.'[5] Miller collected cannon balls on his estate and while he was up at
Oxford he avidly read Civil War pamphlets. The Edgehill
tower sought to romanticize the event and to present history
in Thomson's words 'unwarped by party zeal.' There was a
view over the battlefield from the guardroom tower, where
visitors were presented with a sheet locating positions while
they were entertained to cold collations. Some friends, like
George Lyttleton of Hagley, preferred to keep romanticizing
and the serious business of eating apart. 'Mrs Lyttelton will
like to dine at the house better than at the Castle, and my
stomach prefers hott meat to cold, though not my taste; so,
if you please, we will dine at the foot of the hill;' but others
were enthusiastic. 'Surely Edgehill fight was never more
fortunate for the nation than it was lucky for Mr Miller,'
wrote Shenstone, and Richard Jago praised Miller's tower in
his poem *Edgehill*.

> Its adverse Side a Precipice presents
> Abrupt and steep! Thanks, Miller, to thy Paths
> That ease our winding Steps! Thanks to the Rill
> The Banks, the Trees, the Shrubs, th'enraptured Sense
> Regaling, or with Fragrance, Shape, or Sound,
> And stilling, ev'ry Tumult in the Breast!
> And oft the stately Tow'r's, that overtop
> The rising Wood, and oft the broken Arch,
> Or mould'ring Wall, well taught to counterfeit
> The waste of Time, to solemn Thought excite,
> And crown with graceful Pomp the shaggy Hill.

So virtue paints the steep Ascent of Fame,
So her aerial Residence displays.
Still, let thy Friendship, which prepar'd the Way,
Attend, and guide me, as my ravish'd Sight
O'er the Bleak Hill, or shelter'd Valley roves.
Teach me with just observance to remark
Their various charms, their storied Fame record.
And to the visual join the mental Search.

The distant Edgehill tower above the battlefield, planted out with trees in significant spots, can be seen from the terrace at Farnborough laid out by Miller for his neighbour Holbech. Miller became famous for his sham ruins and castellated towers he put up for his friends such as the Sham Castle at Bath for Ralph Allen or the tower at Hagley for Lyttelton, which the envious Horace Walpole felt bore 'the true rust of the Barons' Wars.' In view of Lyttelton's remarks on Miller's Edgehill entertainments, the Hagley ruined tower was presumably not used for the purpose of romantic picnics.

Miller's Gothic buildings were always seen in relation to landscape and it was landscape which was the eighteenth century obsession. The early part of the century saw it as the preoccupation of gifted amateurs, but as the century advanced the interest became widespread and attitudes more standardised. Addison's 'polite Imagination' developed into a 'fine taste' which was the criterion by which every well-bred gentleman was judged. The appreciation of landscape and architecture and art was not merely a 'pleasure of the Imagination' but a moral sense. It was Shaftesbury who had given the lead in exploring the principles of discerning taste and in linking aesthetics to the moral sense. In *The Moralists* (1709) he wrote: 'what is beautiful is harmonious and proportionable; what is harmonious and proportionable is true; and what is at once both beautiful and true is of consequence agreeable and good.' Taste flourished in the stability of the age and the culture of Shaftesbury's neo-classical ideas. Connoisseurship came to replace conviction and scholarship, and the Dilettanti Society, formed by those who had made the Grand Tour, had more standing than the Royal Society. Chiswick could do more for culture and the intellect than Oxford, and the world of fashion spoke louder than the dormant universities.

1 The study of physic … Gaddesden's 'Rosa Medicinae'
Written at Merton College in 1309. In Gaddesden's own words: 'as the
rose overtops all flowers, so this book overtops all treatises on the practice of medicine.' (Chapter 3.)

2 A knot pattern: embroidery by Queen Elizabeth I
A prayer book embroidered for Katherine Parr c. 1544, when Elizabeth
would have been about eleven years old. Designs for embroidery, frets,
plaster ceilings and garden knots shared common sources. (Chapter 3.)

3 The Botanic Garden: entrance depicted by Ackermann
The Physic Garden (as it was originally called) was founded in 1621;
the gateway was built by Inigo Jones's master mason Nicholas Stone in
1632–3. From Ackermann's *Views of Oxford*, 1814. (Chapter 3.)

4 *Renaissance symmetry at St John's College*

The Canterbury Quadrangle at St John's College with arcades and garden gateway aligned on the front quadrangle. (Chapter 3.)

5 Hogarth's Line of Beauty: path at Exeter College

Path at Exeter following the fashionable serpentine curve that leads the eye 'a wanton chase'. From W. A. Delamotte: *Original Views of Oxford, its Colleges, Chapels and Gardens*, 1843. (Chapter 9.)

6 Picturesque treatment of the old chapel at Balliol

Delamotte (1843) shows the Balliol chapel given a ruined, picturesque effect by rampant vegetation. This early 16th-century chapel was soon to be replaced by a 'true style' 13th-century Victorian restoration. (Chapter 9.)

7 Balliol today: the chapel garden

The new Fellows' garden with the addition of the Devorguilla tomb, to offset
the Butterfield chapel of 1856. (Chapter 12.)

FLORA

GRÆCA

Sibthorpiana.

CENTURIA PRIMA.
1806

MONS PARNASSUS.

8 'Flora Graeca': masterpiece of botanical illustration

The work of John Sibthorp, the fourth Sherardian Professor, was illustrated by Ferdinand Bauer and published after Sibthorp's death in 1796.
In addition to the superb botanical illustrations, Bauer produced a
delightful title page for each of the ten folio volumes with a Greek
landscape painted below the flower-enwreathed title. (Chapter 11.)

Although it was Shaftesbury's neo-platonic idea of 'Beautiful Nature' that gave the philosophical basis to the midcentury idealised landscape gardens, the decision as to what constituted beautiful forms was taken on empirical lines. Ideas of Taste fluctuated and Hogarth wrote *The Analysis of Beauty* in 1753 with a view to establishing what shapes and forms were universally pleasing. He ridiculed the Connoisseurs and the theory of ideal Beauty and demonstrated, in the manner of Addison, that Beauty was in the eye of the beholder and suggested that what the eye particularly relished was being lead 'a wanton kind of chase.' Waving and serpentine lines were universally acceptable as forms of grace and dominated ideas on landscape gardening as well as on Georgian furniture and decoration. They were already to be found in the Rococo fashion of ornament which drew inspiration from natural objects, such as shells, flowers and seaweed, in which the line wandered freely.

Some time in the eighteenth century the Fellows of Exeter changed the straight garden path, shown in *Oxonia Depicta*, 1733, to make an 'S' curve, clearly to accord with the Line of Beauty. Not only would the eye, according to Hogarth, be led a 'wanton kind of chase' by the serpentine line but from the pleasure it would give to the mind it 'makes what would else be toil and labour, become sport and recreation.' The Fellows and visitors are obviously enjoying the walk on the sweeping curve painted by W.A. Delamotte. Exeter had always been confined and forbidden to have a 'bowling allee or tenniss court' in the proximity of the Bodleian Library, but in the eighteenth century it learned to take advantage of the nearness of buildings of such architectural merit. The south side of the Divinity School gives great distinction to the Exeter garden and the terrace walk at the end of the garden has breath-taking views over Radcliffe Square. It is also very pleasant to secure a seat in Duke Humphrey's library which overlooks the Exeter garden, for, as Erasmus had said, there is nothing nicer than having a library overlook a garden.

Edmund Burke, in 1757, writing in his *A Philosophical Enquiry into the Origin of Our Ideas of the Sublime and the Beautiful*, extended Hogarth's artistic analysis of Beauty to

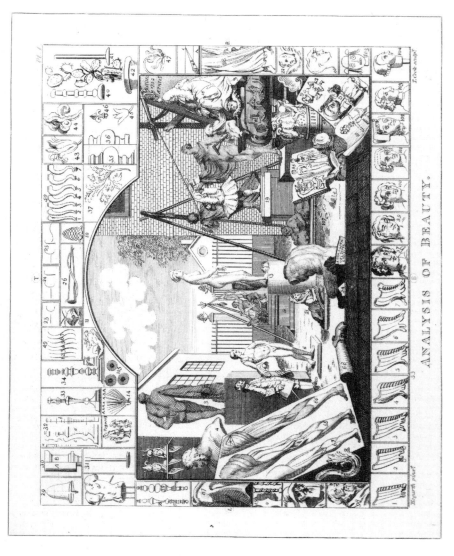

9.3 The Line of Beauty

The title page of Hogarth's *The Analysis of Beauty*, 1753. The serpentine line seen here in classical statuary, Georgian candlesticks, Chippendale chair legs and, satirically, in women's stays, was much used in landscape gardening.

a philosophical enquiry and further stabilised eighteenth-century attitudes to the psychology and perception of beautiful forms. For the theory of landscape gardening Burke's definition of Beauty as smoothness and gradual variations was as important as Hogarth's serpentine line. 'Among all the figures in Architecture, there are none that have a greater Air than the Concave and the Convex,' Addison had stated.[6] This was now adapted to landform. Eighteenth-century guide books always point out the Concave and the Convex slopes that are to be appreciated in a landscaped garden. The essential ingredient in a landscaped garden, alongside the beautiful smooth forms and the waving lines, is the greenness. This too was greatly influenced by the empirical ideas fostered at Oxford in the time of Locke and Addison. The latter had insisted that green was the most restful colour to the eye. Following on Locke's theories that 'that great Modern Discovery, which is at present universally acknowledged by all the Enquirers into Natural Philosophy: namely that Light and Colours, as apprehended by the Imagination, are only ideas in the Mind, and not Qualities that have any Existence in Matter,' Addison had stressed the essentially visual nature of colour and set out to show that green was the most restful colour to the eye. 'The Rays that produce in us the idea of Green fall upon the Eye in such a due proportion, that they give the animal Spirits their proper play:'[7] David Hartley, writing in *Observations on Man*, (1749), had pointed out that 'the middle colour of the seven primary ones and consequently most agreeable to the Organ of Sight is also the general colour of the vegetable kingdom.' It seems as though Nature had anticipated Newton, Locke and Addison.

Lancelot Brown, known as 'Capability Brown,' became the professional practitioner of mid-century landscape gardening ideas. His work was the epitome of stabilised beauty and the recognisable harmony of beautiful forms, all in the colour 'most agreeable to the Organ of sight.' Brown has left an indelible mark on Oxfordshire. To the south of Oxford he worked at Radley, Nuneham, Rycote and Henley Park and to the north at Kiddingtom, Adderbury and Blenheim. The landscape of Blenheim, undertaken in 1765, is undoubtedly a masterpiece, and, as Vanbrugh's palace had been at the beginning of the century, was very influential on taste in Oxfordshire. Oxford did not actually consult the great man himself but some colleges which were still with formal gardens made Brownian improvements within their ground. Cambridge, on the other hand, did consult Capability Brown.[8] Having deformalised the Wilderness at St John's College in 1779 and given the Fellows lawns and trees sweeping down to the Cam, Brown presented the University with a scheme for landscaping the Backs as a whole. In the scheme the Cam was to have been made into a lake and Kings College would have had the central position as the great house in the Brown landscaped park. Whatever reaction Kings College had to the proposal, the other colleges bordering the Cam were unwilling to be relegated to adjuncts in the park, and the plan for suggested improvements, like so many others in both Universities, was scrapped and put in the archives.

Oxford's riverside walks were more extensive and more rural than those in Cambridge and it was the feeling of walking in country scenes, as described by Addison in the Magdalen and Christ Church walks, that was to be preferred above landscape improvements. Colleges such as Merton overlooking Christ Church Meadow appreciated the prospect of the adjacent country from terrace walks in the seventeenth-century manner. Brownian ideas in Oxford were rather the deformalising of gardens than the improvement of the surrounding countryside. At New College it meant the grassing over of the parterres in the 1760s and at Wadham, Balliol and St John's the planting of informal groves. Trinity remained formal until the nineteenth century.

Brown usually worked on landscapes of several hundred acres and, in Oxford college gardens, it was a question of adapting Brownian principles to a few acres. St John's managed so well that several guide books have attributed their garden to Capability Brown. Thomas Frognall Dibdin in his *Reminiscences of a Literary Life*[9] recalled the days when he used to sit day after day with Johnson and Boswell in the gardens and groves of St John's which he called 'a very paradise of their kind.' He added a note that 'These are the work of Brown, and if ever Cowper's precept of giving "ample space to narrow bounds" were realised, it has been in these delightful gardens. It was said, that when George III paid his first visit to Oxford, he declared that his dominions did not contain such a specimen of gardening skill, and yet they are confined within a boundary of four acres.'

The gardening skill which impressed King George was in fact the combined effort of the local nurseryman, Robert Penson, and the Fellows. St John's had taken the transition from the formal Williams *Oxonia Depicta* garden of stilted trees and clipped evergreens to Brownian landscaping in easy stages. By the time Isaac Taylor's plan was published in 1750 the deviations from Nature, so despised by Joseph Addison, had disappeared and the trees were growing naturally. The accounts show that flowering trees and shrubs had been introduced in the 1740s. Robert Penson, who owned nursery gardens in St Ebbes and St Clements, the latter near to the Botanic Garden, supplied trees and shrubs for the gardens in 1772 and '73.[10] The site of one of his nurseries is still commemorated by the street name of Penson's Garden. In 1774 he submitted plans for a new layout, but until the wall between the two gardens was removed in 1778 it was not possible to offer a unified scheme. Shortly after work had begun to naturalise the inner grove, *A New Pocket Companion for Oxford* remarked that the college still retained the names they formerly had of the outer and inner grove. The outer, which once had the stunted elm walks, was still laid out in regular walks and grass plots, but the inner grove on which Penson had worked had been transformed. In the words of the Pocket Companion, 'the inner Grove is of quite a different Cast to this, being so contrived as not to satiate the Eye at once, but its various Parts present themselves gradually to view. No spot is calculated to yield a more pleasing variety.' St John's had successfully carried out Alexander Pope's three recommendations for landscape gardens, variety, surprise and concealment of bounds.

In the 1790s there were new brooms on the Balliol Governing Body who set about the naturalising of their Grove, and orders were placed with Penson and also with Tagg of the Paradise Gardens for a number of trees and flowering shrubs, hornbeams, white hawthorns, syringas, honeysuckle, Lombardy poplars, viburnum, euonymus, laburnum, bird cherries, lilacs, wayfaring trees, thorns, acacias, guelder roses, spindle trees, hypericum, mountain ash, almonds, sweet-briars, laurestinus and ponticum rhododendrons. Dog's-tooth violets, crocuses and crown imperials were also ordered for underplanting.[11] As the eye was led up to the pinnacles and battlements of neighbouring towers and turrets while walking along the gravel paths through the flowery grove, the Balliol grove must have been a delightful retreat.

When Wadham decided on being fashionably naturalised they preferred to consult Blenheim rather than to rely on Mr Penson, the local gardener. They had been changing the garden with Dr Wilkin's mount and Wren's experimental bee hives little by little over the years, and not without the usual college arguments. A resolution in the Convention Book of 1730 that the clipped trees should be replanted has a note added. 'This does not confirm the causeless and expensive alterations in ye Garden.'[12] The mount was not removed until 1755 after the statue of Atlas had blown down in a high wind and been broken to pieces. In 1795 the double walls between the two gardens and some outbuildings were removed and the way was clear for a more ambitious scheme (the sour commenter in the Convention Book of 1730 having presumably, like Atlas, left the Wadham scene by them). In 1796 the Fellows approved a plan of alterations recommended by Mr Shipley, the Duke of Marlborough's gardener, who was said to be a pupil of Brown. Many trees were cut down. The Civil War earthworks were kept as a terrace walk but extensive lawns could be laid with unimpeded views to the country to the north, which one hundred years later would become a flourishing North Oxford suburb.

Oxford, with its famous skyline of domes and spires, provided views for at least one of the nearby landscaped gardens of surrounding Oxfordshire country houses. Nuneham Courtenay was chosen by Lord Harcourt in 1758 as the ideal site for his Palladian villa, on an easy hillock near the River Thames with a distant view of Oxford, which resembled Poussin's view of Rome from the surrounding hills. Like so many other English milords, the young Earl had been greatly taken by all he had seen on his Grand Tour, the actual Italian landscape of the classics, the paintings of mythologi-

9.4 Nuneham Park, 1775

Paul Sandby's drawing of Lord Harcourt's villa, built above the Thames
to give a view of the distant spires and domes of Oxford.

cal landscapes by Claude and Poussin, Italian architecture and
antiquities. He became the first President and a founder of
the Dilettanti Society, formed for those who had travelled
in Italy and sought to promote a feeling for Italy in England.
He wanted to create a landscape garden which would evoke
the Arcadian scenes of the Italian landscape painters. The
ancestral home at Stanton Harcourt to the north of Oxford
was low-lying and lacked the materials for landscaping. The
Earl chose an ideal site for his purposes five miles south of
Oxford, where he could live out the ideal of the cultivated
man retreating from the burdens of public life, as advocated
by the ancients and idealised by Pope.

In the making of ideal landscaped gardens it was a necessary first step to remove scrub to expose the beautiful landform and to clear any outbuildings which impeded the view.
In order to create the Nuneham landscape Earl Harcourt had
to remove an entire village.[13] One old widow who was heart-
broken at the thought of leaving and joining her companions
in the new turnpike village was allowed to remain. After her
death, when the cottage was pulled down, a poem by the
Poet Laureate was inscribed on a tree in praise of her virtue:

> Tho' Thames before her flowed, his farther shores
>   She ne'er explored, contented with her own.
> And distant Oxford, tho she saw its towers
>   To her ambition was a world unknown.

Oliver Goldsmith, who had witnessed the removal of the
village in 1761, later wrote an indictment of Lord Harcourt's
kind of landscape gardening in *The Deserted Village*[14] and
commiserated with the old widow who had been left as
'the sad historian of the pensive plain.'

The 2nd Earl Harcourt, who inherited in 1777, had always
deplored his father's high-handed action. He was the friend
and patron of Rousseau, whom he befriended during his
exile in England. He made a small flower garden[15] at Nuneham as a copy of Julie's garden from *La Nouvelle Héloïse* and
inscribed Rousseau's words on a seat: 'Si l'Auteur de la
nature est grand dans les grandes choses, il est très grand
dans les petites.' William Mason was the creator of this garden; the Nuneham flower garden, so delightfully painted by
Paul Sandby, started a cult of the informal flower bed, which

9.5 The Carfax Conduit

The Jacobean top of the old conduit was removed from the centre of Oxford in 1787 and made into the architectural feature in Lord Harcourt's landscaped garden at Nuneham.

had been excluded from Brownian landscapes. The St John's
College beds of groups of shrubs and flowers, shown in the
1783 Almanack, are clearly part of the Nuneham cult.
Capability Brown landscaped Lord Harcourt's park in 1782,
one of his last commissions. A ruined tower was intended to
provide the architectural feature on Brown's hill, but when
in 1787, the Carfax Conduit which stood in the middle of
Oxford had to be removed. Lord Harcourt, who had just been
made an honorary D.C.L. by the University, begged that he
should take away the Jacobean ornaments and erect them on
a new Conduit base in place of the intended tower. A piece
of genuine Oxford antiquity would, he thought, be of more
interest in his landscape park than a Gothic ruin. The Earl
was an antiquarian and helped to provide material for local
topographical books. He was an artist and patron of the
Picturesque, a movement which was to have a great influence
on gardening in the last decade of the century. It was William
Gilpin, the Picturesque Traveller, who did much to influence
the high phase of landscape gardening.

10

The Picturesque movement

William Gilpin, the pioneer of the Picturesque, entered the Queen's College in January 1740. He finally left Oxford in 1748 after taking his M.A. He later told his friends that all he had gained at the University 'was from reading books, which he might have read anywhere,' but he did visit Blenheim and Stowe and study art collections and enjoyed the view from his bedroom window. In his Memoir[1] he said he had 'chambers in an old part of the College which had formerly been occupied by the Black Prince.' In letters to the family he describes the New College garden with its parterres, 'Arches, Pyramids and Pillars hewn out of Yew-Tree,' and shady walks and arbours. He describes the immediate view in detail in a letter to his aunt on 27 March 1742, and goes on to describe the scene beyond on the picturesque principles that were to become a life's obsession:

> As Objects now begin to lessen, you must expect a fainter Description, agreable you know to the Rules of Painting. Beyond the Gardens then the next Thing is a most beautiful Grove which at once charms both your Eyes and Ears. The one is charm'd by the Linnet, the Thrush and the hoarse Musick of Crows and Rooks, than which no noise is more agreable to one: the other by Deer playing among the Openings of the Trees, and a noble new Building which is so shaded and cover'd with Oaks and Elms that it appears to me like an old romantick Castle rising out of a Wood, or if you please a Scaleby. My View is bounded in Front

by this Grove; for Variety upon each Side there is an Opening
into a most delicious Country, which abounds with Green Fields,
Trees, Spires, Villages, and in short wants nothing but a little
more Water, and two or three of your Scotch Mountains to make
it a most compleat Prospect.[2]

In everything he saw or read, William Gilpin called in the
painter's eye. He was taught to draw by a gifted father and
kept up his hobby all through his life. He spent part of his
youth at Scaleby Castle and at Carlisle where his father was
garrisoned.[3] Castles and border soldiers played an influential
part in Gilpin's picturesque imagination and he always
longed to return to his beloved Cumberland. Looking out of
his Queen's window on to the Oxford city wall he wrote:
'This wall to another spectator would afford no pleasure nor
indeed to me upon any other account than as it puts me in
mind of those at Carlisle.' His view of venerable objects was
always picturesque rather than romantic.

William Gilpin defined the Picturesque as 'a term expres-
sive of that peculiar kind of beauty, which is agreeable in a
picture.' The first published suggestion that a new pleasure of
the Imagination was the contemplation of a scene with the
eyes of a painter came after a visit to Stowe from Oxford.
This *Dialogue upon the Gardens ... at Stow* (1747), dis-
cusses the picturesque compositions to be noted in Lord
Cobham's landscape garden. Observation was linked with
reading and he found a great pictorial sense in Virgil, whom
he called 'a great master in Landscape.'

After his ordination the Rev. William Gilpin was for many
years a schoolmaster at Cheam and he was at pains to cultivate a 'picture-making faculty' in his students when they
read the classics. In a notebook[4] he listed for them what he
found picturesque in Virgil's *Aeneid* — a hero resting after a
battle, glittering armour, a sea nymph pushing a ship, the sea
in a storm, a wolf running off in fear, a rocky and woody
scene. Many of the ideas he lists as picturesque were heroic
attitudes suitable for a history painting, which is consistent
with the use of the word in the early eighteenth century and
his own statement: 'By Picturesque I mean precisely nothing
more than such ideas as can be formed into a picture.' Gilpin
was himself largely responsible for the change of emphasis

in the term Picturesque, so that by the end of the century it was used almost exclusively to describe scenic beauty.

From developing a 'picture imagination' when reading it was a short step for Gilpin to suggest that this same faculty would be an agreeable accompaniment to travel. In 1768 he published an *Essay on Prints* for the instruction of the large new public for whom cheap prints had become available. He showed how to apply the principles of painting to the examination of prints to enable the layman to appreciate such matters as 'design, disposition, keeping and the distribution of light.' In the Cheam school holidays he travelled to out-of-the-way places 'in search of picturesque beauty' and, for his own amusement, recorded with descriptions and on-the-spot sketches what he found to be 'pencil-provoking' in the Wye Valley, the Highlands, the Lakes and other regions of picturesque Britain. Gilpin was persuaded by the 2nd Earl Harcourt and William Mason to publish his Tours, which by the end of the century had become extremely popular, especially with the improvement of roads. The enjoyment of pictures and the appreciation of scenery in the Gilpin manner became inseparably linked, so that anyone with pretensions to taste was seen, like the Tilneys of *Northanger Abbey*, to be 'viewing the country with the eyes of persons accustomed to painting and deciding on its capability of being formed into pictures.'

The tourist was taught to analyse the landscape and to see how variously Nature 'worked up' the scenery in the different regions visited. By proving that the homeland was picturesque, or worthy of painting, Gilpin broke the spell of idealised Italian landscape, which had been the model for painting, poetry and landscape gardening in the first half of the century and opened the way for a British School of landscape painting. William Gilpin did not himself apply his argument for the Picturesque, developed through the analysis of prints and travel, to the creation of real landscape.[3] When the 2nd Earl Harcourt inherited Nuneham in 1777 he had tried unsuccessfully to persuade his friend to take the living so that he could superintend the picturesque improvements of the landscaped garden. William Mason, whom Gilpin described as a 'man of taste, sentiment, delicacy and virtue

with very picturesque ideas'[6] made a picturesque Tour
throughout the garden for Lord Harcourt featuring the
windings of the river, the Carfax Conduit, the Thamesside
villages and the Berkshire downs, which can still be seen
today.[7] The Earl wrote his own guide book giving the picturesque stations at which to view the framed vistas in
typical Gilpinesque style:

> On the left there is a narrow opening that admits a view over the
> underwood, and the trees in the foreground, apparently uniting
> with a clump in the garden below, leading the eye to the other
> masses of wood till it reaches Oxford, which is framed by trees
> and shrubs.[8]

Oxford itself had its own excursions into the Picturesque,
where gradually picturesque effects came to be preferred to
beautiful forms in the landscaped college gardens. The
death knell was sounded for the green tunnels and vegetable
sculpture except at Trinity College where the formal garden
was still thriving in the first decade of the nineteenth century.
In 1843 W.A. Delamotte lovingly depicted the picturesque
period of Oxford college gardens in his *Original Views of
Oxford, its Colleges, Chapels and Gardens.* The view of
Balliol Chapel from the garden with its ivy-mantled tower
was worthy of a part in any Gothic novel and was 'pencil-
provoking' enough for any addict of the Picturesque. Sanderson Miller had anticipated picturesque vision by seeing buildings in relation to landscape and noting with due relish the
pinnacles and towers of Oxford 'embosom'd high in tufted
trees.' Humphry Repton observed that 'there is nothing
more interesting as a picture than the combination of Trees
and Buildings; they assist and relieve each other in forming
that picturesque Whole, which Painting endeavours to imitate,
and for which Oxford has long been celebrated.'[9] New
towers appeared even in the nineteenth century which
could be used to advantage as picturesque features in college
gardens. St John's and Wadham could enjoy framed vistas of
the high tower of the Ruskinian University Museum from
their gardens.

Worcester College made picturesque virtue out of necessity
and has the only true landscaped garden in Oxford, having its

own designed piece of water. The College, under its present name, dates only from 1714, but some of the buildings are among the oldest in the University and the row of buildings called the cottages dates from before the dissolution of the monasteries in 1539, when the old Gloucester College was suppressed. An arch from the monastic buildings is sited by the lake adding a romantic touch of history to the picturesque scene. Although the college buildings were completed by the 1770s, landscaping of the grounds was not undertaken until the beginning of the nineteenth century and then the decision was taken partly for practical reasons. The college's frontage to the Thames had been cut off by the extension of the Oxford Canal in 1790. The Canal Company was dilatory about draining the bordering land in spite of an undertaking given to the college when the land was transferred. In 1817 the Fellows asked for the necessary arrangements to be made to convert the swampy, evil-smelling area into a lake and they agreed to plant trees. The Oxford Guide of 1821 highly commended the college's efforts in the laying out of 'three acres of ground with great taste, embellished with a large sheet of water, well stocked with fish.' Richard Greswell, a later Bursar, who had also taken an active part in the planting of Port Meadow, was responsible for the planting of the fine specimen trees on the lawns. The Provost's lodgings were virtually a Palladian country house and the nineteenth century engravings and the fine water colour by Le Keux depict the Worcester College scene as a country house in a picturesquely planted landscaped garden.[10] Another parklike feature is the curly barge board added to the gable end of the monastic side of the Quadrangle and seen from the landscaped garden. The picturesque gable resembles a cottage orné when seen from the 'hanging garden' which is brought up to the level of the upper floor by a banked terrace. This mound is variously said to be made from the excrement of

---

10.1 Worcester picturesque landscape (overleaf)

Showing the garden front of the Provost's Lodgings looking like a Palladian country house, and the gable end of the old monastic building with its cottage orné effect.

the monastic long room latrine, the stones and rubble of the dissolved monastery and the spoil from digging out the lake. Other cottage orné effects are to be seen in the University Parks with the two delightful lodges and even the Cricket Pavilion treated as a picturesque park adjunct.

The most picturesque scheme envisaged for Oxford was, however, rejected. In 1801 the Fellows of Magdalen College invited Repton to submit one of his famous Red Books for the improvement of the College. Repton took on the mantle of Capability Brown whose technique he modified to accord with the picturesque attitudes of the 1790s. His method was to paint a picture of a place as he found it and by means of hinged flaps show what it would look like after his picturesque improvements were executed. The plans and recommendations were bound with red morocco and Repton's greatest advertisement was that these handsome volumes were left on library tables to be seen by other envious landlords. Repton was concerned that an academic society might not treat his Red Book manuscript in the same way and that it might be hidden in the stacks, so he took steps to make his own arrangements in writing to the College:

Sir,
    In answer to the honour of your Letter of the 16th Jan, the plans which you are so good to mention in terms of commenda-tion, can nowhere be so properly disposed as in the College lib-rary to which they relate — and if my part of the plans proposed, meet the approbation of the Society I shall be happy to assist in carrying them into execution — in the mean while as I should be sorry to have them entirely laid upon the shelf of the Library without making them publickly known — I shall request leave of the College to let me shew them to some few personages and perhaps to the King himself if I can procure an Audience for that purpose — I should also wish to have leave from the College to copy one of the Drawings on a larger scale for the purpose of exhibiting it at the Royal Academy — and when the Society shall have had leisure to inspect them — I will trouble you to cause the book to be carefully packed in a box and directed to me at the Salopian Coffeehouse, Charing Cross London.
        I have the honour to be Sir
            Your most obedient humble Servant
                                H. Repton[11]

The Red Book includes a dissertation on Grecian and Gothic architecture which Repton afterwards reprinted in his *Observations on the Theory and Practice of Landscape Gardening* in 1803. The architectural designs in the book were by his son John Adey Repton. The frontispiece has a vignette of two young men in gowns and mortar boards, seated on some learned treatises; they are unconvincingly accompanied by gardening implements and a theodolite. In the centre is a drawing of a gateway at the far corner of the deer park, made out of an old square tower. Repton observed in his commentary that 'as the College boundary Wall is very massive, the gate should rather partake of the ponderous character of a castle, than of the more elegant species of Gothic Architecture.'

Repton made much of the fact that Magdalen alone had the materials for landscaping but in all the schemes that had hitherto been considered the College had never seen itself in a picturesque light enjoying and contributing to the Cherwell views. 'In the various plans which have been suggested by architects only, there seems to have been a total disregard to these local circumstances and advantages which are possessed by Magdalen, over every other College in either of our Universities . . . in every design which I have seen for Magdalen, the Command of Property seems to have been neglected and no advantage taken of the adjacent Meadow, and trees or the River Charwell which flows through the premises; but the View towards the East has always been sacrificed, to form an Architectural Quadrangle, which would exclude all benefit from the adjoining territory . . . Redundance of water is natural to the situation, it would surely be advisable to display this in one broad than in many narrow channels.'

The proposal to landscape the Meadow and to make it visible from the principal rooms of the College and at the same time to render the college a picturesque Gothic building in the composition entailed some rather drastic alterations to the Founder's architecture. The north side of the quadrangle was to be stripped of its upper storey and retained as a screen and the whole of the east side of the cloister was to be removed to achieve the desired effect. The before and after drawings showed the 'improvements.' Passions were roused when the Fellows who had rooms in the portions of the cloister which were to be sacrificed in the interest of the Picturesque lifted Repton's overlay and saw the intention. Repton had not taken into account the difference between improvements projected for one owner of a country house and proposals for a collegiate body. Hawksmoor, who had had considerable experience, expresses the feelings of professionals who are forced to deal with college governing bodies and their corporate decisions: 'I must confess your owne affairs are best known to yourselves, and must therefore submitt the executions of them to your own wisdomes.'[12]

Addison's beloved walks were left unchanged and Repton's proposals for picturesquing an ancient cloister were put away on the library shelf, as he feared. By 1823 the project, which had been aided and abetted by Repton's partner John Nash, had become history and J.C. Buckler wrote:

> Mr Repton a landscape gardener and Mr Nash a well-known professional architect, severally produced volumes of designs for the disfigurement of Magdalen College and the disposal of its pleasure grounds, touched, it is true, with the artist's magic pencil and secured in cases of red morocco and gold, yet, by their preposterous absurdity, not to enlarge on their ruinous splendour, consigned to an oblivion from which I shall not risk their escape, by bestowing on them any further comments.

A mere View was to Mr Buckler a hateful word, 'Who, save, alas, the Sons of Magdalen,' he thundered, 'would consent to remove or mutilate one wing of a large mansion because it impeded some pretty object from the view of the other?'[13]

J.C. Buckler represented the turning point in taste and feeling. After the Romantic Movement fictitious ruins ceased to be built. Only pilgrimages to real abbeys and Scott's border towers would satisfy the romantic sense of history. Taste, which had meant picturesque taste in the last decades of the eighteenth century, and feeling were merged in the appreciation of venerable objects; what was 'pleasing to the eye' had also to be 'delightful to the mind' to satisfy the romantic traveller. In Oxford John Chessell Buckler, who styled himself an architectural antiquary, was a pioneer in the field of the accurate and detailed recording of standing structures. He and his father were prolific topographical artists and there are over 12,000 of their drawings in the British Museum. In Oxford he recorded details of tie-beams and joints in timber-frame buildings and he undertook sympathetic restorations of old buildings.[14] He became a practising architect; his approach was an intensely scholarly one inspired by a deep knowledge of Oxford buildings. Like Sanderson Miller he went round Oxford with his eyes open, but his observations went deeper and were archaeological rather than picturesque. Of the architecture of Magdalen he wrote in 1823: 'the facts and observations here presented, result from the frequent and long residences in Oxford, and a deep veneration for the ancient Architecture of England, which the Author has diligently examined, in order to define, if possible, its essential characteristics, and to acquire a just knowledge of its governing principles.' This report was, he felt, a duty owed to antiquity written, he said, 'in the hope of stimulating the Guardians of Magdalen College to preserve inviolate its splendid architecture.' There had been other abortive attempts to improve Magdalen's cloister since the relegation of Repton's Red Books to the dark recesses of the library. Their history was summed up by Buckler in these words:

> The assaults on the architecture of Magdalen College have been more numerous than those on any other of the renowned Colleges in Oxford, but without the amount of mischief which might be expected. Fortunately, so much time was passed in former years in contention and controversy, that before the subject proposed was talked into tangible shape, it died away and expired without regret.

Buckler's talents as artist, recorder, archaeologist and architect were invaluable and contributed to the strength of Gothic Revival as a movement. He deplored Victorian 'innovations' to medieval architecture and his own additions to old buildings now have a weathered authentic feeling, the gatehouse tower of Jesus College, the rose-window at Iffley church, and for his own college, Magdalen, the Library, which was built as a school room for Magdalen College school.

A sense of history and the feeling that essential characteristics of a building should be respected gave a new meaning to the expression 'in keeping,' which had hitherto only been used in a pictorial sense of the relation of near and distant objects. A new feel for congruity and sympathetic treatment for the surroundings of historic buildings, readily understood today, brought with it an interest in old-fashioned gardens. Returning to Oxford in 1807, Robert Southey visited the gardens he had known in his Balliol undergraduate days. The New College formal gardens had just been destroyed and drawings of the time show that the Mount had begun to acquire a picturesque growth and trees were growing naturally. Southey shows the romantic attitude of a love of the familiar scene even though he acknowledges it represented a garden of somewhat whimsical taste.

> We visited the gardens . . . the College arms were formerly cut in box, and the alphabet grew round them; in another compartment was a sun-dial in box, set round with true lovers' knots. These have been destroyed more easily as well as more rapidly than they were formed; but as nothing beautiful has been substituted in their places, it had been better if they had suffered these old oddities to have remained. One proof of their predecessors' whimsical taste, however, has been permitted to stand; a row of trees, every one of which has its lower branched grafted into its next neighbour, so that the whole are in this way united.

Trinity College did not disappoint for all the old familiar topiary and yew panelling were still intact.

> The garden here is remarkable for a wall of yew, which encloses it on three sides, cut into regular pilasters and compartments. D. cried out against it; but I should lament if a thing which is so perfect in its kind and which has been raised with so many years of care — indeed so many generations — were to be destroyed, because it does not suit with the modern improved taste in gardening. You would hardly conceive that a vegetable could be so close and impervious, still less that anything so unnatural could be so beautiful as this really is.[15]

In *The Doctor* Southey recounts the fortunes of topiary yews which had been left to grow naturally as fashions changed and had recently been put back to a formal shape which 'belonged to old times' and were remembered by the family in childhood days. 'This was with them a matter of feeling, which is a better thing than taste.' The Trinity topiary garden, which (remarkably enough) even Humphry Repton admired, survived intact through the landscape and picturesque phases of fashion but was finally defeated by the demands of more relaxed leisure and recreation, particularly the needs of croquet playing. Some of the overgrown yews once clipped into panels can be seen through the grille on Parks Road.

11

Horticulture in the university

In the eighteenth century plants had been treated as elements in a landscape composition by the great designers and there was a tendency to banish flowers to the kitchen garden. At the beginning of the nineteenth century, in response to a growing feeling that horticulture had been neglected in the cult of the Picturesque, the Horticultural Society of London (later the Royal Horticultural Society) was formed. At their first meeting in April 1805 it was regretted that there was a lack of scientific information about horticultural matters and they emphasized the importance of the selection of good forms of plants and attention to the design and construction of greenhouses. John Claudius Loudon, the influential conductor of the Gardener's Magazine, felt obliged to remonstrate when William Sawrey Gilpin, the Rev. William's nephew, published his *Practical Hints on Landscape Gardening* in 1832 without even mentioning horticulture. 'Mere picturesque improvement is not enough in these enlightened times,' said the editor of the comprehensive *Encyclopaedia of Gardening*, 'it is necessary to understand that there is such a character of art as the gardenesque as well as the picturesque. The very term gardenesque may startle some readers, but we are convinced, nevertheless, that this is a term which will soon find its place in the language of rural art.'[1] Loudon had appropriated the word 'gardenesque' to mean 'as a gardener would like' in the same way as picturesque had been used to mean 'worthy of painting' or 'as a painter would like.' The new steam-heated greenhouses and the introduction of exotic plants from all over the world gave new dimensions to horticulture. Loudon's gardenesque style was calculated 'to display the individual beauty of trees, shrubs and plants in a state of nature.'

11.1 Island flower beds

'View of Lord Harcourt's Flower Garden at Nuneham...' by Sandby, 1777. Published in Copperplate Magazine, 1778. William Mason's informal flower garden was very influential, particularly in college gardens, where island flower beds became popular.

To some extent the picturesque shrubbery and flower beds of William Mason's garden at Nuneham, which Loudon had seen and admired, had anticipated the gardenesque ideas. The Nuneham island and promontory beds with their hollyhocks, pinks, arbutus, willows, small magnolias, and other flowering shrubs grouped together are echoed in the St John's College gardens, which were painted as early as 1781 by M.A. Rooker for the Oxford Almanack. The Physic

Garden in Oxford had, in any case, kept alive an interest in floriculture and as new and wonderful worlds were opened to the plant collectors the material they brought back by way of seed and herbarium was nurtured and collected as it had been since the days of the elder Bobart. It has been calculated that by 1800 the number of introduced plants had risen to something like 14,000, compared with the 1,600 plants, species and varieties collected by Bobart by the middle of the seventeenth century.

William Sherard, the botanist, who called himself 'the drudge of all the gardens in Europe' greatly added to Oxford's plant collections. He was a Fellow of St John's and a lifelong friend of the younger Bobart. During the years 1703–15 Sherard was British consul at Smyrna and he returned to Oxford with many plants from Greece and Asia Minor. Some of the plants found their way to his brother Dr James Sherard's botanic garden at Eltham and some to the Oxford Physic Garden. William Sherard had also travelled extensively in Europe and studied botany in Paris and Leyden and had collected what was, according to Linnaeus, the finest herbarium in Europe. He met the leading men of science and brought Dillenius of Darmstadt to England. The latter subsequently produced a catalogue of the Sherard Eltham garden. Sherard had set his heart on reforming botanical teaching in Oxford, and when he died in 1728 he bequeathed his books and herbarium to the University and endowed a Chair of Botany, stipulating that his friend Dillenius should be the first professor, and that thereafter the appointment should rest with the Royal College of Physicians and not with the University. The Sherardian Professor of Botany, C.D. Darlington, writing in 1971, blamed the plans accepted by the University in 1734 as setting the stage for 'the long continuing struggle between two contrasted ways of attacking the study of plants, the descriptive and the experimental, grounded respectively in the herbarium and the garden, and alternately advanced by successive Sherardian Professors.'[2] Darlington was himself a committed experimental exponent.

Botanical illustration gave added interest and incentive to plant collecting, and to the study of botany by description.

Dillenius, who favoured the descriptive rather than the experimental method, was artist as well as botanist and illustrated his own books. His *Historia Muscorum* had 85 illustrations and 250 of his coloured drawings of fungi were never published. In 1736 the Swedish botanist Linnaeus visited the Physic Garden and met Dillenius, who disapproved of the young man who was attempting to upset the whole science of botany as it was then understood. When they came to a wall of the garden on which the ivy-leaved toad-flax was growing Linnaeus was asked to give his opinion on the controversial structure of the plant.[3] He gave such a masterly analysis of the plant and its structural affinities with the family to which it is now assigned that Dillenius was exceedingly impressed and offered to share his house and salary with him if he would stay in Oxford as his assistant. Linnaeus did not accept the invitation but he later dedicated his *Critica Botanica* to the Oxford professor and named the genus *Dillenia* after him, for as he handsomely said, 'the genus Dillenia being of all plants the most distinguished for beauty of flower and fruit like Dillenius among botanists.'[4]

Humphry Sibthorp, the next Sherardian Professor, made little impact on botany in Oxford and it was reputed that he only gave one lecture during the thirty-seven years he held the Chair. He did, however, seek to strengthen the association between the cultivation and illustration of plants by appointing the botanical artist Georg Dionysius Ehret as Head Gardener. Ehret was immensely skilled in drawing sections and details of plants and his beautiful paintings on vellum earned him a high reputation as a flower-painter. He entered Oxford Physic Garden in 1750 but resigned the following year finding, it is said, the petty jealousies of university life uncongenial. The climax of botanical illustration was Oxford's *Flora Graeca* undertaken by Humphry Sibthorp's son, John Sibthorp, the fourth Sherardian Professor.

Soon after John Sibthorp was appointed Professor of Botany in 1784 he travelled to Vienna to study the Dioscorides Codex, the first Englishman to have done so.[5] The illustrations enabled him to verify the traditional application of the Ancient Greek plant names but the next step was to identify correctly the plants of the Dioscorides herbal by

visiting Greece, Cyprus and Asia Minor where the plants had
been gathered. In Vienna Sibthorp met the Austrian Ferdinand Bauer, one of the greatest botanical artists of all time.
Bauer accompanied him on his first voyage from 1785-7
but he found the Oxford Professor too inconsiderate a master
to go with him on the second voyage in 1794-5. However, he
did faithfully carry out Sibthorp's publishing instructions
after his death in 1796. Sibthorp bequeathed his estate to
the University of Oxford, directing that 'all the profits and
rents from it should be applied to publication of a work for
which I have collected the material, to be entitled *Flora
Graeca* and to consist of ten folio volumes, each volume to
consist of 100 plates.' In addition to the beautiful and
botanically accurate plant illustrations, Bauer produced a
delightful title page for each volume with a Greek landscape
painted beneath the flower-enwreathed title.[6]

The appointment of Charles Daubeny as Professor in 1834
radically changed the direction of the work of the Physic
Garden. In the days of the Bobarts it had always been experimental, linking botany, medicine and practical gardening,
but, as Professor Darlington pointed out, the appointment of
the Sherardian Professor, with its concentration on the Herbarium and descriptive method, took away from the experimental interest of the Garden. Teaching was also at a low
ebb, which was accentuated by the Sibthorps' long absences.
When Joseph Banks, the future Director of Kew, was up at
Oxford from 1760-3 he could find no tutor in botany, but
finding one in Cambridge brought him back to Oxford
triumphantly. Mr Israel Lyons only stayed a short time, however, and returned to Cambridge. Although Daubeny had
been appointed by the Royal College of Physicians, and the
original Frames of the Statute relating to the Sherardian
Professorship enjoined that plants employed in medicine
should be grown in the Garden, he saw no reason to be confined by the purposes implicit in the title Physic Garden and
petitioned for a change of the name to Botanic Garden.[7] Part
of the Garden should become available for the purposes of an
Experimental Garden, for ascertaining 'the effects of soils, or
of chemical agents, upon vegetation, and for other researches
of a similar description.' The study of plants in the interest of

11.2 The Botanic Garden

The name Physic Garden was changed to Botanic Garden after Daubeny's appointment as Professor of Botany in 1834 and a new emphasis was placed on experimental gardening.

science and industry was brought into the ideas of the newly-formed British Association for the Advancement of Science which aimed at giving 'a stronger impulse and more systematic direction to scientific enquiry – to obtain more general attention for the objects of science and the removal of any disadvantages of a public kind which impede its progress.' Daubeny was elected President of the British Association in 1836, having been a founder member of the Association in 1831. He was steeped in its Victorian views on progress and the dissemination of knowledge. He was the first Secretary of the Ashmolean Society, founded in 1828, and the meetings, which were often held in his rooms, were for the interchange of 'observations on subjects connected with natural history, experimental philosophy and other branches of modern research.'[8] He later founded a Daubeny Club to bring together those working at or interested in Natural Science.

In the Botanic Garden, now so-named, Daubeny removed the double yew hedge that traversed the centre of the garden, which he said only harboured vermin, and reorganised the gated squares in which the drug plants had been kept. A fine range of glass houses was built on the banks of the Cherwell with tanks for aquatics. Daubeny's water lilies, *Nymphaea 'daubenyana'*, were very popular with visitors. Additions were made to the gardener's house, new rooms added to the library and the garden raised and levelled. Inundation of the Garden had always been a problem, in spite of Danby's initial efforts, and the plants were frequently up to their necks in water. William Baxter the Curator took advantage of the situation by cultivating grasses and every species of the British willow and the Baxter *Salicetum* became famous.[9] As Dillenius before him, he studied mosses and fungi which first attracted his attention as a gardener in the Oxford 'damp and mildewed environment.' Baxter, a Scotsman, had, like Bobart, given practical instruction in botany to the undergraduates, especially in the days of Daubeny's predecessor Dr George Williams, who, although described as an elegant scholar, was no teacher. All this changed with Daubeny, and Baxter enjoyed the same relationship of Professor and experimental gardener as had existed between Morison and Bobart. Baxter went on to publish in 1871 a book on *British*

Phaenogamous Botany, or figures and descriptions of the genera of British flowering plants in six volumes.

Daubeny had come to botany through chemistry and this became obvious in his policy for the Botanic Garden. Daubeny had succeeded Kidd as Professor of Chemistry in 1822 and in 1840 became Professor of Rural Economy, extending his interests to agriculture. The Daubeny Laboratory in the Botanic Garden was built by Magdalen College in 1848 with Roger Bacon's dictum 'sine experienta nihil sufficienta sciri potest' over the entrance. In the garden plots were laid out to test the mineral requirements of crops. Daubeny set up the first experiments with chemical fertilisers in this country, and by 1843 one of his pupils, John Bennet Lawes, had gone on to found the great agricultural experiment station at Rothamsted.

Daubeny is chiefly remembered in Oxford as a pioneer in the theory of evolution. He gave a party in the Botanic Garden for the victorious Darwinians after the famous debate between Huxley and Wilberforce at the British Association meeting in Oxford in 1860, held in the new University Museum. Professor Daubeny was President of the Zoology and Botany Sections and introduced the debate. He himself gave a paper on 'The Final Causes of the Sexuality of Plants with particular reference to Mr Darwin's work on "the Origin of Species by Natural Selection." ' The herbaceous plants in the plots in the Garden had for some time been arranged in evolutionary sequence by Daubeny, and his botanical and zoological studies were related. He was famous for the monkeys he kept in cages in the Danby gateway, which used to be shown to guests after dinner, and were occasionally to be seen walking down the Iffley road.

The University Museum, opened just in time for the British Association meeting, was Oxford's new temple of natural science, and much of the material from the old Ashmolean Museum in Broad Street was transferred there. It marked a new era of science holding its own in the University. The brilliant dawn of experimental science in Commonwealth Oxford had been eclipsed by the return of clerical orthodoxy and Anthony Wood had noted that in 1683 Christ Church men chose not to come to see the arrival of the Tradescant rarities from Lambeth which were to form the basis of scientific collections in the university. It was not without good reason that William Sherard had laid down that the Chair of Botany he wished to endow should never go to a cleric. As the Huxley–Wilberforce debate was to highlight, science and theology were on opposing sides on the question of evolution, as they had been before in the realm of natural science. Only when J.S. Duncan, curator of the Ashmolean Museum in 1826, began to arrange his objects to show the argument of Dr Paley's Natural Theology could they see the possibility of natural science and orthodoxy being reconciled. Duncan's avowed intention was 'to induce a mental habit of associating natural phenomena with the conviction that they are the media of Divine manifestations.'[10] He even thought it necessary to introduce the concept of Botanical Theology or the Evidences of the Existence and Attributes of the Deity collected from the appearances of Nature, although botany had usually been exempted from clerical disfavour and nobody was going to suggest that man was descended from a foxglove.

Canon William Buckland, the first Professor of Geology, set out to reconcile the new information available on geology with the biblical account of the creation. John Keble agreed with Buckland's Mosaic cosmogony and went as far as to add that 'when God made the stones he made the fossils in them.' Professor Buckland's house at Christ Church, surrounded as he was by every divine manifestation of Creation, became legendary. W. Tuckwell in his *Reminiscences of Oxford*, published in 1900, recalled the home at the corner of Tom Quad, where he used to visit the Buckland children.

> The entrance hall with its grinning monsters on the low staircase, of whose latent capacity to rise and fall upon me I never quite overcame my doubts; the side-table in the dining room covered with fossils, 'Paws off' in large letters on a protecting card; the very sideboard candlesticks perched on saurian vertebrae; the queer dishes garnishing the dinner table — horseflesh I remember more than once, crocodile another day, mice baked in batter on a third day — while the guinea-pig under the table inquiringly nibbled at your infantine toes, the bear walked round your chair ad rasped your hand with file-like tongue, the jackal's fiendish yell close by came through the open window.

It was as Ruskin observed, a 'benevolently cheerful doctrine of Divinity' practised in the Buckland home. The children were as eccentric as their father and Frank once took a bear along to a Daubeny garden party dressed in a cap and gown and introduced him to Sir Charles Lyell, the man whose *Principles of Geology* were to confound the Buckland cosmogony.

Charles Daubeny was the 19th century counterpart of the seventeenth-century man of universal curiosity. An obituary tribute in 1868 commenting on the breadth of his interests saw 'the fruits of a life chiefly spent in tranquil intellectual occupation, under the fostering wing of one of those great semi-monastic establishments which are peculiar to this country; and however slight their intrinsic value, considered as contributions to the stock of human knowledge, may be, they will serve at least to show, by their number and variety, what may be accomplished by persons gifted with greater energy and more profound attainments through the aid of foundations, in which an exemption from domestic cares and a liberal provision for all the reasonable wants of a celibate life, afford such facilities for the indulgence of either literary or scientific tastes.'[11] He had a zeal for scientific education, giving scholarships at his own college Magdalen and science medals for the school. When he came to Oxford there was no British Association, no local Natural History Society, no museum, nor public lectures to any but professional students. Under his guidance the Rules of the Ashmolean Society provided for honorary members to include 'Gentlemen not of the University, possessing a taste for Science or Literature.'

The Botanic Garden was always a link between town and gown and this was strengthened by Daubeny's patronage of the Oxfordshire Horticultural Society, founded in 1830, which held two summer shows in the Garden. The Society became the Royal Oxfordshire Horticultural Society after the visit of Prince Albert to Oxford for the 1847 meeting of the British Association. In the mid-eighteenth century there was great florist activity in Oxford, and Florists' Feasts were held at various inns in the city and surrounding towns.[12] The term florist is now applied to one who sells cut flowers for decoration and grown commercially, but from the seventeenth to the nineteenth century it referred to the cultivators of flowers

9 Repton's Red Book: the proposals for Magdalen

a. The grounds before improvement. Repton prepared the Red Book for the Fellows in 1801 and requested it be displayed in the library.
b. After the proposed improvements. The design took advantage of the natural abundance of water in the area to float a lake and open up the college to the landscape. But Repton was turned down. (Chapter 10.)

10   Worcester: the medieval atmosphere
An archway of the dissolved Benedictine monastery opens on to the landscaped
Worcester garden. (Chapter 10.)

11 Worcester: the lake

The three-acre garden was laid out by the college without professional advice. It embodies the well-established principles of Pope's 'variety, surprise and concealment of bounds', free flowing lines, a lake whose size is not immediately discernible and a path inviting the visitor forward, so leaving 'room for the imagination to work'. (Chapter 10.)

12 Worcester: cottage orné

By the addition of curly barge boards to the gable, a trellised porch on the window and a raised garden, an upstairs set of rooms enjoys the effect of a picturesque cottage in a park. (Chapter 10.)

13 Christ Church: the Deanery garden, by J. M. W. Turner
Watercolour by Turner, probably from the 1790s. Later the Deanery garden
was to be the scene for many of Lewis Carroll's Alice stories. (Chapter 12.)

14 Christ Church: the Broad Walk

Christ Church Meadow, still grazed by cattle, has kept its ancient rural aspect in the heart of the city. The Broad Walk, a favourite place for promenading, was described — and depicted — by Delamotte in 1843 as 'like the cloisters of a cathedral to shut out the world.' (Chapter 16.)

SICUT LILIUM

15 *'Convent Thoughts': the Pre-Raphaelites at Oxford*

Painted by Charles Collins in 1851 in the garden of the University Press for Thomas Combe, the University Printer, a High Churchman and patron of the Pre-Raphaelites. (Chapter 12.)

16 Wood Croft, Boars Hill: a woodland garden near the city
Created in recent years by the eminent plant physiologist, the late Professor
Geoffrey Blackman, F.R.S. (Chapter 15.)

for their beauty rather than for their medicinal properties, which was the province of the herbalist. Bobart was one of the first generation of florists who grew plants for their beauty rather than for use. There was a growing desire to arrive at perfection of form and colouring in such florists' flowers as carnations, pinks, tulips and auriculas even before the intensive cultivation to produce new varieties obsessed nineteenth century horticulture. Writing in 1676, John Rea extolled the virtues of Bobart's auriculas:

> the red of scarlet-colour Auricula as of divers sorts, one of the best I know, is called Mistris Austin's scarlet, it hath large leaves, a strong upright stalk, bearing a great truss of fine scarlet flowers, with snow-white eyes; divers other excellent flowers have been raised in Oxford by Mr Jacob Bobart, Keeper of the publick Garden.[13]

Some pressed specimens of the auriculas raised by the younger Bobart are preserved in his *Hortus Siccus* and in other collections of the Herbarium.

Oxford was frequently mentioned by Rea and his son-in-law Samuel Gilbert, whose *Florist's Vade-Mecum* reached its third edition in 1703, as a place where choice new florists' flowers were raised, particularly the favourite auriculas. The colleges were not without corners for florists' flowers in their gardens as individual members became interested in the cult. John Rea observed that the 'noble kind' of auricula called 'Mr Good's Purple' was raised by Mr Austen of Oxford and given to Mr John Good of Balliol College. 'It is a strong plant with large leaves, a tall stalk bearing a great truss of many fair, fine rich purple flowers with snow-white eyes that will not wash yellow with rain.' In April 1775 there was an advertisement in *Jackson's Oxford Journal* for the sale of tulips that belonged to the Rev. Dr Tottie of Christ Church where they could be seen in flower forming 'the finest collection of tulips in England, annually enriched by importation of the best flowers from Holland.'[14]

The fascination of florists' flowers, with their stripes, lacing and double forms, and the joy that a cottager or artisan with the smallest of back yards could experience led on to the formation of clubs and shows, where they could be seen by fellow enthusiasts. The Rev. Dr Tottie of Christ

Church and the humblest Oxford tradesman could have exchanged floral secrets at the flower shows held at the Town Hall in the 1780s, and by the late 1820s clubs had been founded all over the country. The ecstasy of the prize-winner at a florist's show is captured by Crabbe in *The Borough*:

> His was the prize, and joy o'er-flowed his heart
> This, this is beauty! cast, I Pray, your eyes
> On this my glory! see the grace — the size!
> Was ever stem so tall, so stout, so strong,
> Exact in breadth, in just proportion long;
> No kindred tint, no blending streaks between;
> This is no shaded, run-off, pin-eyed thing,
> A king of flowers, a flower for England's king.[15]

As well as Professor Daubeny's patronage of the local horticultural society and its shows, hospitality to horticulture was given by the colleges. Those with gardens allowed tents to be set up for exhibits, and the Queen's College, lacking the facilities for a garden venue, allowed a show to be held in the main quadrangle. When the University Parks were being laid out in 1863 under the direction of James Bateman of Magdalen College, who had had considerable experience in landscaping his own estate at Biddulph Grange in Staffordshire and was also a great plantsman, it was suggested that the cricket pavilion should be combined with an arcade for flower shows. There was general approval for Bateman's overall plan for the parks but exception was taken by the Vice-Chancellor and some others to the 'costliness and inutility' of a permanent Arcade for flower shows.[16]

Oxford became famous for carnation growing and the Professor of Astronomy, Professor Pritchard, was one of the cult's most enthusiastic supporters.[17] He grew thousands of carnations in the garden of the Observatory, most of which he had obtained from E.S. Dodwell of 18, Stanley Road, off the Iffley Road. In the 1880s Dodwell, a famous raiser of new varieties of carnations, started the 'Oxford Union Carnation and Picotee Society' which held annual exhibitions in his garden. When Professor Pritchard was over eighty he went up the Iffley Road to the Dodwell show at 1.00 pm, returned to his Observatory to lecture at 3.00 pm and went back to his florist friends at 4.45 pm. College servants and gardeners were often enthusiastic members of the local societies and as early as 1838 the Wadham gardener created a device to decorate the Town Hall for a Grand Dahlia Show with the city and university arms, Victoria and a crown in fruits and flowers, mainly dahlia blooms.[18] Dahlias and chrysanthemums became popular for autumn flowering as so many of the florists' flowers were early flowering and limited the time for shows. The 25-inch to the mile Ordnance Survey maps of Oxford show the proliferation of nursery gardens and greenhouses, commercial and private, in the city to cater for the new zeal for horticulture.

12

Victorian Oxford

Romanticism, when it came to Oxford, that most medieval of English cities harbouring the hopes of young ideals, was bound to be a heady mixture. Matthew Arnold, who lived through these intoxicating, intellectually turbulent times as an undergraduate at Balliol and a Fellow of Oriel, summed up its enchantment when he became Professor of Poetry, in these immortal words;

> Beautiful city! so venerable, so lovely, so unravaged by the fierce intellectual life of our century, so serene! . . . and yet, steeped in sentiment as she lies, spreading her gardens to the moonlight, and whispering from her towers the last enchantments of the Middle Age, who will deny that Oxford, by her ineffable charm, keeps ever calling us nearer to the true goal of all of us, to the ideal, to perfection, – to beauty in a word, which is only truth seen from another side . . . Adorable dreamer, whose heart has been so romantic! who hast given thyself so prodigally, given thyself to sides and heroes not mine, only never to the Philistines! home of lost causes, and forsaken beliefs, and unpopular names, and impossible loyalties![1]

By the time Matthew Arnold wrote this eulogy in 1865 the 'adorable dreamer' and 'home of lost causes' had seen the Oxford Movement, Reform, Ruskin, High Gothic architecture, William Morris, the Pre-Raphaelites and Wonderland.

The two undergraduates who came most under the spell of Oxford's romantic medievalism were William Morris and

148

Edward Burne-Jones. They came up to Exeter in 1853, the year of Matthew Arnold's legend of the Scholar Gypsy. Burne-Jones wrote home enthusiastically: 'Oxford is a glorious place; godlike! at night I have walked round the colleges under the full moon, and thought it would be heaven to live and die here.' Later when he was in despair about his work he returned to Oxford 'having a great belief in the effect its ancient peace would bring me, and every day drew in the gardens there – a whole forest of trees, grasses, flowers, anything.' For William Morris Oxford was 'an abiding influence and pleasure in my life' and he and Burne-Jones revelled in the cloisters of New College, Mob Quad, the illuminated manuscripts in the Bodleian Library, the flowers in the meadows, the college gardens, the grey-roofed houses, the winding lanes, the sound of many bells. It was a full-blooded romantic approach to history which sought out the memories and the legends and related them to the place. Oxford had remembered the martyrs Latimer, Ridley and Cranmer in the Martyrs' Cross erected in 1841 and the feeling that began with the rejection of Repton's plans for landscaping Magdalen and the naming of Addison's Walk was intensified. Writing in 1839, Thomas James lamented that 'beautiful as are St John's Gardens, who would not exchange them for the *very* walks and alleys along which Laud, in all the pardonable pride of collegiate lionizing, conducted his illustrious guests, Charles and Henrietta? Who does not grieve that we must now inquire in vain for the bowling-green in Christ Church, where Cranmer solaced the weariness of his last confinement?'[2] Matthew Arnold, reviving Glanvill's story of *The Scholar Gypsy* and its memories in *Thyrsis*, captured the magic of 'that sweet city with her dreaming spires' as seen from the surrounding hills. The local scene so well-known to Oxonians was given a poetic life – the Cumnor hills, the stripling Thames at Bablockhythe, Godstow, the Fyfield elm and the Hinksey ridge whence could be seen 'the festal light in Christ Church Hall.' It would now be impossible for a tourist brochure to be printed without reference to Arnold's 'dreaming spires,' a phrase which enraptured romantic Oxford.

The Gothic tradition, so essential to the image of dreaming

spires, had never died out in Oxford, so that the expression Gothic Revival is not as applicable to Oxford as to other parts of the country. High Gothic architecture in Oxford, however, was linked to the Oxford High Church Movement. The Oxford Society for the study of Gothic Architecture was founded in 1839, following Pugin's *Contrasts*, published in 1836, which promoted Gothic as the only true style being both English and Christian. Loud were the rejoicings when the new Anglican convent in the Woodstock Road went up opposite the Horse and Jockey in Early English Christian style rather than in pagan classic architecture. Pugin himself designed a Gothic gateway at Magdalen to replace the Renaissance one which resembled the Nicholas Stone archway of the Botanic Garden across the road, but this in its turn was taken down and replaced by the present one in 1885. Most colleges had Victorian Gothic additions but the only new blatantly ecclesiologically Gothic foundation was Keble College, erected in the 1870s in memory of John Keble, the inspirer of the Oxford Movement. The architect, William Butterfield, was much favoured by the Ecclesiologists, and his building, the first brick college in Oxford, has always been violently controversial. The polychrome patterns of chequers, diapers and zigzags in the red brick have been irreverently referred to as 'streaky bacon' by generations of undergraduates. The two quadrangles are not completely closed and the walk through the openings provides the same space and movement experience as through 18th century Peckwater Quad at Christ Church. Butterfield stipulated that the centre of the main Liddon Quadrangle should be grassed and sunken, which offsets and gives even greater feeling of height to the triumphantly towering Tractarian chapel.

Butterfield advocated dark yews, hollies and evergreen shrubs to offset his buildings. The new chapel he built for Balliol in 1856 in his favourite striped buff and red stone was planned not only for its effect in the front quad but also from the new Fellows' garden which surrounded it. The Fellows' garden had not previously been enclosed from the grove and the rest of the college gardens. The Butterfield garden drew attention to his own contribution to the college's architecture and is in effect a chapel garden. Some of his earliest letters to the college insist that the gardener should get on with the turfing and levelling of the garden and getting in the roots of ivy. 'There is no time to lose in such matters,' he wrote. The dark green elements are emphasized as a necessary accompaniment. On December 13th 1856 he wrote:

> I have left a private terrace for the Fellows with a low wall. In front of this I have shewn low trees, as hollies and other dark evergreen shrubs. In the recess at the North end of the ground Eastwards of the Stables I have shewn a large formal shrubbery. To this I would remove any trees from the present gardens, which are in the way of the new plan, and which will bear removing. I would intermix yews with them for the sake of winter appearance. I should like yews in all other places when I have put Y against a tree. It is just possible that some of these may be overshadowed by existing trees in which case it would not be worth while to put them in. But I feel that the College would be made very much more cheerful in winter by some good dark foliage. It is a mistake to connect yews with Churchyards only. I saw last autumn in Herefordshire an avenue of Scots Firs and Yews alternately of a mile long and very old and handsome and Herefordshire is full of yews everywhere, to the great improvement of the scenery in winter.[3]

The effect of the picturesque landscaped chapel so delicately portrayed by William Delamotte was transformed by the Butterfield improvements of the 1850s. The taste of the age approved the demolishing of the genuine early 16th century chapel to be replaced by a 'true style' thirteenth-century Victorian chapel which might, or rather ought, to have been there at the time of the original foundation, in the view of the Ecclesiologists. A decade later Alfred Waterhouse revived the front facade of Balliol in would-be thirteenth-century castle collegiate which Oscar Wilde thought might be confusing to visitors. 'C'est magnifique,' he is supposed to have said, 'mais ce n'est pas la gare.' The Fellows' garden received additions from both the Butterfield and Waterhouse demolitions of old Balliol. There is a doorhead with quatrefoils from the old chapel and stone bosses from the original gateway entrance to the college. The bits and pieces piled together make a centrepiece for the garden, sometimes facetiously called the Devorguilla tomb after the Lady Devorguilla wife of John de Balliol, who in 1284 bought the original three tenements and land on which the college was built.

The Gothic Revival led Oxford to renewing its remembrances of pious founders' intentions. This was nowhere so apparent as at Christ Church which had never given Wolsey his heart's desire for his Cardinal College — a bell tower as commanding as that of Magdalen. Partly through piety and partly through necessity, the bell tower was finally erected by G.F. Bodley in 1878. Gilbert Scott, who in 1860 had given Exeter a brand new medival chapel modelled on the Sainte Chapelle in Paris, was called upon in the 1870s to 'restore' parts of the cathedral. In the course of his survey he advised that the bells were too heavy for the cathedral tower and that the tower should be strengthened or the bells taken and out and put into a new belfry. The belfry was called Wolsey's Tower, and a statue of the Cardinal was placed above the entrance to the fan-vaulted staircase which forms the basement of the tower. The decision to erect the belfry might have been the end of remembering the Cardinal's aspirations if an interesting discovery had not been made when a new entrance to the cathedral from the quadrangle was created by Dean Liddell. It had been decided to narrow and lower the terrace at the same time and this revealed the foundations of the buttresses of Wolsey's projected cloisters, which had been buried by John Fell in his planning of elegant regularity for the quadrangle. Fell's classical balustrade had already been removed, except on the St Aldate's front, and replaced by the battlements and pinnacles, which it was said the Founder would have had if he hadn't fallen from favour at the crucial moment for his college, and some members of the Government Body felt that they should go the whole way in re-gothicising the quadrangle by erecting his intended cloisters. In view of the fact that Wren's masterly tower had been designed to complete a cloisterless quadrangle with rhythmic arcades and a great feeling of space, this was a strange idea, to say the least, but Wren was out of favour with Gothic Revivalists.

The cloisters were not built and their archaeological remains were encased in the stone walls which project at right angles to the terrace. The impression of the Great Quadrangle today is still of the spaciousness and uniformity of the Renaissance, and the Victorian Gothic is played down. The decision not to erect the cloisters and so irrevocably alter the appearance of the Quadrangle was not arrived at without much debate in the Governing Body and a letter from one of its members to the Pall Mall Gazette speaks volumes on the difficulties of decision-making through a large Committee, where there are as many opinions, expressed at length, as there are members.

> Sir,
>
>   Visitors to Oxford who may chance to enter the great Quadrangle of Christ Church cannot fail to be struck by the changes now taking place. The central lawn is fringed by a series of long low walls. At first glace one might suppose them to be buttresses of the terrace wall; it is only when one begins to realize their number, their unnecessary length, and the entire want of reasonableness in their presence, that passive acquiescence gives place to a feeling of vague astonishment. But the strangeness of their appearance is as nothing compared with the strangeness of the arguments advanced in their defence. They are a necessary evil; they are an unquestionable good; they would cost more to remove than to keep; they would cost only a trifle more to keep than to remove; they are not retained with a view to erecting cloisters, but they have an artistic value in themselves, but will serve hereafter as foundations for the buttresses of cloisters; they have an archaeological interest; they are a pleasing novelty; we should wrong the memory of Wolsey if we did not preserve this record of what he wished to do; we should wrong our successors if we did not provide for everything they may possibly wish to do.[4]

The stone wall projections over the grass of the quadrangle do mystify visitors from time to time and a guide of a coach tour was heard to pronounce them 'the tombs of Christ Church dons,' a remark which would have greatly amused the writer of the letter to the Pall Mall Gazette. This was none other than the Rev. Charles Dodgson, better known as Lewis Carroll, who had vociferously opposed all Dean Liddell's so-called improvements. In his skit *The Vision of the Three T's* on the 'Beautifying of Thomas his Quadrangle,' Cardinal Wolsey had himself returned to view the alterations and completion of his intended college as the Victorians thought he wanted it and collapsed moaning into Mercury, his broad-brimmed betasselled hat left floating like a boat on the water. In this same basin, as a prelude to Wonderland, the Buckland children had stoon on a turtle before it was sent down into the kitchen to be made into soup for a banquet and had exercised the family crocodile on a string when word had been given that the Dean's carriage had left Christ Church. It was for Dean Liddell's daughters, however, that the real Wonderland was invented and the Deanery garden, which is the background to so many of the Alice stories is the most famous of all Oxford's gardens.

Charles Dodgson, a maths tutor at Christ Church, first met Alice Liddell in 1856, soon after her parents had moved into the Deanery from Westminster. He was sub-librarian at the time and used to watch the children playing from the library windows which overlooked the garden. He later joined them to play croquet and invented a game called Croquet Castles which was published in 1863. Walks to the Botanic Garden to see Daubeny's giant water lilies, to feed the ducks on Worcester lake and see the Magdalen deer, boating trips on the Thames and visits to the new Museum all contributed to the magic moments of fantasy in a Wonderland based on Oxford reality. Still to be seen are Alice's door in the Deanery garden which was kept locked and only used by the Dean to pass through the garden next door as a short cut to the cathedral, and the chestnut tree on which Dinah the cat, alias the Cheshire cat, used to sit and listen to the story-telling. It is not clear who ordered the wrong roses for the Deanery garden and was so soundly reprimanded — perhaps Pat the Irish gardener who pronounced arm as 'arrum' — or if the rabbit hole was in the garden or out on the river bank at Godstow, but it was undeniably at Christ Church, through the Alice books, that Lewis Carroll captured for all time the wonder of childhood and its 'unending happy summer days.'

The innocence and wonder of childhood was essentially a Pre-Raphaelite image shared by John Ruskin, Alice's drawing master, who appears in Wonderland as an 'old conger eel, that used to come once a week' to teach 'drawing, stretching and fainting in coils.' Children should for ever be playing on daisied lawns under chestnut trees, but Ruskin was aware that every little girl did not have a Deanery garden to grow up in. G.W. Kitchin, a Christ Church friend of both Ruskin and Carroll, told the story of how one little girl was given a dream cottage garden. 'One day, walking near Radley, Ruskin's attention was caught by a group of little girls playing in the road, and he went and talked to them. One of them attracted his special attention. He asked her why she was playing in the dust? Had she no garden at home? Did she love flowers? What her name was? And she replied modestly, with wonder in her eyes. On reaching home, he gave orders to his solicitor to look out for, and buy a cottage with a garden in Radley and have a deed of gift of it made out in the little girl's name which was done accordingly, and she, full of wonder, with her astonished parents, entered at once into possessing it.' Kitchin commented pessimistically, 'I hope the cottage was well tied up, and that it has not already been turned into beer.'[5]

John Ruskin's influence on education, morals and art was enormous, and nowhere more so than at Oxford where he was Slade Professor of Art during the years 1870-79 and 1883-84, and published eight volumes of his lectures. Together with Pugin he was mainly responsible for the intense moral issues behind the Gothic Revival, and he was the apologist and chief supporter of the Pre-Raphaelite Movement. It was he who was largely responsible for the Pre-Raphaelite connection with Oxford. When he was at Christ Church during 1837-39 he had rooms in Peckwater and always regretted that he did not have 'an oriel window looking out on a Gothic chapel.' The Tractarians, the Pre-Raphaelites and the Gothic revival architects were united in a passion for the Middle Ages, whose 'last enchantments' were to be found in Oxford. When the Pre-Raphaelites, Rossetti, Morris, Burne-Jones and Val Prinsep, were depicting deeds of chivalry on the walls of the Union Debating Hall, William Morris wore chain-mail. They had taken up their swords against the shoddy materialism of the Victorian age and vowed to return to the ages that did not disappoint. Morris and Ruskin soon parted company from ecclesiology, being concerned not so much with the way that Gothic architecture and ritualism were associated, but with the genuine craftsmanship of the cathedral builders. Morris

12.1 Natural art history in the Ruskinian Oxford Museum
Fresh plants were brought over from the Botanic Garden every morning for the carvers to copy. This capital was carved from *Hypericum calycinum.*

fulminated against Victorian 'restorations' which led him to found the Society for the Protection of Ancient Buildings in 1877, and pleaded with the guardians of Oxford to preserve that most beautiful of all cities which, with its surroundings, would, if we had a grain of commonsense, have been treated like a most precious jewel whose beauty was to be preserved at any cost.

Oxford's Natural History Museum, completed in 1860 in time for the British Association meeting, although inspired by Ruskin's favoured Venetian Gothic, was conceived in the spirit of traditional craftsmanship. Ruskin, who had attended lectures by Professor Buckland and Daubeny, believed in natural history in the form of natural art history. The ornamentation of the Museum would prove the dictum that 'Nature is the art of God' and Ruskin wrote ecstatically to his collaborator Sir Henry Acland, 'Such capitals as we will have I hope to be able to get Millais and Rossetti to design flower and beast borders — crocodiles and various vermin — such as you are particularly fond of — Mrs Buckland's 'dabby things' and we will carve them and inlay them with Cornish serpentine all about your windows.' Ruskin boasted that the Museum was the first building in Europe since the fifteenth century which had fearlessly put to trial the old faith in Nature. Floral decoration was a speciality and Ruskin lovingly quoted Sir Walter Scott on the decoration of Melrose Abbey.

> Spreading herbs and flowerets bright,
> Glistened with the dew of night
> No herb nor floweret glistened there
> But was carved in the cloister arches as fair.[6]

The wrought-iron ornaments in the large spandrels of the Museum girders are interwoven with branches of lime, sycamore, chestnut, walnut trees and shrubs and in the trefoils briar, passion flowers and ivy. The Irish brothers O'Shea collected fresh plants from Daubeny at the Botanic Garden every morning before they began to carve the capitals. One of his water-lilies and even a Venus fly-trap can be picked out in the decoration. All the workers were to be united by the honest zeal of the medieval craftsman and no swearing was allowed. Art was the expression of man's pleasure in labour. Ruskin put up with his own hands one of the brick columns

in the interior of the Museum but it was later found necessary to demolish it and get a professional bricklayer to re-erect it.

Morris and Ruskin both held strong views that art was not for the few and gave lectures at working men's societies and campaigned for social reforms. Ruskin felt that energy should have fruitful results and deplored the waste of time his undergraduates spent in amusement and the tyranny of games. The Hinksey road project has passed into history as a Ruskinian social experiment. Believing that their energies should be directed to useful social schemes, the Professor took out a volunteer gang of undergraduates in flannels with spades, picks and barrows to make a new cart road at Ferry Hinksey on ground hallowed by the Scholar Gypsy. The party bent on proving the dignity of labour included the young Oscar Wilde, Alfred Milner, and Arnold Toynbee. When they had finished they were to sow the banks with wild flowers and make the rural walk 'far more beautiful than any college gardens.'[7] The locals were to be persuaded to keep geese and donkeys on the green and small prizes were to be offered to children for well-kept doorsteps and the cultivation of moss.

The road was hopeless and the only level piece was said to have been done by David Downs, the Ruskin gardener summoned from the family home at Denmark Hill. The surveyor was able to report to Edward Harcourt, the anxious landowner, however, that the 'young men have done no mischief to speak of.'[8] Shrimpton's the booksellers in Broad Street displayed for some time a caricature of the Slade Professor with a pick and shovel and a caption President of the Amateur Landscape Gardening Society.

There was a lot more to the legacy left by Ruskin and Morris than medieval dreams and abortive social landscape schemes. When after Ruskin's death an Oxford college

---

12.2 Ruskin's road building experiment at Ferry Hinksey
The Slade Professor took out a volunteer gang of undergraduates in flannels with shovels, picks and barrows to make a new cart road on ground hallowed by the Scholar Gipsy. The road proved hopeless.

framed on his principles and called by his name was founded, G.W. Kitchin of Christ Church, who had been amused by the Radley cottage garden episode, saw Ruskin College as growing 'into a great power for good, because it aims specially at bringing the working world into closer relations with the ancient Oxford.' It is to William Morris and his power of making the past part of the present that all preservation societies owe the concept of visible history. He had a deep appreciation of vernacular architecture and was instrumental in preserving the Great Coxwell Barn and other rural buildings which had 'grown up out of the soil and the lives of those that lived in it.' His ideas on honest workmanship and the unity of the arts were passed on in the Arts and Crafts Movement. 'Have nothing in your houses that you do not know to be useful, or believe to be beautiful,' William Morris had said in an address on The Beauty of Life delivered at the Town Hall, Birmingham in 1880. Arts and Crafts brought in the vogue for simple settles, honest chests and tapestries. In the design of fabric Nature was to be followed as the O'Sheas had carved Nature in the Oxford Museum in the mood of Melrose. Ruskin and the Pre-Raphaelites had urged painters to study plants and paint them as they grew. Many Pre-Raphaelite paintings have backgrounds of Oxfordshire flowers, drawn with great detail and accuracy. 'Convent Thoughts,' by Charles Collins (see plate 15), was painted in the garden of the University Press in Walton Street at the invitation of Thomas Combe, the Printer to the University, who was a High Churchman and patron of the Pre-Raphaelites.

The Ruskin-instructed artists had learned to paint the heather and harebells as they grew nestling in the rocks, and Nature was seen to produce her own exquisite miniature rock gardens. The artificial rock garden at St John's College, one of the first of its kind, was greatly admired by lovers of the minutiae of Nature in Pre-Raphaelite art. The dainty flowers nestling in the local coral ragstone had a bejewelled effect which delighted, and as one admirer described it, 'the outline of whorl-leaf of the tiny, delicate, filigree-like plants that cling to the grey stone, and the thousand points of colour, white and grey, mauve and heliotrope, orange and brown, with which it is spangled' was seen as a new garden art.

Its creator, Dr Bidder the Bursar, had faced an old wall with rock work giving pockets for alpines and with underground water to keep them fresh. Reginal Farrer, the 'Father of English Rock Gardening,' who had started his own rock garden in the Ingleborough hills, used to visit the St John's rock garden regularly when he was an undergraduate at Balliol and, after he had himself become famous for his book *My Rock Garden*, written in 1908, he sent Dr Bidder a root of *Potentilla farreri*. The widely-travelled Fellows brought back rock plants from Albania, the Himalayas and New Zealand. The Vice-President brought back a little double campanula from Iceland and the President of Trinity added a gentian from Monte Generoso. The garden still flourishes although the rockery layout has been changed, and there is an inscription on the wall in memory of its creator. 'To the memory of Henry Jardine Bidder B.D., 1847–1923. Fellow, Tutor, Bursar, Vicar of St Giles, Keeper of the Groves. This rock garden which he made and loved is his monument.'

13

The North Oxford Victorian suburb

The Oxford Victorian mixture of Tractarianism, Reform, Ruskin, High Gothic architecture, the Pre-Raphaelites, Arts and Crafts and Wonderland spilled over into the North Oxford suburb. Although Ruskin referred to it as 'the elongating suburb of married fellows on the cock-horse road to Banbury,' a number of civic dignatories and prosperous tradesmen had already established themselves before the dons appeared. The latters' 'unholy rush to the altar' began in 1877 when the celibacy ban was lifted and, as they were required to live within a mile and a half of Carfax, there was a scramble for up and coming North Oxford.

The delights of living in an Oxford 'rus in urbe' were already apparent in Park Town, which, according to the advertisements, possessed 'all the advantages of a situation in the country, combined with the comfort and the security of a town.' A private trust had appointed Samuel Lipscomb Seckham as architect of the 'elegant villas and terraces,' which were completed in 1855, and William Baxter, former Curator of the Botanic Garden, to lay out 'ornamental gardens and pleasure grounds well stocked with trees and flowering shrubs.'[1] Baxter, like the Bobarts before him, had used his experience at the Botanic Garden to take on private work advising on garden layouts. His central garden at Park Town is Loudonesque in style, the semi-formal design being dictated by the regularity of the Crescent, each house of which would have equal enjoyment of the layout. He planted specimen conifers as he had done in Rose Lane outside the Botanic Garden and at Headington Hill for Morell the brewer who had built a house there on the grand scale in 1861.

Park Town, designed by one architect with communal gardens, stables and mews and with strict conditions laid down in title deeds for preserving the uniformity of its design,[2] was in the classical planning tradition of Cheltenham, Bath and Leamington. Attitudes had changed by the time St John's College decided to develop their North Oxford land. In 1859 a local architect, E.G. Bruton, who was diocesan surveyor and a designer of parsonage houses, read a paper to the Oxford Architectural Society on the value of medieval precedent in planning modern domestic buildings as well as

13.1 Classical Park Town with communal centre garden
Park Town, designed by one architect, was completed a few years before the Gothic suburb was planned.

churches and collegiate architecture. One of the first houses
to embody the new Oxford thinking was no. 55 Banbury
Rd, built in 1864 for the Rev. R. St John Tyrwhitt, a disciple of John Ruskin.[3] Both he and the architect of his
house, E.G. Bruton, were much concerned with the development of art education in Oxford. Tyrwhitt was himself an
amateur artist and had worked with William Morris on the
murals of the Debating Hall and had also decorated the walls
of the geology lecture room in the University Museum with a
representation of the Mer de Glace. His red brick house in the
Banbury Rd has a striking Ruskinian doorway with a carved
tympanum attributed to J.H. Pollen of Merton College, who
had also assisted Morris in the painting of the Union murals.

The Seven Lamps of Architecture was the guiding light in
North Oxford and the suburban houses went up in Ruskin's
'honest materials' of brick and stone with a high standard
of workmanship and no roughcast or cemented exteriors.
Ruskinesque polychromatic brick arches and carved stone
capitals modelled from living foliage, in the spirit of Scott's
Melrose, can still be seen along his 'cock-horse road to
Banbury.' The 'last enchantments of the Middle Ages,' both
feudal and monastic, received a new lease of life in North
Oxford, where members of the Arnold family lived. Bell
towers, tracery, angle-turrets and even a garderobe extension
appeared in the Gothic suburb. Creeper-covered doors with
branched Gothic hinges step straight out of a Morris tapestry
of the Romance of the Rose.

The St John's estate of Norham Manor was conceived as a
park suburb filling in the area between the existing Park
Town and the University Parks, which were being laid out
adjacent to the University Museum, completed in 1860.
The houses on the south side of Norham Gardens set into the
perimeter of the park were undoubtedly the pick of the
estate. They could enjoy the landscape sweeping up to the
Gothic museum tower while their gabled and turreted houses
presented a picturesque appearance when viewed from the
park. In 1860 St John's appointed William Wilkinson as
supervisor, but not sole architect, of the estate, and within
his plan there was plenty of scope for individual taste.
Wilkinson saw the house in relation to its setting as he

13.2 Ruskinesque house on the Banbury Road

Creeper-covered walls at no. 55, a Gothic door, polychromatic brick arch, iron finial and carved foliage capitals.

clearly demonstrated in his *English Country Houses*, 1875, and in this he was in the Picturesque tradition. Four of the illustrations in the book were of his North Oxford houses, which were shown as country houses in their own right. The suburb was planned with individual and varied gardens, but a condition was laid down that the flowing setting should not

13.3   A Gothic fantasy on the Norham estate
'Gunfield', seen from the University parks, built in 1874 by Wilkinson's pupil, Frederick Codd.

be broken by high boundary walls in front gardens. North Oxford, like Butterfield, believed in dark green to offset red brick buildings and the low brick walls in the front gardens topped with evergreen hedges and large trees are still a most distinctive feature of the area.

Gee, the nurseryman, whose splendid greenhouse still survives, set up in the Banbury Road to supply the garden suburb. Ferns and spikey plants in pots to echo spikey finials and gables were much in demand, as were the specialised carnations sold by Joseph Bates,[4] a florist and nursery gardener who set up the Parks Nursery by the Parks to be near the new Victorian colleges and suburb. There was no lack of interest in scientific gardening with professors exchanging notes about soil analysis, the carbon content of the North Oxford atmosphere, and contrivances for heating and watering their greenhouses. The Waynflete Professor of Chemistry laid out the garden of his Ruskinian house at 15 Norham Gardens with the help of his father-in-law, Dr Alfred Smee, FRS, the eminent eye surgeon and ecologist, whose book *My Garden, its Plan and Culture together with a general description of its Geology, Botany and Natural History* aroused a great deal of enthusiastic interest when it was published in 1872. The garden was divided up into a series of different sections — a fern glen, a saxifrage, sempervivum and sedum garden, an American garden and an alpinery mound. Cartloads of plants were sent up from the famous Smee garden at Carshalton, and never a day passed without instructions to his daughter about planting lavender under the peach trees, covering the verandah with wisteria or the mound with scillas, and putting peat around the American plants.[5]

Dr Smee complained of the way his son-in-law, Professor Odling, had treated the part of the walk near the park, which he said 'is like a hedge and looks vulgar.' He urged his daughter to increase her efforts to make 15 Norham Gardens into a 'miniature Carshalton garden.' Alfred Smee was of the school of William Robinson whose views expressed in *The Wild Garden* and *Home Landscape* influenced the vogue for naturalizing of bulbs and the planting of hardy exotics in a natural setting. Dr Smee's daughter was not, however, prepared to go all out for her father's glen gardening. A croquet lawn was absolutely essential in North Oxford. The game was comparatively new to Oxford when Lewis Carroll introduced the croquet scenes in *Alice's Adventures in Wonderland* but it soon became an absorbing family game and a little Alice can be seen before a hoop in the Wilkinson drawing of a house in Norham Gardens. 'Tell your husband he was right about the axis of the croquet lawn,' Dr Smee grudgingly admitted in one of his daily gardening letters to his daughter and the eminent authority on the eye conceded that 'as the hoops of the game are placed geometrically, it is offensive to the eye to have curved lines in relation to them.'

Croquet was only one of the respectable dissipations of Norham Gardens and the Banbury Rd, the area covered by the opprobious name of the 'Parks system' by the Fellows who did not succumb to matrimony.[6] Tea parties and amateur theatricals flourished, perambulators increased and cats stalked out their territories as brick wall after brick wall went up in the fashionable suburb. As the Mauds, Alices, Enids and Beatrices grew into children Lewis Carroll, who himself preferred not to forsake the Christ Church Common Room for the permanent matrimonial delights of North Oxford, was constantly called in to entertain with Mad Hatter tea parties or to read 'The Hunting of the Snark.' On receiving an At Home card with Tea 4–6 p.m. written in the corner he hastened to reply that he feared that even an inveterate tea drinker could not drink tea from 4–6 p.m.[7]

The University Parks became as popular a resort for the citizens of Oxford as the college gardens and Christ Church Meadow had always been. The park had been laid out to the plan of James Bateman of Magdalen College with a cricket ground, ornamental walks, a bathing place and a bridge over the Cherwell.[8] In the 1860s, unlike today, the buildings surrounding the park were highly picturesque, the Tower of the Winds, Keble Chapel, the University Museum, the lodges and even the cricket pavilion. In Ruskin's day science could be confined in picturesque buildings and the chemical laboratory attached to the Museum was built as a replica of the Abbot's kitchen at Glastonbury and discharged its 'noxious fumes' from its furnaces through medieval chimneys. Today, alas, the buildings required by Nuclear Physics and Engineering in the Science Area are not picturesque adjuncts to a landscaped park. The University Park provided healthful exercise for North Oxford families and ample scope for civic activities. For Queen Victoria's Jubilee in 1887, 7000 children were entertained to tea in the Park and the enterprising mayor organised tea for all provided by two engines working tanks into which 86 lbs of tea were shovelled, with 70 taps disgorging from lengths of pipe.[9]

The North Oxford Victorian suburb predates other garden

suburbs by at least a decade. It was not planned as a total community like Bedford Park with shops, reading room and pubs, since it was linked to Oxford, which had its own commerce, culture and entertainment. A new church of SS. Philip and James was built to accommodate the new High Church community, however. This was on a site given by St John's College, who nominated their Bursar as the first incumbent. Street's church, affectionately known as Phil and Jim, dominates the area between the Banbury and Woodstock roads, and the Bursar was in a good position to see that the terms of the leases were carried out to the last letter. Leaseholders of St John's are forbidden, amongst other things, to keep pigeons which might eat the mortar from the red brick houses; they are also forbidden to hang out their washing, but this decree was temporarily relaxed in the Second World War and no subsequent Bursar has remembered to reinstate it.

Although much has been lost, there are still delights for the walker in North Oxford, particularly in the Spring when there is a riot of flowering trees alongside the evergreens. A young future Poet Laureate[10] cycling through the area with 'Kant on the handle bars, Marx in the saddlebag' was moved to sing:

Belbroughton Road is bonny and pinkly bursts the spray
Of prunus and forsythia across the public way.

The Victorian favourites, laurustinus, mahonias, aucubas, hollies, berberis, arbutus, pampas grass and yuccas still abound and here and there can be glimpsed a fern-patterned cast-iron seat, a pre-Raphaelite statuette in a shrubbery, a length of rope-shaped brick edging, fossils or strange archaeological ornaments brought back from a donnish holiday or salvaged from a college restoration.

The large scale Ordnance Survey maps of North Oxford made in the 1870s together with the estate agents' advertisements give a detailed picture of the layouts of the gardens. Carriage sweeps flanked by ornamental flower beds and enclosed with brick walls and iron palisades, indoor ferneries and conservatories galore, some heated by flues from fires in the communicating rooms and some by little stoves outside the glasshouses. Flowers were confined to shrubberies, her-

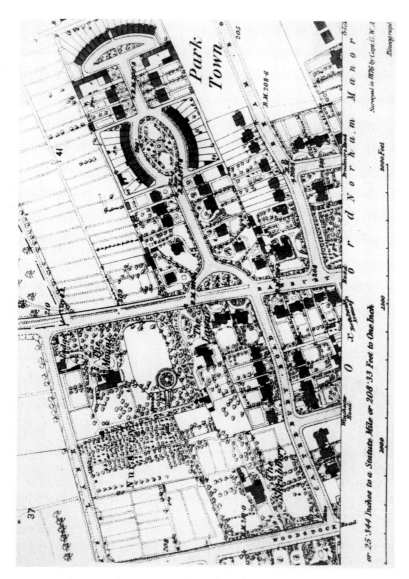

13.4 The Ordnance Survey of North Oxford in 1876
Showing the layout of Park Town and also the three houses, The
Mount, The Shrubbery and The Lawn, which were taken over by
St Hugh's College (see chapter 14).

baceous borders or to the popular island beds. These were usually semi-circular or kidney-shaped and edged with low box or hooped wire framing, and the flowers were graded up from small plants at the edge to a tree, usually weeping, in the centre of the bed. Such a bed can be seen in the Wilkinson illustration and the little Victorian Alice meets up with an isolated island bed in her Adventures with the Live Flowers. It had 'a border of daisies and a willow tree growing in the middle.' 'Aren't you sometimes frightened at being planted out here with nobody to take care of you?' Alice enquired. 'There's the tree in the middle,' said the Rose. 'But what could it do, if danger came?' Alice asked. 'It could bark,' said the Rose.

There was real danger in living on the Norham Manor estate in its early day and the occupants of the first two houses, Professor Goldwin Smith in no. 7 Norham Gardens and Professor Montagu Burrows in no. 8 used to stretch a cord between the two houses to signal if assistance was needed and finally persuaded the Paving Commissioners to give them a street lamp.[11] Professors had been allowed to marry even before the 1877 statute and an almost continuous band of Professors soon came to occupy the best houses overlooking the University Parks. The Wilkinson illustration is of no. 13, the home of Sir William Osler, Regius Professor of Medicine, a house admired and illustrated by Viollet-le-Duc as an example of nineteenth-century architecture based on Gothic art. As the dining room and the drawing room were side by side, the hall had to be given scope for a processional route of taking the ladies in to dinner and for the ladies to withdraw in a becoming fashion after the meal.

Hardly had the academics settled in to North Oxford than a sinister development took place. Not for long did their ladies see themselves as the perfect Victorian wives and mothers processing in to dinner. They wanted to take part in what Oxford had to offer intellectually. It was Women's Education and not Votes for Women that concerned them. As early as 1866 certain wives and sisters of Oxford professors had obtained permission to attend some of the university lectures and even to have some special classes for women. After a set of lectures by Ruskin on Italian Art in 1873,

13.5 No. 13 Norham Gardens

Built in 1868 by William Wilkinson, who designed his Norham Manor suburb as a series of country houses. Illustration from Wilkinson's *English Country Houses*, 1875.

Mrs Creighton, who lived in a house ominously called Middle-march, called together a committee of women to campaign for higher education for women. The celibate dons in their college Common Rooms must have been triumphant when the committee produced a theory of equal rights of husband and wife in intellectual pursuits with the suggestion that the care of the one-year-old baby should be shared, turn about, by the mother in the morning room and its father in his study.

Mrs Creighton was assisted in her proselytizing for women's education by Mrs Humphry Ward, the niece of Matthew Arnold, who was later to write her widely-acclaimed novel *Robert Elsmere* in the Arnoldian tradition; and by Mrs Kitchin, Mrs Max Muller and the two sisters of Walter Pater. The Women's Movement coincided with the cult of aestheticism in Oxford, which was not surprising with Walter Pater, its high priest, living in Bradmore road on the Norham Manor estate. Aestheticism took over from the Pre-Raphaelites but the pursuit of beauty, nature and art was to be a sufficient end in itself and not tied up with Ruskinian moralising. The North Oxford women wore aesthetic colours of sage green, peacock blue and ochre – the 'Greenery Yallery' satirised by Gilbert and Sullivan – but they scorned ideas from Belgravia and Mayfair and emphasized that the fashion of their movement for plain lines and Liberty gowns sprang from William Morris and Burne-Jones. They did not wish to be upholstered like armchairs as their mothers were but draped like women to portray the beauty of motion. Their aesthetic costume looked particularly well on the croquet lawns. 'Most of us were very anxious to be up-to-date and in the fashion, whether in aesthetics, in housekeeping or educa-tion,' wrote Mrs Humphry Ward, the wife of a Brasenose don, in her *Writers' Recollections*.[12]

They furnished their houses with Morris wall papers, spindle-legged chairs, and old chests and cabinets in hand-worked oak on which they stood blue pots. They arranged a very few well chosen flowers in vases with a simple, yet newly conscious oriental art. Pampas grass was particularly favoured in a tall vase against a green wall or de Morgan tiles. It was the Paters of no. 2 Bradmore Road who were the first to have William Morris wallpapers in Oxford, but the Humphry Wards at no. 17 soon followed suit and there were soon few North Oxford houses without walls covered with his flower designs of marigolds, blackthorn, honeysuckle, willows, corncockles, snakes' heads or sunflowers. House and garden were united as never before. The garden came into the house with the Morris papers and fabrics and, literally often, with the ubiquitous creepers. The drawing room opened on to a flower-filled conservatory or wisteria-covered verandah and the dining room led on to a cool fernery. The pampas grass *Cortadena selloana*, only introduced in the mid-nineteenth century, grew out in the garden in the island bed and was arranged inside the house aesthetically. The emancipated young women were part of the floral scene as well. 'We used to grow sunflowers in crewel on our blue-green serge dresses,' recalled Mrs Humphry Ward, the chronicler of North Oxford's aesthetic days. Old-fashioned flowers had been encouraged by Tennyson and the Pre-Raphaelites and in a contribution to the Oxford and Cambridge Magazine in 1856 William Morris lovingly described all the native flowers which would have grown round a medieval abbey, including his favourite, much-copied sunflower, nasturtium — and passion flowers which the monks would never have known. 'At the other edge of the lawn, near the round arches, were a great many sunflowers that were all in blossom on that autumn day; and up many of the pillars of the cloisters crept passion flowers and roses;' and in a great garden beyond there were 'trellises covered with roses, and convolvulus, and the great-leaved fiery nasturtium; and specially all along by the poplar trees were there trellises, but on these grew nothing but deep crimson roses; the hollyhocks were all out in blossom at that time, great spires of pink, and orange and red, and white with their soft downy leaves ... lush green bryony with green-white blossoms, that grows so fast, one could almost think that we see it grow.'[13]

The William Morris cult was essentially a reaction to shoddiness and ostentation, and a belief in the unity of the arts. In the garden it meant an 'old-fashioned' look with a return to straight walks and yew hedges, if appropriate, to assist the effect of the building. Like Ruskin, Morris advocated a 'natural combination of flowers' and both agreed with Sir Walter Scott that 'nothing is more the Child of Art than a garden.' A house springing out of the turf in the approved eighteenth century fashion was a dishonest deception. William Morris divided his garden into compartments hedged by sweet brier and wild roses and Scott and Ruskin revived the term pleasance for the garden. Ruskin loathed showy flowers like dahlias and tulips, which he said should be avoided like garlic, and in general condemned the bigger and better horticultural cult. He saw some Victorian flower gardens as 'an assembly of unfortunate beings, pampered and bloated above their natural size, stewed and heated into diseased growth, corrupted by evil communication into speckled and inharmonious colours; torn from the soil which they loved, and of which they were the spirit and glory, to glare away this term of tormented life among the mixed and incongruous essences of each other, in earth they know not, and in air that is prison to them.'[14] All Ruskin's admonitions were couched in biblical wrath and few in North Oxford who professed to follow in his footsteps would have dared to indulge in gaudy bedding out schemes. His admonitions followed through volumes of text are apt to be contradictory, even on gardening, however, and in general, gardening styles at the end of the nineteenth century had become eclectic, some following historical precedents and others striving towards a new naturalism to accommodate the many new plant introductions from Japan and America. Apart from the Pre-Raphaelites' flowery medievalism there was no precedent to follow in laying out the gardens of North Oxford Gothic houses, since the history of feudal times was no help when it came to the middle class and suburban life style.

When Gothic had run its course and the first Queen Anne building on a large scale went up in North Oxford the time had come for a traditional accompaniment in the garden. The women had triumphed in their battle for education and in 1879 Lady Margaret Hall and Somerville Hall were founded 'for the reception of women desirous of availing themselves of the special advantages which Oxford offers for higher education.' Lady Margaret Hall, called after Henry VII's mother, 'A scholar, a gentlewoman and a saint,' started life in a Norham Gardens house with a North Oxford Gothic portal, but in 1881 a small Queen Anne building was erected and in 1896 Sir Reginald Blomfield went to work in earnest on a Queen Anne extension in 'honest' red brick. Blomfield felt strongly that it was the architect and not the gardener who should be responsible for the design of the garden, and that the garden should harmonise with the house by echoing architectural themes. In his influential *The Formal Garden* of 1892 he advocated the modest formality of the late seventeenth century. William Robinson, the authoritative editor of *The Garden* and author of *The Flower Garden* and *The Wild Garden*, immediately took up the cudgels in *Garden Design and Architects' Gardens* in 1892 and thundered that it was 'barbarous, needless and inartistic' to make gardens harmonise with architecture. The battle was enjoined between architects and gardeners. John Sedding, an architect and member of the Art Workers' Guild, did much to try and bring the two sides together in his ideas on *Garden-craft Old and New*. The terrace, sunken garden, clipped yews and aligned paths of the Lady Margaret Hall garden which harmonise with his Wordsworth Building certainly suggest that here, at least, Blomfield had made his point that the architect should be responsible for the main lines of the garden design.

14

Arts and Crafts

Victorian gardening had been essentially eclectic in style with a continual battle between those who advocated wild, natural or glen gardening, like William Robinson and Alfred Smee, and those who followed Sir Reginald Blomfield, whose architectural eye saw formality as the only answer to resolving the relationship of house and garden. Ruskin and Morris and the Arts and Crafts lobby wanted the best of both worlds, truth to nature and traditional gardencraft. It was left to Gertrude Jekyll and Edwin Lutyens to give the new century a new style, which would reconcile architects, gardeners and craftsmen.

The eighteenth century had worked out the principles of landscape gardening with 'poet's feeling and painter's eye'[1] and vast tracts of land, wood, water, groves, valleys, and glades had been made into landscape pictures. Nineteenth century gardens were on a smaller scale but could take advantage of the wealth of new plants collected from explorations in the Himalayas and the Far East. The azaleas, winter-flowering jasmine, and new rhododendrons in particular could transform woodland gardening. The painter's eye was once again needed to create a landscape with flowers, but this time it was an eye deeply appreciative of colour that was called for, and the vision to mass the varied colours in natural groupings. The Arts and Crafts understanding of materials would also be essential as the new pictorial gardener must also be a plantsman with a knowledge of where to grow plants and when they would flower in the designed colour scheme. William Robinson had pleaded that the beautiful new plants such as *Lilium auratum, Primula japonica*, chrysanthemums, and the so-called Japanese anemone, should be integrated into flower borders and not displayed in collections. The garden artists had to 'choose from ten thousand beautiful living things; to study their nature and adapt them to his soil and climate; to get the full expression of their beauty; to grow and place them well and in right relation to other things, which is a life-study in itself, in view of the great numbers of the flowers and flowering trees of the world.'[2]

Such a garden artist in the Arts and Crafts tradition was found in Gertrude Jekyll, herself a disciple of Morris and Ruskin, whose hatred of the Victorian age of mass production she shared. She studied art at the South Kensington School of Art and was a friend of Hercules Brabazon, to whom she acknowledged her debt in learning 'colour beauty.' Ruskin had once said that Brabazon was 'the only person since Turner at whose feet I can sit and worship and learn about colour.'[3] Miss Jekyll's advice was widely sought after for impressionistic colour scheme planting. Finally in 1908 she set down many of her ideas in *Colour in the Flower Garden*, which included schemes she had already planted for friends and clients. She emphasized that no colour stands alone and that its real value was brought out in relation to the colours beside it. Her borders were often planned with cool colours at either end, working up to fiery colours in the middle, offset by yellow or copper foliage. Dark yews were used as a backcloth to enhance flowers of delicate colour and the shape and texture of foliage. For azaleas Miss Jekyll recommended white at the lower and more shady end of a group with pale pinks and soft yellows to follow, building up to the deepest crimson, flame and burnt orange colours. Detailed instructions for flowering changes are given. White everlasting pea planted behind delphiniums and *Clematis jackmanii* behind the pea and when the stalks of the delphiniums become bare and the foliage turns yellow the everlasting pea to be trained over the stalks which have been cut short. The clematis is brought over to take the place of the pea in the middle of August when it has stopped flowering. Gypsophila to follow oriental poppies, to be followed in turn by trailing nasturtiums to cover over the patches of gypsophila when it has gone brown.

The attention to detail, lovingly given in her gardening books, proves her friend William Robinson's belief that true artist-craftsman gardening was 'a life-study in itself.' Miss Jekyll only came to gardening after her involvement with the Arts and Crafts Movement, her study of painting and her own participation in such crafts as silver engraving and embroidery. When her eyesight began to fail and she had to give up close work she turned her attention single-mindedly to gardening. Her embroidery as well as her painting had given her a training in design and colour combinations. She supported Morris in the aims of his S.P.A.B. and had learned from him to appreciate local vernacular traditional crafts. She later published her study of Surrey crafts and her childhood memories of cottage life in *Old West Surrey*, published in 1904. She rescued from destruction all kinds of household objects which were even then becoming obsolete, including some fine examples of Wealden ironwork, which now form the Jekyll Collection in the Guildford Museum. There was an increasing demand for commuter houses in West Surrey after the arrival of the railway and she made a passionate plea for the protection of the old vernacular buildings which were being destroyed to make way for them.[4] The listing and protection of buildings legally was far off when she said, 'to retain them untouched, to preserve them from decay or demolition should be felt our duty. I feel sure that in another hundred years this will be known more widely and felt more strongly even than now.' Like William Morris, she was deeply aware that the harmony between domestic buildings and their landscape sprang from the intimate relationship between the soil and the local building materials – a harmony which she saw was being disrupted by the easy rail transport of mass-produced slates and bricks.

Her interest in vernacular architecture was further stimulated by her friendship with the young architect Edwin

Lutyens which by the end of the 1880s had flourished into a partnership. Lutyens was also a native of West Surrey and had learned much about its architectural traditions from a Godalming builder. Driving round the narrow lanes together in Miss Jekyll's dog-cart they sketched and photographed vernacular details which appealed to them; a buttressed wall, a patterned chimney, the angle of a building which, although the result of chance, was pleasing, the galleting in the mortar courses, tile-hung cottages which probably traced their origins back to the design of Flemish weavers. 'Eye and brain must be alert to receive the impression and studious to store it to add to the hoard of experience,' wrote Gertrude Jekyll, but for her it was the accompaniment of flowers with the domestic buildings which was especially noted and later assimilated into her garden designing; lavender and hollyhocks by an old weather-boarded barn, snapdragons along a brick wall, cottage porches wreathed with roses, ferns in dipping wells and herring-boned patterns of brick and ironstone in the garden paths, and old millstones embedded in paving.

At Munstead in 1896 Lutyens planned a new house for Miss Jekyll which gave expression to their belief in vernacular tradition; not a mere picturesque imitation of old forms but built in the spirit of West Surrey craft workmanship which allowed capacity for fresh development to meet changing needs. Built in the local stone and timber, Munstead Wood was described by its owner as 'designed in the thorough honest spirit of the good work of old days and the body of it so fashioned and reared has, as it were, taken to itself the soul of a more ancient dwelling place. The house is not in any way a copy of an old building, though it embodies the general character of old structures in the district.' When Miss Jekyll had planted a garden round the house, leading it back naturally into the landscape from which its fabric had been taken, William Morris's ideal of a homestead which was part of the continuous life of the earth had been achieved. The Lutyens house and Jekyll garden were to influence architecture and gardening for decades to come.

The Jekyll garden, although inspired by the Surrey scene, was easily adapted. Helen Allingham of Witley, a friend of

Gertrude Jekyll, has made familiar to us the actual scenes which inspired woodland cottage gardening, where sunken lanes, sandy paths, and cottage gardens blended with heath and woodland. Gertrude Jekyll idealised the cottage garden, as the eighteenth-century landscape gardeners had idealised the rural scene, but her stylised cottage gardens were intimate and inward-looking and the attraction of the setting of the house was not dependent on long views or improved rural landscape; the new vernacular house was surrounded by a planted garden and the garden melted imperceptibly into the woodland. Like the Lutyens house, the Jekyll garden embodied traditional ideas but at the same time was forward-looking and adapted to new ideas. Jekyll herbaceous borders were the old mixed borders of the cottage garden but allowed her to develop her impressionist planting schemes. Edwin Lutyens provided an architectural frame of walls, paths, steps, rills and other features within which she could plant informally but without the excesses of wild gardening. The combination of architect and craftswoman gardener was an innovation and had a far-reaching effect on the relation of house and garden.

Oxford produced its own Miss Jekyll in the form of Miss Annie Rogers, Custos Hortulorum of St Hugh's College. Miss Rogers spent her life in Oxford and had had no contact with country craft like Miss Jekyll, but she was a follower of William Morris and the Arts and Crafts Movement, had attended Ruskin's Art lectures, and was one of the chief protagonists of women's education.[5] She was the daughter of the Drummond Professor of Political Economy who was a close friend of the Rev. Charles Dodgson. The latter photographed her and told her many stories, and she was shown *Alice's Adventures Underground* while it was still in manuscript.[6] The young Annie had more in mind for herself than the Alice of the book and was determined to embark on higher education. In 1873, when she was seventeen she entered for and won an exhibition to Worcester College, who were dismayed to find that the initials A.M.A.H. had stood for Annie Mary Anne Henley. The Professor's daughter was rejected but she started her campaigning for the education of home students and the year before the first women's halls

were opened she saw the founding of the Society of Oxford
Home Students, later to become St Anne's Society and
College. Annie Rogers had already proved by her Worcester
exploit that statements such as J.W. Burgon had made when
preaching a sermon at New College in 1884 were unwise. To
the women present he fulminated, 'Inferior to us God made
you: and inferiors to the end of time you will remain.'
Shortly afterwards a chastened undergraduate recorded in
verse, which it is to be hoped that J.W. Burgon read:

> I spent all my time with a crammer,
> And then only managed a gamma,
> But the girl over there,
> With the flaming red hair,
> Got an alpha-plus eaily — damn her.[7]

As well as working for the Home Students, Annie Rogers
was a tutor at St Hugh's College and when the college moved
into its new buildings in 1916 she immediately assumed
responsibility for the garden, and its care became an absorbing interest to the end of her life. Normally committees
supervise Oxford college gardens but Miss Rogers, like Miss
Jekyll, was a formidable law unto herself. Nobody objected
to what was seen as 'enlightened despotism' in the garden as
it grew yearly in beauty under her guidance.[8] She read all
the gardening books avidly. William Robinson's Flower
Garden, Reginald Farrer on Alpines and Bog plants and the
English Rock Garden, Gertrude Jekyll on Wall and Water
gardens, Eden Phillpotts on Shrubs, W.J. Bean on Trees. She
read up on pruning hardy shrubs from the RHS journal and
kept copious cuttings from the *Gardener's Chronicle* and
Gardening Illustrated. Such gardening magazines were aimed
at the discerning middle-class gardener who actually gardened,
and this included an increasing number of devoted lady
gardeners. The *Gardener's Chronicle* had begun in 1841
under the direction of Paxton and Lindley, price 6d. It was a
high-water mark in the annals of gardening as Lindley sought
to make it 'a weekly record of everything that bears on
Horticulture, or Garden Botany, and to introduce such
Natural History as has relation to Gardening, together with
Notices and Criticisms of every work of importance on the
subject.'[9] *Gardening Illustrated*, begun in 1879 by William

Robinson, was an instant success. Annie Rogers read and noted and ordered and acquired plants from friends with or without their knowledge. A fat green book belonging to the Custos Hortulorum preserved at St Hugh's has alphabetical lists of addresses and garden plants on the same page. It is sometimes difficult to see whether 'very sweet — thin out late summer' refers to a rock rose or a North Oxford don beginning with R. It has also been suggested that all the surnames in the book were of gardening enthusiasts from whom cuttings could be obtained at the suitable period indicated. The college gardener was often taken along with her on such visits and walked behind her along the herbaceous border filling his pockets with cuttings from plants surreptitiously indicated by Miss Rogers. The Bidder rock garden at St John's was a special delight, and college porters were warned that although a blind eye might be turned on an odd snip here and there, if Miss Rogers was seen to appear with her umbrella, a favourite receptacle for cuttings, she must on no account be left on her own.

The St Hugh's garden may now look as though it had been planned as a whole, but it was made up from a number of existing gardens belonging to North Oxford houses, acquired over a period of thirty-five years. These were houses belonging to prosperous citizens of Oxford, built in the 1840s before High Gothic and married dons appeared on the scene. The Mount, acquired by St Hugh's in 1913, was built for the solicitor and Town Clerk and known locally as Quillville. It was then so isolated that the owner always carried firearms walking home from Oxford. The next occupant kept a fox chained on the lawn. Another house in Woodstock Road, acquired much later by the College, called The Shrubbery and now the Principal's house, was originally built for Thomas Mallam, Mayor of Oxford in 1847.[10] He began life as a tobacconist but later became an auctioneer, when he acquired, amongst other things, an unwanted Tudor ceiling for which he had a new room built on to his house. His preoccupation with the acquisition of wealth and property gave rise to the local name for his house as Quidville. The third large North Oxford garden to be incorporated into St Hugh's grounds was that of The Lawn, and the original yew hedge

14.1 The building of St Hugh's, c. 1913

The Mount, originally built for the Town Clerk of Oxford in the
1840s, had large grounds which became part of the college gardens.

dividing it from The Mount next door, and seen on the OS map, is part of the present garden.

Amazingly the work of building the neo-Georgian college went on during the Great War and the students were able to move in from their cramped quarters in Norham Gardens in 1916. The garden was given over to wartime food production, including the keeping of pigs, but Miss Rogers' thoughts were always on the planning of a college garden which would bring together the old gardens that had been inherited. The head gardener from The Mount was taken into the college's services and was warned that it was Miss Rogers' instructions that were to be carried out in future. He returned from a visit to the dell to announce that the old tramp working there had better be thrown out. 'That *is* Miss Rogers,' he was calmly told. Annie Rogers, like Gertrude Jekyll, believed that gardening ladies should be weather-proof and prepared for anything. She always wore stout boots, an old mackintosh and a kind of trilby hat when working in the garden. Like Miss Jekyll she kept her kind heart concealed under a formidable expression and was, of course, an ardent feminist. She wanted the very best for her home students and on one occasion approached the young Gilbert Murray to give some tutorials for her. He rather diffidently asked about payments and on being told that a certain Mr Smith was paid 10/-d an hour he indicated that that would be acceptable. 'You misunderstand me, Mr Murray,' said the redoubtable Miss Rogers, 'Mr Smith is one of my better tutors.' During the War, when sugar was at its scarcest, a neighbour came in to borrow some lumps for an unexpected visitor. 'Man, I suppose?' enquired Miss Rogers. 'Parson, I expect? Thought so.'

The flagged terrace to the college's garden front is 60 yards long and 20 yards wide and it was here that Miss Rogers developed her flair for colour-related planting. Along the long south front of the redbrick building, which was covered with wall shrubs and climbers and sheltered by the shallow wings from wind and frost, tender plants such as passion flowers and pomegranate survived. The terrace itself was laid out, not as a rock garden, but as a tapestry of low-growing plants in beds raised slightly above the paving.[11] When Eleanour Sinclair Rohde visited Miss Rogers in the

early 1930s she found that 'the varied colours of the helian-
themums (nearly forty varieties), alpine phloxes, saxifrages
(chiefly the encrusted kinds), sedums, veronica (various species), fragaria lucida, saponaria ocymoides, potentillas,
thymes, genista sagittalis, oenothera taraxacifolia, convolvulus mauritanicus, etc, suggest the charming phrase in the
Paradisus – "the place will seem like a peece of tapestry of
many glorious colours to encrease every one's delight."' The
tapestry and bejewelled effect would have delighted Annie
Rogers, a devotee of Morris and Ruskin and the Pre-Raphaelite
love of depicting the minutiae of Nature. Some of the St
John's plants brought back from far-flung parts for the
Bidder rock garden had a new lease of life in Miss Rogers's
Paradise. Inset in the terrace beds were Italian cypresses and
pots of agapanthus and at the western end of the stone path
a sundial and rose pergola.

Miss Rogers delighted in collecting flowering trees and
shrubs for the garden. The *Magnolia soulangeana* on the
main lawn was given by the students to celebrate the 1918
armistice and Miss Rogers instituted the custom by which
each new member of the Council presented a tree to the
garden. This custom continues and each new Fellow now
presents one. Many features of the old gardens were brought
into the new college garden by Miss Rogers. The mount
which had given the Banbury Road house its name had been
demolished with the building. Judging by the Ordnance
Survey map this was quite a sizeable feature, perhaps a copy
of that in New College garden, made with the spoil from
digging the cellars of the house. This part of Oxford, the
unenclosed land north of St Giles' Church, was known as
St Giles Field and since the sixteenth century gravel for
road repair in Oxford had been extensively dug leaving the
land pitted with holes and trenches. One such pit had been
turned into a fernery by the Vicar of St Margaret's, the last
tenant of The Lawn before it was acquired by St Hugh's, and
another pit at The Mount had become an ornamental dell.
All these features of both gardens, wild garden, orchard, dell,
shrubberies, winding paths and mature trees were brought
together by Miss Rogers. A nut walk was underplanted in the
Jekyll fashion with drifts of daffodils and other Spring

flowers, and violets and periwinkle encouraged along the winding paths of the wild garden. In 1932 the college acquired more land as part of The Shrubbery and here can still be seen the remains of the Edwardian garden with the huge low greenhouse and tanks for Sir George Whitehead's orchids and a sunken garden.

Eleanour Sinclair Rohde gave pride of place to St Hugh's garden, which was not merely a spring or summer garden, but full of interest the whole year round. *The Times* of November 10 1932, when reviewing her *Oxford's College Gardens*, noted that she had given 'a well-deserved tribute to Miss Anne Rogers, who has made the terrace garden at St Hugh's one of the beauties of modern Oxford.' The book was given to Miss Rogers inscribed 'To the Custos Hortulorum with the love and respect of St Hugh's College.' Annie Rogers was killed in St Giles in 1937 in the way that many people feared she would one day end her life, as she appeared to have a total disregard for motorised traffic. A sundial was erected at the entrance to the terrace in memory of the Custos Hortulorum with an inscription by Professor Myres: 'Floribus Anna tuis faveat sol luce perenni.' In her will she had left her gardening bible, the Country Life *Century Book of Gardening*, to Mr George Harris, the Head Gardener of St Hugh's College, who had been her greatly valued helpmate in the creation of Oxford's finest garden between the wars.

The art of Jekyll gardening could be learned from the study of the detailed planting plans and advice in Gertrude Jekyll's books *Wood and Garden* (1899); *Wall and Water Gardens* (1901); *Colour in the Flower Garden* (1908); *Gardens for Small Country Houses* (1912); *Garden Ornament* (1918). Oxford could not directly absorb the Surrey vernacular style and the heathland gardening, but it was much influenced by a nearer and more indigenous cult — the charm of the Cotswolds. Many new buildings in Oxford went up with Cotswold slates and squared rubble limestone and old-fashioned Cotswold manor gardening with roses round even baroque arches appeared in the colleges. The garden of the Provost's Lodgings at Worcester College was actually laid out by Alfred Parsons RA, who was one of the famous Broadway set consisting of Edmund Gosse, Henry James, Edwin Abbey,

John Sargent and Mary Anderson, who were the original pro-
moters of Cotswold charm.[12]

William Gilpin had seen nothing in the Cotswold landscape
which would characterise it as a picturesque region. He found
its meadows and downy appearance featureless and disliked
the dry stone walls which separate the fields, but did not
seem to notice the stone villages. Cobbett too found the
Cotswold country poor and dull with little to please the eye.
In 1876 William Morris and Edward Burne-Jones stayed at
Lord Coventry's Broadway Tower, which an Oxford colleague
Cormel Price had leased, and were enchanted with the
village nestling in the valley. The Cotswold tour became
particularly attractive to Oxonians but it was really the
image of the Cotswolds as seen through American eyes that
captured the imagination.

Harper's Magazine of New York had sent over a team of
illustrators to depict the English scene and two of their
number, Edwin Abbey and Frank Millet, discovered Broadway. Soon there was a colony of artists, including the painter-
gardener Alfred Parsons, who settled at Luggers Hill. Henry
James, who had already published *The Passionate Pilgrim*
in 1875, in which he poured out the feelings of an American
seeing for the first time the land which embodied his natural
affections and the literary and artistic associations of a lifetime, wrote an article on 'Our Artists in Europe' for *Harper's
Magazine*.[13] Alfred Parsons was an Englishman, but he
featured in the Henry James article because he had visited
America and had, the author felt, 'learned so well how
Americans would like England to appear.' He knew 'exactly
the England that the American imagination, restricted to
itself, constructs from the poets, the novelists, from all the
delightful testimony it inherits.' Alfred Parsons certainly
delighted in the rural picturesque, particularly the type of
vignette later used for 'highways and byways' local books;
meadows and lanes, dovecotes and tithe barns, orchards,
streams, cottages and smocked countrymen, but it was in
the depiction of the old Broadway gardens that Henry James
felt he excelled himself, 'the garden walls, the mossy roofs,
the open doorways and brown interiors, the old-fashioned
flowers, the bushes in figures, the geese on the green...'

Alfred Parsons was happiest when painting flowers, and in particular that most English of all flowers, the rose. He is best known for his illustrations of Ellen Willmott's *The Genus Rosa* and for his illustrations for William Robinson's *The English Flower Garden* and *The Wild Garden.* An unusual depiction of a rose is his pub sign for 'The Rose Revived' at Newbridge showing a rose in a glass of beer. He painted many gardens including Miss Willmott's at Warley Place and also designed gardens featuring roses and old-fashioned flowers. Henry James was delighted with the garden he designed for him at Lamb House, Rye, calling Alfred Parsons the 'best of men as well as best of landscape-painters and gardeners.'[14] At Wightwick Manor, a house with Ruskin and Morris influences, Alfred Parsons designed a garden with lawns, borders, golden yew hedges, and a circular arbour covered with pink roses and purple clematis. He relished the literary associations of flowers, and plants were brought to the Wightwick garden from Tennyson's Farringford and Morris's Kelmscott Manor. At Court Farm, Broadway, where he designed the garden for the famous Edwardian actress Mary Anderson, he was able to incorporate the old stone out-buildings with moss-grown roofs into the design. Lilies under pleached limes, tiny planted courtyards and peacocks cut on yew hedges completed the old-fashioned look and seemed a perfect setting for a Kate Greenaway child.

Alfred Parsons was a cousin of Emily Olive, the wife of the Provost of Worcester College, Dr Daniel, and it was through the Daniels that the Cotswold garden image came to the colleges of Oxford. The Revd. Dr Charles Henry Daniel was Oxford through and through. He was, as the Oxford Magazine recorded, 'a true scholar by instinct and acquirement and an artist by genius.' In 1859 he was Librarian of the Union when the famous Pre-Raphaelite painting of the murals took place. He was tutor, Bursar, Librarian, Chaplain and finally in 1903, Provost of Worcester College. He was responsible for the decoration of the hall and chapel as carried out to the design of William Burges and wrote a history of the college. Dr Daniel was a pioneer in private printing, which he took up seventeen years before Morris embarked on the Kelmscott Press. A charming book from the

Daniel Press in Fell's seventeenth-century type, was *The Garland of Rachel*, (1881), being poems by 'divers Kindly Hands' which included Austin Dobson, Edmund Gosse, Robert Bridges and Lewis Carroll, for Rachel Daniel's first birthday. The printer's work was by Dr Daniel, the head-press by Alfred Parsons, and illumination by Mrs Daniel. Emily Daniel was herself an artist and on one occasion in June 1895 printed the posters and programmes for a charity performance of Alice in Wonderland in which Rachel was Alice and her sister Ruth, the Dormouse. The performance was to take place in the Worcester College garden and Mr Dodgson was seen shyly hiding in the shrubbery as he watched the rehearsals.[15] At the last moment he expressed disapproval of people paying to enter the grounds, which was resolved by the college by allowing the audience to come in free but paying to go out. A truly Carrollian solution.

When Dr Daniel became Provost in 1904 he asked Alfred Parsons to redesign his garden. The Daniels had a Cotswold cottage near Stow-on-the-Wold and a boat near Bablock-hythe and the Rose Revived, and were only too willing to have a Cotswold garden in the Alfred Parsons style. There was a sundial in the centre of the garden and round it beds of roses, pinks and snapdragons. All the beloved 'old-fashioned' flowers, the delphiniums, tiger lilies, peonies, sweet peas, wallflowers, larkspur and irises grew happily in the shelter of the stone wall that separated the Provost's lodgings from the main quadrangle. It had that element of Parsons gardening which Henry James referred to as a 'nook quality.' Not content with bringing the romance of Cotswold manor gardening to the garden concealed behind the wall of the Provost's lodgings, Dr Daniel extended the roses round the door image to Henry Keene's classical buildings on the North side of the Quad, and the fan-lighted door of the Provost's lodgings at the end of the terrace was embowered with flowery creepers in true old-fashioned Cotswold cottage style. The effect today is viewed with mixed feelings.

Dr Daniel was a scholarly follower of the Arts and Craft Movement which had led on from the Ruskinian revolt from academic theory. The Art Workers Guild had been formed in 1884 to promote 'the Unity of all the Aesthetic Arts,' backed by William Morris, and when painters, weavers, wood-engravers, printers, illuminators and others all joined forces, a new impetus was given to the ideals of craftsmanship. They believed that the knowledge of the craft was fundamental to a designer. The young Lutyens, Sedding, Lethaby and Voysey were dedicated to Arts and Crafts principles for architecture, Hamo Thornycroft in sculpture, Walter Crane in decorative arts. John Sedding and Alfred Parsons were both founder-members of the Art Workers Guild and they and Gertrude Jekyll extended the same ideas to garden-making. Blomfield had been ridiculed by William Robinson as a garden designer who knew nothing about his materials — plants.

Some Arts and Crafts details appeared on Edwardian houses as North Oxford extended northwards. Voyseyesque arched porches, projecting eaves and leaded casements can be seen on houses in the Woodstock Road, and sale catalogues at the beginning of the twentieth century advertise these as having paved walks, circular lily ponds, pergolas, loggias, and terraces with ornamental stone seats. Balustrades were out of fashion. There was to be a unity between house and garden by linking the materials used for steps and walls with that used on the house, in the Lutyens manner. This can be seen at Rhodes House where the stone steps match the stone used for the window surrounds.

Rhodes House, by Sir Henry Baker, was the first building in the University to be built to look like a Cotswold manor house, as opposed to the Daniel treatment of giving an eighteenth-century college the Cotswold look through rampant planting. While it is true that the entrance to Rhodes House from South Parks Road is too imperial-looking, with its pillars and copper-domed rotunda, to reflect Cotswold charm, Sir Herbert, who had worked with Lutyens on grand public buildings in Delhi, wanted the entrance front to be fitting for a 'seat of classical learning' and as a memorial to Cecil Rhodes in 'the Oxford he loved.' Rhodes House on the garden side is seen as a seventeenth-century manor house with hipped roof of stone slates and mullioned windows. Sir Herbert Baker felt that the building, which was begun in 1926, should represent the 'traditional craftsmanship of the stone-building shires of Oxford and Gloucester,' and inside

14.2 Rhodes House, by Sir Henry Baker, begun 1926

The garden front resembles a Cotswold manor house with hipped roof, stone slates and mullioned windows. In the Arts and Crafts tradition there is an artistic unity between the house, its interior decoration and the garden.

Morris fabrics and honest Arts and Crafts furniture were used. On one of the walls hangs the William Morris tapestry of the Romance of the Rose bequeathed by the architect as a Kelmscott finishing touch.

Sir Herbert Baker, who was a friend of Miss Jekyll's, maintained that the early work of Edwin Lutyens was inspired by her sense of the 'harmony of Art and Life.'[16] The house, its interior decoration and the garden must be an artistic unity. Sir Herbert had sought Gertrude Jekyll's advice on the laying out of the garden of Groote Schuur, the house he designed for Cecil Rhodes in South Africa, and also for his own garden at Owletts, Cobham, Kent. There is no direct evidence for having consulted her about the garden for Rhodes House but certainly today the broad herbaceous border in front of the Wadham stone wall has a Jekyll character.

Somerville College in 1933 was the next college to acquire a Cotswold look. Like the other women's colleges Somerville started with an older house, in their case Walton House on Walton Street, and developed piecemeal as benefactors appeared. The entrance from the Woodstock Road through a round-arched gateway leads to a small squared-rubble Cotswold stone quadrangle, which is quite a contrast to the rest of the college through the next archway.

The Oxford Magazine of May 1936 welcomed 'the first Lutyens college in Oxford' but, apart from a pedestal to support Mercury in the Tom Quad fountain at Christ Church, Campion Hall was to be Edwin Lutyens's only commission in Oxford. Lutyens was always at pains to design special features for his clients' needs and relished the idea of purpose building for a Jesuit college. William Morris's S.P.A.B. and the Oxford Preservation Trust wanted the old Micklem Hall on the Brewer Street site preserved. Lutyens added a gable to it and used it as a guide for the design of the new hall, using materials matching the old house and the city walls opposite on the narrow street. The courtyard within reveals a Cotswold manor looking onto a masonry-edged pond, all contained within a small area. Campion Hall is masterly in its reticence of a new building fitting in to an old street scene. Many people are in fact unaware that Campion Hall is a Lutyens building until they look closer at the fine craft workmanship to be seen in the details of the building.

15

Boars Hill

Gertrude Jekyll and William Robinson might well have been thought to have said the last word in woodland gardening. Miss Jekyll had described in *Country Life* how the garden and woodland landscape should be united through harmonious planting.

> The scheme of gardening has been kept very simple. It was evident that the beautiful stretch of forest ground deserved to have its own sentiment preserved as much as possible and that where it met the garden it would be well that the two should join easily and without any sudden jolt, therefore the planting between wood and lawn is of easy groups of such shrubs and trees as first suggest woodland; crabs and amelanchier with plantings of double-flowered bramble and double gorse and some of the wilder of the rambling roses. By degrees as the clumps or brakes approach the lawn, they have a more garden character, some are of rhododendrons and one at some distance from these is of azaleas.[1]

There was, however, still a further stage to go in the understanding of woodland gardening beyond the horticulturist's love of plants or the sensitive eye of the landscape painter. The ecological approach, the interrelationship between plant life and the environment, only came to be studied in the twentieth century. Geoffrey Blackman, who was to be Sibthorpian Professor of Rural Economy at Oxford from 1945–1970, was one of the first to try to bring the benefits of a wider ecological understanding to gardening. While he was lecturer in Ecology at Imperial College, London from 1935 until 1945 he expressed this view in an article on 20 February, 1937 in the *Gardeners' Chronicle*, of which he was associate editor for five years:

> Horticulture might well be defined as a study of plants in a man-made environment, and ecology as a study of plants in the tranquillity of Nature untouched by man. Clearly, these two subjects have a great deal in common, but even though it is often implied, it is seldom stated that ecology has a direct bearing on horticulture or, for that matter, horticulture on ecology. Yet research workers in both fields are attacking similar problems, with only this difference, that the ecologist chooses to conduct his experiments 'where every prospect pleases and only man is vile.' Ecologists in the past have directed their attention principally to discovering what factors govern the distribution of vegetation throughout the world. They have, perhaps, thought in terms of continents rather than in square yards and acres, units more familiar to the gardener. Yet, in spite of this, we can learn a great deal from the principles they have established.

Professor Blackman's own researches on plant nutrition, weed destruction and the introduction of new crops were to have a major influence on agriculture and horticulture after the 1930s. The question he had originally asked himself, the answering of which was to have such far-reaching effects and to lead to a Fellowship of the Royal Society, was, 'Why do bluebells grow in woods?' It was a question that would have delighted the seventeenth-century Oxford empiricists, who knew the value of asking the right questions. The answer seems simple enough. Bluebells will grow very happily in full sunlight as on the little rocky islands off the coast of Brittany, but detest being trampled by animals in meadow land. They grow well in deciduous woods because they flower early in Spring when there is ample light before the canopy shades them and little competition from other plants. The effects of light on plant growth and competition, distribution of species in woodland communities and nutrients were all to become life-long studies which influenced not only all future ecological researches but made Geoffrey Blackman an outstanding woodland gardener.

The Blackmans first found a house on top of Putney Hill

in wild woodland, unbelievably covered with bluebells, and started to plant rhododendrons between the trees. The War stopped gardening pursuits as Geoffrey Blackman was occupied in applying biology and ecology to the task of increasing food production. He recruited a team, often called the 'Blackman boys,' many of whom are now botanists of international fame and heads of botany departments. Geoffrey Blackman was responsible for the cultivation of sunflowers as an oil seed crop.[2] The sunflower, so beloved by William Morris and the ladies of North Oxford for aesthetic purposes, was now to add commercial horticulture to its functions. Selective weed control, used to increase wartime cereal production was to revolutionise the maintenance of garden lawns. Geoffrey Blackman, a great lover of wild flowers, always regretted that his successful researches had destroyed the poetic image of cornfields full of scarlet poppies and after the war, when motorways were being built, he pressed for grass islands to be left in the centre to encourage the seeding of wild flowers. The life's work that followed the question about the bluebell often took Professor Blackman far afield. He gave advice to the Rubber Research Institute in Malaya, where he was responsible, with the help of his Oxford team, for introducing the use of hormones to increase the flow of latex from the trees. Even after retirement he was asked by the United States to investigate the ecological effects of herbicides used in the Vietnam war and to advise on the aftermath of defoliation.[3]

When Geoffrey Blackman was given the Sibthorpian Chair he refused to live in North Oxford, the traditional home of Oxford professors, because it did not have rhododendron soil and he and his wife, Audrey, had set their hearts on continuing the woodland gardening they had begun at their Putney Hill home. He was soon made, appropriately, Keeper of the Groves at St John's College, of which he was a Fellow, and turned his attention to making an ecological study of the grounds. The problems of where to live and how to make the college grounds suitable for his kind of woodland gardening were solved simultaneously. The answer to both was Bagley Wood, which had been owned by St John's since the sixteenth century.[4] West Wood House on its outskirts was rented from

15.1 A study in persuasion

A sceptical St John's gardener (Mr Munday) listens to the professorial Keeper of the Groves (the late Professor Geoffrey Blackman). Model by Audrey Blackman.

the college for the home of the Sibthorpian Professor, and cartload after cartload of leaf mould was transported from Bagley Wood to St John's College for the new Keeper of its Groves, who used it to good advantage to transform the lime-soaked Oxford soil into a suitable habitat for woodland gardening. The gardener was a little disconcerted at the arrival of Bagley Wood and the new professorial broom and often needed persuasion before accepting the advanced views of the Keeper of the Groves on nutrients and weed control.

Geoffrey Blackman was delighted to receive from Denis Wood, an old colleague who was now in the family business of Woods of Taplow, a quantity of prize rhododendrons which had just been on exhibition at Chelsea Flower Show. The Professor worked round the clock digging holes in the West Wood garden to receive them; professional gardeners have often been amazed at his capacity for digging and clearing even after a busy day in his Department. He seemed impervious to cold, wet, time or hunger. West Wood also received some of the original Kingdon–Ward introductions from hitherto unexplored mountain regions where India, Burma and China meet. Geoffrey Blackman had a great admiration for Frank Kingdon-Ward and delighted not only in his rhododendron introductions but in the many Primulas, Gentians, Lilies and Meconopsis which enriched woodland gardening. Writing in the *Gardeners' Chronicle* (Geoffrey Blackman had said: 'The garden is a mirror of man's adventurous spirit, the plants in it reflect his conquest through the ages of impenetrable forest and precipitous mountains,' and Frank Kingdon-Ward's publications read like any adventure in a Persian tale: *The Land of the Blue Poppy* (1913), *The Mystery Rivers of Tibet* (1923), *The Riddle of the Tsangpo Gorges* (1926), *Plant Hunting on the Edge of the World* (1930), *Assam Adventure* (1941), *Burma's Icy Mountains* (1949).

Geoffrey Blackman was only too pleased to review Kingdon-Ward's *The Romance of Gardening* (1935) for the *Gardeners' Chronicle*, since it was a point of view he shared. Mr Kingdon-Ward, he said, 'brings out the true meaning of the word romance — the spirit of adventure and the touch of remoteness from the drab turmoil of everyday life.' He dwelt on the trials and tribulations of the plant collector in the wilds, realising that 'he must first know all the many thousand species in cultivation that he is likely to find in the region. He must be able to recognize them when they are in flower, and have a quick eye for vegetative forms. He cannot collect plants, for there are no means of sending them quickly to civilization, and therefore he is restricted to collecting seeds. To secure these he must perforce wait for his plants to flower or must continue his journey and judge when the time and the seeds are ripe for his return.' Geoffrey Blackman also found romance in raising these tender plants and in the 'triumph of nurture over nature,' as he put it, and in helping such Kingdon-Ward introductions as *Meconopsis betonicifolia* and *Primula florindae* from Tibet to feel at home in England. 'Just as the collectors who have brought the seeds home have had successes and failure, so the gardeners who have striven to raise these unknown plants, have sometimes succeeded and sometimes failed.' The challenge of scientific enquiry and experiment was a romantic concept for Geoffrey Blackman and in concluding his review of *The Romance of Gardening* he quoted his favourite lines from *Romance* by Joseph Conrad: '. . . passed through so much, good chance and evil chance, sad hours and joyful, all lived down and swept away into the little heap of dust that is life. That, too, is Romance.'[5]

Geoffrey Blackman was always a romantic, quoting Wordsworth frequently in scientific papers and with a passion for fast cars. He celebrated his sixtieth birthday by buying an Aston Martin. At the end of the impressive scientific achievements recorded in *Who's Who*, Professor G.E. Blackman's recreations are listed as 'Gardening with the Ericaceae and collecting watercolours.' His appreciation of the visual arts was, as with Gertrude Jekyll, a great asset in planning colour beauty in a woodland garden. Living in Bagley Wood appealed to his romantic sense, for was this not the very spot in the *Scholar Gypsy* where 'on the skirts of Bagley Wood' the gypsies had pitched their tents 'above the forest-ground call'd Thessaly?' It was here, for good measure, that St Frideswide had hidden with her maidens when pursued by the heathen king and it is said to be the Bagley Wood foliage which is represented on the carvings of her shrine. It was to Bagley Wood, also, that the Pre-Raphaelites had come from Oxford on their 'truth to nature' painting sessions.

In 1967 the Blackmans left the St John's house on retirement and bought their own house on the other side of Bagley Wood on the way to Boars Hill. It was here at Wood Croft that Geoffrey Blackman made the garden of his dreams, the culmination of a life's study of the interrelationship of plants and their environment. Here was another wilderness to be tamed on the other side of Bagley Wood and to it were transferred Denis Wood's Chelsea Flower Show rhododendrons and the Kingdon-Ward introductions. Once more huge holes were dug and leaf mould brought from every part of the Scholar Gypsy wood, and the precious rhododendrons were dropped into their new homes from a forklift truck. Bluebells once more appeared to greet the Professor who had learned from their life style about the ecology of woodland communities. There was an additional bonus at Wood Croft, for there had been potters as well as gypsies in the wood and the sunken claypits filled naturally with water and their banks could be planted with bog-loving primulas and astilbes. The historical connection with potters at Wood Croft, Geoffrey Blackman's last garden, is a particularly happy one and partakes of William Morris's concept of the 'continuous life of the world.' Audrey Blackman is herself internationally famous as a ceramic artist. Her lifelike porcelain figurine compositions achieve their remarkable character through stance and gesture. The 'Study in Persuasion' shows the Keeper of the Groves caught in the act of trying to suggest to a determined head gardener that scientific methods might be introduced into St John's College gardening.

Professor Blackman died on 8th February, 1980 but his garden lives on as a memorial to him. It was something of an understatement for *Who's Who* to record Geoffrey Blackman's recreation as 'Gardening with the Ericaceae.' Mr McDermott, the greatly valued weekend gardener, (who during the week worked on the nightshift at British Leyland) had helped from the beginning to create the Wood Croft garden out of a jungle and had seen Bagley Wood, not so much tamed, as willingly made into an ecological garden. He summed up Geoffrey Blackman's achievement in these words: 'The Professor set it going and it created itself. He put the plants in their rightful places, where they wanted to be, and it's now so relaxed that I am quickly led towards any plant that is unhappy. The Professor set the clock and everything seems just to go on. What he's done is going to last for ever.'

15.2 The creation of Wood Croft
Professor Blackman and his gardener, Mr McDermott, planning his woodland garden. 'The Professor set the clock and everything seems just to go on'.

Another eminent Oxford academic, who brought his own special skills and knowledge to gardening, had settled higher up on Boars Hill in the days when it was still sparsely populated. He was Sir Arthur Evans, FRS, the archaeologist of Knossos fame, who from 1884 to 1908 was Keeper of the Ashmolean Museum. He was a direct descendant of Ehret, the eminent flower painter who for a short time had been head gardener at the Botanic Garden, and was interested in plants as well as in antiquities. He collected foreign plants, not so much for the beauty of their form, as Kingdon-Ward had done, but for their historical interest and associations.

He like Geoffrey Blackman, was a romantic at heart and work for him was an adventure.

As an undergraduate at Brasenose he made many excursions to Boars Hill in search of the Arnold haunts in *Thyrsis* and the *Scholar Gypsy*.

> Tonight from Oxford up your pathways strays!
> Here came I often, often, in old days —
> Thyrsis and I; we still had Thyrsis then.

Twenty years later he built a house, Youlbury, on the south-west end of Boars Hill, and carried out experiments in acclimatizing plants brought back from his archaeological travels. He built a dam across the combe to hold up the waters of a spring in the hillside and formed a lake and, according to his sister, made a secret garden where the spring rose 'a little sanctuary of stillness hidden by bamboo bushes planted with trembling rushes and white fritillaries, with clumps of frail Japanese iris that looked like flights of butterflies.'[6] He made plantations of Scots and Douglas firs on top of the hill and in leaf mould in the warm Greensand hollows he was able to grow plants more generally associated with Mediterranean gardens, fuchsias and camellias, the Mediterranean heath, magnolias, *Solanum jasminoides*, a Japanese lemon and a loquat and a mimosa which grew twenty feet high.

Of special interest to the archaeologist gardener was the clump of stone pines grown from seed in a sheltered part of the Youlbury woods. The stone pines had both romantic and historic associations and Sir Arthur delighted in telling visitors that he had collected them in the very wood that Dante had described as the 'celestial forest' in his *Purgatorio*, which Byron had hailed as 'Ravenna's immemorial wood, Rooted where once the Adrian flowed o'er.' Sir Arthur Evans had found cones of the stone pine in the wells of Roman Silchester and realized that the so-called 'umbrella' pine, beloved of Italian landscape painters, had been cultivated in the area some seventeen centuries before he had planted his Youlbury clump.[7]

Sir Arthur was keenly interested in youth and encouraged walks and fieldwork by stimulating interest in the archaeology of the area, and was a keen conservationist and champion of rights of way. In 1914 the Youlbury Troop of Boy Scouts was formed and he allowed the woods to be used as a training area and international camping centre. He showed the Scouts the art of signalling on the local Beacon and left them wide-eyed with his stories of revolts and brigands he had encountered in the Eastern Mediterranean. He kept in contact with his young friends after they left and after the Great War erected a sundial at Youlbury bearing the names of those who had been killed with the inscription;

In loving memory of a Youthful Band
Who played as Children Among these Woods and Heaths,
And shared at Youlbury in Joyous Hours
In the Great War For their Country's sake and for Mankind
They fell before their Time.
But, wherever they now lie, Here they are never far away.

Boars Hill attracted a remarkable community of poets in the post-War years, John Masefield, Robert Graves, Edmund Blunden, Robert Nichols and Gilbert Murray. Robert Bridges, the Poet Laureate, had come to live there as early as 1907 and remained until 1930. Sir Arthur Evans was a particular friend of Robert Bridges, but was accepted by all as a man of letters as well as of learning. There was a great deal of interest in his work on his great book about the Palace of Minos, which was written as Bridges, in his last years, was writing his *Testament of Beauty*. Robert Graves's first residence in Oxford had been at Somerville College, which had been turned into a wartime convalescent home and when, after the war, he became an undergraduate he pleaded his ex-service lungs as a reason for living five miles out of Oxford on Boars Hill. In *Goodbye to all that* (1929) he describes the relief and tensions of the war-shocked community on Boars Hill. Bridges drew up the recantation of wartime hatred against the Germans, and Gilbert Murray, Regius Professor of Greek, campaigned for the League of Nations. Robert Graves and his wife opened up a shop on the Robin Hood lines of full price to the well-to-do and cut price for the villagers. Sir Arthur Evans's gardener's wife presented difficulties as they were never sure whether her purchases were for herself or on behalf of her employer.

Robert Graves and Edmund Blunden felt reluctantly that there were too many poets on Boars Hill and that it was rapidly becoming a tourist attraction. John Masefield shut himself up in a garden hut, surrounded by gorse, and only appeared for meals. It was in fact a direct result of following the vision of Matthew Arnold that had made Boars Hill popular in the 1870s. At first the literary pilgrims sought the actual spots in *Thyrsis* when he had described his return to the Hinksey Ridge after the death of Arthur Clough to renew the search for the elusive spirit of the scholar gypsy. They too asked;

> Runs it not here, the track by Childsworth Farm
> Past the high woods, to where the elm-tree crowns
> The hill behind whose ridge the sunset flames
> The signal-elm, that looks on Ilsley Downs,
> The Vale, the three lone weirs, the youthful Thames?

They were puzzled by the signal-elm standing alone on the ridge, for the only lone tree appeared to be an oak. Sir Arthur Evans pointed out that the oak was 'elm-like' but dismissed the pilgrims' enquiries by saying that 'the poet's vision was, of its nature, ideal, and took in objects in the surrounding country that could never have been visible from any one spot.'[8] When *Rambles with Matthew Arnold* appeared in 1908 illustrated with photographs by the famous Mr Taunt, showing the Tree with a flag on it for the Relief of Mafeking, the controversy and the pilgrimages intensified. A letter in *The Times* of November 22, 1917 from A.C. Bradley testified that he had had it from the Bard himself that the 'signal-elm' was visible from the train a little before it enters Oxford station.

Unfortunately when the land came up for sale in the 1920s speculative builders lost no time in catering for the pilgrims who wanted houses built on the very landscape of 'the loved hillside.' There was then no legislation for the protection of rural amenities and the Arnold haunts, 'spiritual associations which must live wherever the English language is spoken'[9] would have been built over but for the vision and determination of Sir Arthur Evans. In 1928 he persuaded the newly-founded Oxford Preservation Trust to purchase Matthew Arnold's field and other land to safeguard the

Thyrsis views and to try and link it up with footpaths on Boars Hill. While negotiations were going on he adopted assault measures — tall fir poles 14 feet high — to keep off the building and finally when garden walls and trees went up, the excavator of Knossos decided to erect a great Mound which would enable people to see the immemorial view over the treetops.

The 50 feet high Mound on a base 540 feet in circumference stood 530 feet above sea level. It was mainly constructed out of the Upper Greensand bed and stability had been a problem from the outset. Rows of stakes had little effect and after heavy rain the whole of the north-west side slipped down. A second attempt was made two years later in January 1931 and was successfully completed in November 1931, the two stages having taken 20 men 34 months to carry out. On the first attempt horses and carts had been used until the gradient was too steep; then, as the height rose, a tall crane swung strips to the top for the final stage. At the second successful attempt Sir Arthur used small trucks running up inclined rails to complete the Mound.

After dwarf Cornish gorse, the purple Lizard heath and the rosy variety of Dorset had been planted on the side of the Mound to give better cohesion to the Greensand, Sir Arthur Evans saw a marvellous opportunity to develop a new kind of wild gardening in the large areas where the excavations for the Mound had taken place. This would be a garden with flowers, not only the local ones beloved of Boars Hill poets, but representative of the flora from all parts of the British Isles. In Sir Arthur Evans's words:

> Might not a Wild Garden of a new kind be here formed, of native species and purely natural in its scope, though necessarily limited and selective in Character? Such an arrangement, with plants placed according to their habits, straying freely or grouped together for the better display of their mass effect, might indeed in a small way stand to a Botanic Garden of the purely scientific kind in somewhat the same relation as Whipsnade with its free life and movement stands to the Zoo with its captive conditions.

The Youlbury experiments of acclimatizing plants in peaty hollows on the Greensand gave Sir Arthur Evans every hope that a Wild Garden of British plants under Jarn Mound would succeed. The name given to Jarn Mound had been taken from

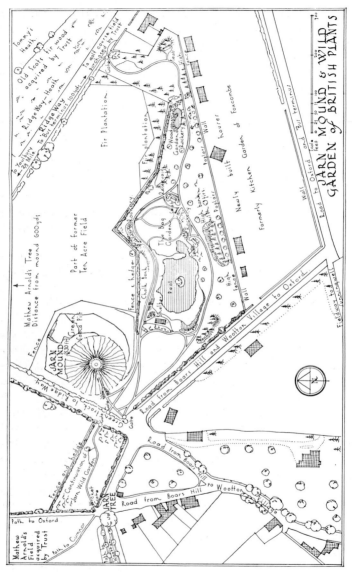

15.3 *The Jarn Mound, made by Sir Arthur Evans*

The Mound and the Wild Garden were part of Sir Arthur's scheme to preserve the immemorial landscape of Matthew Arnold. The map was drawn by Sir Arthur Evans.

the old name of the neighbouring Jarns Heath. Patches of snowdrops, primroses, bluebells, foxgloves, cornflowers and poppies were set along the paths of Jarn Gardens alongside the pink and white mallow which already grew in clumps in the old field. Spindle trees, wild cherries and guelder roses were transplanted from neighbouring woods. The variety in the soil was a great asset as the geological formation of the upper terrace of Boars Hill shows great contrasts and could be exploited. For the flora of the Berkshire Downs, however, chalk had to be carted over to form a bank and on this was grown the lilac blue wild anemone or 'Pasque flower' that grows so well on Ilsley Downs. With it came the chalk-loving box trees that had given their name to Berkshire, 'Beaurruc' being the Anglo-Saxon for box which, as Sir Arthur pointed out, was mentioned by Bishop Asser in his contemporary life of King Alfred.

Dr Claridge Druce, the distinguished Oxford botanist and author of *The Flora of Oxfordshire* (1886), *The Flora of Berkshire* (1897) and *The Flora of Buckinghamshire* (1926) gave every encouragement to the idea of establishing a Wild Garden of native plants and was able to give the whereabouts of some notable local species, some of which had vanished from their original places, such as the larkspur, once common in Boars Hill cornfields, the monkshood and the purple-flowered lungwort (*Pulmonaria officinalis*) which grew in Bagley Wood. A rock garden was made from the hard stone underlying the Greensand, locally known as sand-lag, and from Oolite and Coral Rag from neighbouring quarries, which was soon covered by dwarf periwinkles, Cheddar and Maiden pinks, wild thyme and violets. In reading Sir Arthur Evans's account of the way the wild flowers found their own habitat in the Wild Garden that he had provided for them, one is reminded of Mr McDermott's comments on the Wood Croft garden. 'The Professor set it going and it created itself. He put the plants in their rightful places, where they wanted to be.' Linnaeus's favourite flower, *Linnaea borealis*, that grows in the Scottish and Northumbrian fells, was established in soil laden with pine needles, and the Mountain Avens (*Dryas octopetala*), an Ice Age survival, was placed in a glacial layer of boulders and gravel dumped by the glaciers that had reached Boars Hill during the Ice Age. A bog garden was also formed and into this came the Grass of Parnassus which Druce had confirmed used to grow on boggy ground in the district. The marsh gentian and fritillaries also established themselves well. What particularly delighted Sir Arthur was the realization of his wish to preserve the immemorial Matthew Arnold landscape. His original intention had been to safeguard the view of Oxford, that 'sweet city with its dreaming spires' by purchasing the slopes of Boars Hill and later to erect a Mound as a viewpoint over the surrounding countryside. The Wild Garden was an afterthought but it too had a part to play in immortalizing Matthew Arnold, for, as Sir Arthur said:

> It preserves, within sight of the Tree — and upon the Hill, over-looking the riverside meadows below — the flowers of native growth that find their undying record in *Thyrsis* and the *Scholar Gypsy*. Among the 'store of flowers' here are still seen in their native setting:
> 'the frail leaf'd, white anemone —
> Dark bluebells drench'd with dews of summer eves,
> And purple orchises with spotted leaves —.'
> 'Red loosestrife and blond meadow sweet' flourish round Jarn pond. Both the white and purple fritillaries which
> 'the grassy harvest of the river-fields
> Above by Ensham, down by Sandford, yields'
> are quite at home beside the bog-garden here. The cowslips and primroses, which, according to the poet, had suffered from the ploughboys' team, have had a new domain provided for them in the Wild Garden. The 'Fyfield Tree' — the Witches' Elm — is now only a hollow stump, but the not distant 'wood that hides the daffodils' has out of its plenteous store, spared a few to multiply beside the paths of Jarn.

The Oxford Preservation Trust went on to buy further lands round Oxford to protect the historic views where the eye travels down to the City and campaigned for legislation to preserve the whole of its rural setting. In pursuance of this policy the Trust initiated discussions which led to the Government's approval in principle, in 1956, of a Green Belt for Oxford, varying in breadth from four to twelve miles.[10] Sir Arthur Evans had much earlier agreed with the Oxford City Council that 100 acres of Youlbury should be scheduled as a 'private open space' in accordance with the 1925 Act. Today the Trust still maintains Jarn Mound and the Scholar Gypsy views, and local residents are enthusiastically trying to restore the Wild Garden. Sir Arthur Evans had erected an indication plate on top of Jarn Mound and in his book on Jarn Mound revelled in all the rich historic associations of the places to be seen in the panoramic view, the Confessor's birthplace at Islip, the forest, ridgeways, stone circles, drovers' roads, ancient woodlands, burial places of Saxon kings, the historic battlefield of Chalgrove, Cymbeline's Mount, barrows and Roman Dorchester.

On June 17th 1978 a memorial to the man who had been the inspiration of the imaginative and comprehensive scheme to save Boars Hill was unveiled at the wicket gate entrance to Jarn Gardens.[11] A monolith weighing ten tons had been sent from Tackley pits, reminiscent in is massive ruggedness of the Rollright Stones, the ancient Stone Circle north of Oxford which had always fascinated Sir Arthur Evans.[12] The inscription is simple but says all there is to say about the distinguished archaeologist who loved Boars Hill and its associations.

TO ARTHUR EVANS 1851–1941
WHO LOVED ANTIQUITY, NATURE, FREEDOM AND
YOUTH, AND MADE THIS VIEWPOINT AND WILD
GARDEN FOR ALL TO ENJOY.

16

Christ Church Meadow

Christ Church Meadow and Walks have never been considered merely as the garden environs of the college, but have been held in trust for the citizens, one of whom, a nineteenth century tanner of St Ebbe's, claimed that he had walked round the Meadow 10,000 times in his life. 'I feel thankful,' he wrote, 'for the opportunities I have had, from boyhood to old age, of spending some of the most pleasant hours of my life in walking round this delightful meadow.'[1] They are the City's green lung. 'The scent of these meadows' moisture is the scent of Oxford,' wrote Max Beerbohm from Merton, 'Even in the hottest noon, one feels that the sun has not dried *them*.'[2]

Originally the Meadow was divided by a broad stream, once a tributary of the Thames, called the Shirelake, which was also the County boundary. In the twelfth century the land between the Shirelake and the Priory was known as Prest Hay and the southern part as Stockwell Mead after Galfred de Stockwell who once owned it. In 1346 the Lady Montacute, whose tomb is in the cathedral, gave Stockwell Mead to the Priory of St Frideswide to maintain a Chantry in the Lady Chapel. After the Dissolution, the Meadow, with the Priory and its other possessions, became part of the short-lived Cardinal College. When the college was refounded as Christ Church, Henry VIII pursued a policy of reuniting the Meadow but his intentions were not finally carried out until action was taken by the Dean and Chapter in 1600. By the seventeenth century Shirelake had dwindled to a ditch, which can be seen across the Meadow today.[3]

The Agas map shows walks round Christ Church Meadow which were no doubt, as those at Magdalen, enjoyed by the College for healthful exercise. In 1606 the Disbursement Books show that attempts were made to make these walks more ornamental. The sum of 20 shillings and 4 pence was then paid 'for setting rayles in the walkes,' and in 1624 the sum of 34 shillings 'for setting plants in ye walks.' About this time the Shirelake was drained and ditched. Even in the earliest days of the college's foundation there seems to have been a formally planted walk eastwards from the buildings which was on the line of the present Broad Walk. In the *Journal Book of the Expenses of Cardinal College* there is an entry: 'It appeareth that the walks about Christ Church Medowe were made of the earth that was digged for the foundation of the College.'[4] This walk was swept away during the Civil War, when the Royalist troops trained on the Meadow and earthworks were constructed along the line of the walk. The remains of the bastion shown on Gomme's plan of the defences of Oxford can still be seen, as can the gun emplacement in the lowered medieval town wall to the North of Merton Field. This walk beneath the walls of Merton is called Deadman's Walk after the route taken by Jewish funerals from St Aldate's to the burial ground on the site of the Botanic Garden. It is now a pleasant walk from Christ Church to the Botanic Garden overlooking Merton Field and the Meadow.

At the Restoration Dean Fell set about restoring the Walk as well as the neglected buildings. As in the days of Wolsey, it was débris from the building enterprises that was to form the base of the walk, which was at first given the name of 'White Walk,' later corrupted to 'Wide Walk' and then to 'Broad Walk.' In February 1670 Anthony Wood noted that 72 elms had been planted each side and that an ancient water course on the north side had been stopped up. The wartime earthwork 'Halfmoon Sconce' was not removed immediately. J.B. Malchair, a German who settled in Oxford in 1765 to

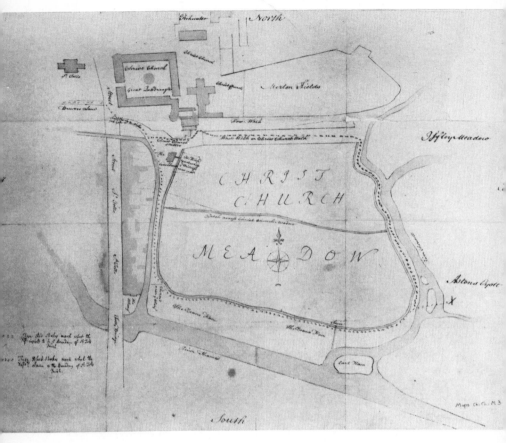

16.1 Map of Christ Church Meadow, 1762

The map shows the Broad Walk laid out in 1668 and the ditch across
the meadow, probably the relic of the Shirelake stream which originally
divided two separate properties. The proposed Meadow Road of the
1950s would have run between the ditch and the Thames.

teach drawing and music drew the Meadow looking through the elm walk to Merton College, which shows the Cherwell walks as treeless.

The vista down Broad Walk ended in rural meadows across the Cherwell, until in about 1780 Professor Sibthorp built himself a house across the river, with a footbridge across to his Physic Garden. A monumental slab in Bath Abbey depicts him in Greek dress, carrying a sheaf of flowers and stepping from the prow of a boat on the Cherwell to enter the gateway of the Physic Garden. Sibthorp greatly admired his house, built with bricks from the clay on the spot and, thinking that Christ Church would also admire 'so beautiful and classical a terminus to the vista of Broad Walk,' confidently applied to the Dean for a studentship for one of his family. 'A studentship?' replied the incensed Dean Jackson. 'My good Sir, I will give you two if you pull it down again.'[5] Cyril Jackson later proposed to build a magnificent classical gateway to the Meadow at the Rose Lane entrance, and designs were made by G. Smith, but the plans were not carried out. St Hilda's College, however, enjoyed the Professor's house, Cowley Place, which became their home in 1893, and through his elegant Venetian windows could look out over the river to orchards and a view of Merton, the Broad Walk and the Botanic Garden. Cowley Grange, next door, was later taken into the St Hilda's buildings. This had been the home of Augustus Vernon Harcourt, a distinguished Christ Church chemist, whose daughter remembers taking sandwiches to her father over Sibthorp's bridge, when he did not want to leave his laboratory for meals. The situation of St Hilda's is as delightful as that of the older Meadow colleges, where countryside and gardens unite.

There is nothing to suggest that Christ Church's governing body had ever considered changing the basic idea of walks round the Meadow with a formal avenue across it in the interest of idealised landscaping or the picturesque. There had never been any scheme for communal landscaping in the manner of Capability Brown's proposal for unifying the surroundings of the colleges at Cambridge which had land bordering the Backs, and no picturesque plan, as submitted to Magdalen by Repton, for floating a lake in the Meadow.

Reflections of Oxford's picturesque architecture, which undoubtedly look very fine in water, were to be left for those occasions when the Meadow was naturally flooded. This used to happen quite frequently in the winter and skating became a favourite pastime for town and gown. Boswell recorded that when Dr Johnson first came up to Pembroke in 1728 his tutor asked for the reason he had absented himself. 'I answered I had been sliding in Christ Church Meadow. And this I said with as much nonchalance as I am now talking to you. I had no notion that I was wrong or irreverent to my tutor.' To which Boswell commented, 'That, Sir, was great fortitude of mind.' 'No, Sir; stark insensibility,' replied Dr Johnson.[6]

The Broad Walk is frequently eulogized in literature and art. William Delamotte in 1843 praised its old-fashioned long perspectives and rejoiced that it had not succumbed to any landscape improvement scheme. In his book on Oxford colleges he said:

> There is nothing in artificial nature (if such a paradox may be allowed) finer than a long vista of trees. It presents at once images of solitude and companionship. We pace the avenue, lessening in dim perspective, with equal delight, whether absorbed in lonely contemplation, or enjoying the conversation of a friend, or watching the figures, especially if ladies be among them (as in the present scene), moving and giving life and happy thoughts to the smooth and level causeway. We are of the old school of landscape gardeners and do not hesitate to avow our partiality to promenades on the dry smooth-shaven green. The Broad Walk of Christ Church presents just such a vista as we have been commending. It is spacious, lined by trees of various foliage, and with the additions of the sky, colour, life, the ceaseless motion of leaves and their rustling sound, seems, like the cloisters of a cathedral, to shut out the world.

Robert Southey saw the vista through the lofty elm arch as 'exemplifying the hypothesis that Gothic church architecture was designed to imitate the places where the Pagan Goths worshipped in the forest.'[7] Looking through the avenue to the spires and towers of Oxford called from him the comment that 'The banks of Ilyssius and the groves of Academus, could never have presented a sight more beautiful.' Mr Verdant Green described Broad Walk as the 'Show Sunday' in Commemoration Week promenade where undergraduates lionised Oxford to family and friends and 'under the delicious cool of the luxuriant foliage, they met all the rank, beauty and fashion.'[8]

Dean Fell's avenue had probably reached its prime towards the end of the eighteenth century and by 1847 it was recorded that some elms were beginning to decay and sixty-five years later, Gunther in his *Guide to Oxford Gardens* declared that the elms 'having reached the limit of their useful life are falling like ninepins before south-westerly gales.' The Broad Walk was extended in 1863 by the planting of further elms at the eastern end. This took place on the occasion of the marriage of the Prince of Wales to Princess Alexandra on March 10th and one of the trees had been planted by Alice in Wonderland watched over by Lewis Carroll and William Baxter. Carroll entered in his diary on that day:

> Edwin and I went into the Broad Walk to see the three Deanery children plant three trees along the Cherwell in memory of the day. Each delivered a short speech over her tree 'long life to this tree, and may it prosper from this auspicious day,' and they named them Alexandra, Albert and Victoria.

Sadly the royal trees, together with all the other elms in the Broad Walk succumbed to elm disease in 1975 and were felled.

Dean Fell had originally planted English elms, *Ulmus procera*, but at the turn of the century the Huntingdon elm had been chosen to fill the increasing number of gaps. In 1976 Mr Ken Burras, Superintendent of the Botanic Garden, was asked to advise on the replanting of the Broad Walk by Christ Church governing body. The elm had been admirably suited to the Meadow setting of Oxford's architecture but the vulnerability of all species and hybrids of the tree to Dutch Elm disease precluded its re-use. In considering the replacement avenue a species tolerant of the soil and high alkaline water table had to be chosen which at maturity would be in scale with the architecture and landscape. A tree which satisfied all the requirements was the Oriental Plane, *Platanus orientalis*, a fine specimen of which already existed along the Cherwell Walk and could be taken as evidence of its ability to succeed under the Meadow conditions.[9] In the garden of the Priory House is probably the largest Oriental Plane in the country, the girth of which was recorded by Gunther as 19ft 3in in 1911. It was planted in 1636 by the orientalist Dr Pococke, who had been chaplain to the Levant Company at Aleppo before becoming Professor of Arabic at Christ Church. Dr Pococke is credited with obtaining the first plants of the cedar of Lebanon and raising them in his Berkshire rectory. A large fig-tree also brought back by Dr Pococke from the East still survives at Christ Church.

The Oriental Plane in the Broad Walk has been planted alternately with its hybrid offspring, the London Plane, *Platanus acerifolia*. This is a most appropriate tree for the Superintendent of the Botanic Garden to have planted, since this hybrid was raised originally at Oxford by the first Curator of the Physic Garden, Jacob Bobart. A direct propagation from Bobart's original tree can be seen at the entrance to the Deer Park at Magdalen College. As with most seedling-raised trees, the Plane is subject to genetic variation which results in forms with different growth habits. A clean trunk, free from side branching characteristics was particularly desirable for the Broad Walk and it was decided to look for a good 'avenue clone' for propagation. Propagation material was obtained from a mature Oriental Plane in a Henley river meadow and from a London plane planted in the 1760s by Lord Harcourt in his landscaped garden at Nuneham.[10]

When the elms in Broad Walk were felled, although the stately avenue was greatly missed, new and breath-taking views of the spires and towers and medieval buildings of Oxford were opened up from the river. A few gaps have been left in the new planting so that vistas can be seen from viewing bays along the Cherwell walks across the grazed meadow. The view from Deadman's Walk which had previously terminated at the avenue is now very extensive and unbelievably 'rus in urbe' in its prolongation across the Meadow and the Thames and to the hills beyond.

A new Poplar Walk was planted by Dean Liddell in 1872 and aligned on the Gothic tower and entrance porch of the Meadow Building. Previously the way to the river Thames was by a rather unsavoury path by the Trill Mill stream, which was little more then an evil-smelling ditch. It was along this path that Lewis Carroll used to take the Dean's children for their favourite boating excursions. On 4th July 1862 on one memorable rowing trip up the river to Godstow he had told them most of the stories which Alice persuaded him to write down for the book to be published as *Alice's Adventures in Wonderland.*

By 1870 boating had become a major pastime in Oxford and the new walk to the Thames was considered to be a great improvement. The colleges gradually formed boat clubs and as Christ Church would not allow club houses in the Meadow the solution was floating changing rooms in the form of houseboats. The London Livery companies had owned elaborate state barges for river pageants which were discontinued and their barges came up for sale. Many of them were towed down the river to Christ Church Meadow and set the pattern for all future college barges. Eights Week, a great rowing and social occasion, is held at the end of May, and there are jubilant celebrations for the college boat that finishes Head of the River.

The gay scene of the ornate boats with their coloured awnings, flagpoles and banners has been splendidly illustrated by Osbert Lancaster on the walls of Randolph Hotel as an episode in Zuleika Dobson, the Max Beerbohm novel, in which the Warden's niece conquers young Oxford so completely that the entire student body drowns itself in the Isis by Christ Church Meadow for love of her. The barges have rotted but an Oxford College Barges Preservation Trust hopes to restore some of them which are now in backwaters and recapture the romantic boating scenes of Edwardian Oxford. The protective railings along the banks have been removed, an action which would delight Ruskin who greatly objected to railings round any part of the Meadow.[11] In 1883 the banks of the Cherwell had been raised and the New Cut made and a bridge was made over the Cherwell to the designs of T.G. Jackson. More permanent boathouses were afterwards built on the island made by the New Cut.

In contrast to the regular planting of Dean Liddell's avenue and the Broad Walk, the Cherwell walks are irregular and rural. Here grow willows, alders, spindle trees, field maple and two fine *Zelkova*, the Caucasian elm introduced into this country in 1760. This type of rural walk in the heart of a city with all its opportunities for what is now called a 'nature trail' would have delighted Addison. The Meadow has always been readily accessible for observing birds and flowers, both by the poetically and the scientifically minded. On 2nd May 1866 Gerard Manley Hopkins wrote, 'Weather cold and raw, chestnut leaves touched with frost and limp. Swallows playing over Ch Ch meadows with a wavy and hanging flight and showing their white bellies. Snakes' heads. Yellow wagtails. Almost think you can hear the lisp of the swallow's wings.'[12] Ruskin also appreciated the near-to-hand Nature which spilled over into the gardens of the Meadow colleges. He wrote from his room at Corpus Christi, when Slade Professor, 'the first quiet and pure light that has risen this many a day, was increasing through the tall stems of the trees of our garden, which is walled by the walls of old Oxford; and a bird (I am going to lecture on ornithology next term, but I don't know what bird, and couldn't go to ask the gardener) singing sweet, momentary notes.'[13]

Artists, including Ruskin, have drawn from nature in the Meadow and the medieval carvers took inspiration from the plants which grew there. There is a meadow columbine carved on the tomb of Lady Montacute, who gave part of the meadow to the Priory. The meadow snakesheads were beloved by the Pre-Raphaelites and can be seen on the St Catherine's window by Burne-Jones. The window is dedicated to Edith Liddell, who died in 1876. She and her sisters had frequented the Meadow walks with Lewis Carroll. Newman and other Tractarians, and later Ronald Knox, were to be seen pacing the walks breviary in hand.

Botanising in the Meadows of Magdalen and Christ Church had always been a favoured pastime. Interest in botany had always been fostered by the Physic Garden and by the habit of mind inspired by Plot's topographical enquiries. All was grist to Dr Plot's natural history mill and an echo was duly noted[14] 'about the east-end of Christ Church new walk, that repeats three or four syllables.' John Locke, the empirical philosopher assiduously collected and identified plants from Christ Church Meadow walks including double marsh marigold, hound's tongue, campion, marsh mallow, bugloss, giant throatwort, hypericum, purple meadow trefoil, stitchwort, fumitory, saxifrage, creeping grass and elecampane. These were pressed into a book which also contained his pupil's Latin exercises.[15] Gilbert White was elected Fellow of Oriel in 1744 and although the natural history observations which won him international fame were made at Selborne, he developed the habit of observing and note-taking in Oxford's empirical tradition with the Meadow to hand. In 1794 Sibthorp published his book on the flora of Oxfordshire, which included a large number of plants found in the Meadow. He was probably helped by his Christ Church friend John Randolph, Professor of Divinity, who was a keen botanist and entrusted with the task of seeing Sibthorp's *Flora* through the press. One Flora or herbarium not completed was that of Dr Wenman, Professor of Civil Law and Fellow of All Souls, as it was recorded in 1796 that he was found drowned in the Cherwell and it was supposed that he fell into the river 'while over-reaching himself in botanising, or in collecting insects for his entomological collections.'[16]

The man who was to do most for the natural history of Oxford was not, however, an academic. George Claridge Druce was brought up in Northampton in straitened circumstances and was apprenticed to a chemist there at the age of fifteen. He had to work twelve hours a day every weekday but got up early to go out and collect wild flowers, which had been an abiding passion through his childhood. He passed his pharmaceutical examinations, learned Latin and was instrumental in founding the Northampton Field Club for like-minded people. In 1879, at the age of 29, he used all his savings to buy a chemist's shop in Oxford at 118, High Street. His great skill as a field botanist was soon appreciated. He used to prescribe for undergraduates for emergencies in his chemist shop and soon became a friend of both town and gown. He served the City Council for forty years continuously and was both Sheriff and Mayor. He was honoured by the University with an honorary degree in 1886 and later made a D.Sc. In 1927 he was awarded a Fellowship of the Royal Society, a rare distinction for a man of no academic training. Dr Druce bequeathed his herbarium of a quarter of a million plants to the Botany School and endowed a curatorship.

Druce's *Flora of Oxfordshire*, published in 1886, was, as he stated on the title page, a 'topographical and historical account.' Of particular interest is his account of the vegetation of the Oxford walls for the *Flora* and subsequently for the Victoria County History. He searched in vain for the navelwort and flixweed that William Coles had said grew on Merton walls in 1657 and he attributed the decline in mural vegetation to the better pointing of masonry, which accounted for the loss of the wall rocket which Dillenius had recorded, the great hone-wort, and a broom recorded by Sibthorp. Dr Druce was, however, able to record many mural plants and today the red valerian, wall rue, spleenwort, hart's tongues, purple toad flax, stonecrops, snapdragons and wall flowers still flourish on the oolitic stone walls around the Meadow. Druce was particularly interested in recording the plants which had escaped from the Botanic Garden and had naturalised on these walls. *Hieracium amplexicaule, Chondrilla juncea, Linaria purpurea* and, most famous of all, Oxford's own weed, *Senecio squalidus*, the Oxford ragwort.[17] Dr Druce investigated and drew his conclusions in a way which would have earned the approval of Plot. He observed that *Senecio squalidus* had been introduced into the Botanic Garden by the younger Bobart and, although Joseph Banks had already noted its appearance in the Meadow while he was at Christ Church in 1760, it did not become widespread until the coming of the railway, when the ragwort spread from the Meadow along the cindered railway cuttings, thriving in conditions similar to the volcanic terrain of Sicily, its place of origin. Dr Druce also noticed how rubbish carted away from the Botanic Garden and deposited on waste ground on the Iffley Road and in the Marston brickyards had been responsible for the establishment of many alien species, such as *Lamium garganicum, Barbarea verna, Potentilla recta, Reseda alba* and *Atriplex hortensis*. He also noted that chalk flora was establishing itself on rubble brought up from Didcot and deposited between the Great Western and L. & N.W.R. stations at Oxford.

Dr Druce relished the historical aspects and associations of plants. On October 19th, the anniversary of the death of St Frideswide, a service is held to honour the patron saint of the

Cathedral and Diocese, the University and City of Oxford. When Dean Liddell preached the sermon in 1889 he was able to refer to the leaves and fruits carved on her shrine in 1289 as identified by Dr Druce: on the south side, the greater celandine, the maple, buttercup and the columbine; on the east the vine and hogweed; on the north the ivy, oak and sycamore; and on the west side the whitehorn and bryony. Sir Arthur Evans acknowledged the help of 'that great authority Dr Claridge Druce' in the making of Jarn Wild Garden. Druce also took a hand in locating the Arnold flora and entered into the Tree saga by establishing that if one climbed the Radcliffe camera and looked in line with St Aldate's spire the umbrella-like stag-headed oak which Matthew Arnold mistook for an elm was clearly visible.

Dr Druce had unbounded energy and enthusiasm and it was said to be not only 'a great joy but a liberal education to botanise in his company.'[18] His great contribution in Oxford and throughout the country was the popularising of field botany, not only by the publication of *Flora* which were field work tools rather than books of literature or art, but by his encouragement of Field Clubs, such as he had pioneered in Northampton. In 1880 he helped to found the Ashmolean Natural History Society and was its first Secretary.[19] He was President four times, led innumerable field excursions, instituted the popular annual Christmas lecture for children and gave lantern lectures. He was always anxious to encourage people like himself who had no academic training to join in the activities of the society. He revived the Botanical Exchange Club, which had once been the Botanical Society of London, where a contemporary ditty ran, 'If the plant is too abstruse, pack it off to Dr Druce.'[20]

Natural history in Oxford after the First World War flourished. Not only the poetic community on Boars Hill, but undergraduates in general were serious and bent on building better worlds for all to enjoy. Two practical visionaries destined to become distinguished ornithologists were E.M. Nicholson, an historian, and B.W. Tucker, who was reading zoology under Julian Huxley. In 1921 they formed the Oxford Ornithological Society and set about co-ordinating voluntary field work activity as Druce was doing in the botanical field. Tucker was the Society's Hon. Sec. and like Druce had tremendous enthusiasm which he communicated to others. In 1927, the year he published *How Birds Live* he opened up a new line of research in the Oxford Bird Census. A trapping station was set up in Christ Church Meadow in the autumn of that year, which was visited four times a day by different people working on a rota system. This established the ringing schemes and other forms of census. The radio was a powerful means of communication and Julian Huxley, in the course of a series of radio talks on bird-watching, requested information of all kinds to be sent in. The Oxford Bird Census then had a paid Director and finally in 1938 the Edward Grey Institute of Field Ornithology was set up in premises in the Oxford Botanic Garden.[21]

The study of the specialized plants in the Botanic Garden and the natural flora, and the fauna, of the Meadow have always been of the greatest importance to naturalists. Such water meadows are becoming increasingly rare as they are drained, ploughed up, re-seeded with higher yielding grasses and fertilised with nitrogen. Christ Church Meadow has been of inestimable value down the centuries and was ably assessed by the German Carl Philipp Moritz who visited Oxford in 1782.

> On Tuesday afternoon Mr Maud took me to the different walks about Oxford, and often remarked, that they were not only the finest in England, but, he believed, in Europe. I own, I do not think, he over-rated their merit. There is one in particular near the river, and close to some charming meadows, behind Corpus Christi College, which may fairly challenge the world.[22]

Such praises notwithstanding, it was proposed in 1965 to build a road through the Meadow to relieve the pressure of traffic in the High Street. Already in 1948 Thomas Sharp had written in *Oxford Replanned*:

> The quietness of Broad Walk is a very lovely thing. If there were any possible way of avoiding its destruction while at the same time solving the enormous traffic problem of the city, it should certainly be taken. But there is no other way. In face of difficulties like these in Oxford, some sacrifice must be made somewhere . . . in place of these losses there can be created one of the most beautiful roads in the world — as well as one of the most necessary.[23]

The fight against the Road through the Meadow became something of a saga, the whole period of the controversy lasting from 1923 until 1974, when it was finally resolved.[24] It made news all over the world wherever men had been to Oxford. A Punch cartoon showed two sheikhs sitting cross-legged in the middle of a desert saying, 'I see they want to put a road through the Meadow.' At one crucial stage in the debate it was found that five members of the Cabinet including the Prime Minister were Christ Church men and a report in the Oxford Mail of 25 September 1956 told the story current in the University that the agenda of a recent Cabinet meeting had read: I) Oxford Roads II) Seizure of the Suez Canal.[25] Public Enquiries came and went with every opinion being consulted. Perhaps the opinion that impressed more than any other was that given by an elderly gentleman with a flowing beard who got up and said, 'It is against the Will of God,' and disappeared.

Geoffrey Jellicoe was asked to prepare a report on the landscape design for the Christ Church Meadow road, if this was agreed to be the only solution to the Inner Relief Road. This removed the hated idea of a Mall, 'one of the most beautiful roads in the world,' where motorists enjoyed from their windows that 'sweet city with her dreaming spires' that 'needs not June for beauty's heightening,' because the proposed Jellicoe road[26] was to be a sunken one further away from the Meadow colleges. No scheme that involved a road carrying heavy traffic, would, however, have compensated for the loss of the peace, tranquillity and timelessness of Christ Church Meadow and finally the Buchanan view prevailed. Unless the High were closed, traffic would continue to use it, but if it were compulsorily closed a relief road could be placed anywhere and did not have to be so convenient and attractive to motorists. The Meadow remains still grazed by cattle as green countryside in the heart of a city. In the words of W.H. Auden of Christ Church:

> May the *Meadows* be only frequented
> By scholars and couples and cows:
> God save us from all these demented
> Plans for a road *Through The House.*[2]

One of the areas which would have been swallowed up, together with Broad Walk, in the proposed Christ Church/ Merton Mall was the memorial garden flanked with an iron grille and stone piers on St Aldates, and laid out axially with Broad Walk with steps leading up to it over the Trill Mill Stream. This garden was laid out in 1925 as a War Memorial and on the ground is an inscription from Pilgrim's Progress. 'My sword I give to him that shall succeed me in my pilgrimage.' An unintentional reminder for future road planners of what has been called the 'bloodiest battle' over an environmental issue.

17

Modern Oxford

Science advanced on all fronts from the last decades of the nineteenth century onwards, and with it the need for more laboratories. It was a critical time for the Botanic Garden, since, after the founding of the University Museum in the Parks area, one by one the natural sciences had put up buildings in the vicinity with obvious mutual advantages. Botany was the only absentee. 'Her presence was urgently required to aid the Palaeontologist with his fossil plants, the Physiologist with material for vivisection without licence, students in general and botanical students in particular with a garden in which they might, without loss of time, gather valuable information and maintain health,' as Dr Gunther recorded. The idea was that five acres might be railed off from the Parks as a 'Garden of Instruction.' In 1873 the Garden Committee consulted Dr Hooker, Director of Kew Gardens, and it was finally resolved to leave the Botanic Garden on the original site and to build new glass-houses. The Botany Department itself did not leave the Botanic Garden buildings until 1952 to become part of the University Science Area, and shortly afterwards a new experimental garden, one acre in extent, on the edge of the University Parks was established.

The Genetic Garden, as it was called, was set up by Professor Darlington, who was appointed Sherardian Professor in 1953. In his inaugural lecture[1] the Professor spoke of his strong conviction that botany was fundamental for the study of life as a whole, and of the new research opportunities in the age of the electron microscope which would have left Robert Hooke in his High Street laboratory amazed. Professor Darlington recalled that the first seven Sherardian Professors had been doctors of medicine and that the Botanic Garden was essential as a repository for drug plants, which meant that botany had been a descriptive study rooted in the writings of classical antiquity. 'Botany therefore developed, in Oxford as elsewhere,' he said, 'towards description rather than experiment. And description, losing connection with its uses grew into a pure science, a science pursued with the purpose of knowing plants for the sake of knowing them.'

Professor Darlington, turning his back on taxonomy, became an outstanding experimental geneticist. The interest in variegation started by Morison and Bobart was scientifically developed in the Genetic Garden. Beds are arranged to demonstrate variegation and genetically-controlled breeding systems.[2] The Sherardian Professor maintained that although botany was not just a tool of medicine as in former days, it could still be studied with advantage by the medical research worker who 'will no doubt hope to study the chromosomes of man. But before he does so he will be well advised to try his 'prentice hand on the larger and more accessible chromosomes of the lilies in our Botanic Garden, and if he does so he is not dabbling in a matter of remotely historic academic interest. For it was the chromosomes of the snakes head lily obtained from Christ Church Meadow, twenty years ago, which showed how the chromosomes of man recombine in heredity.'[3]

Fittingly, it is a garden outside the Botanic, formerly the Physic Garden, which commemorates Oxford's greatest contribution to medicine, the foundation of the science of antibiotics through the discovery of penicillin. It was given by the American Lasker Foundation in 1953 and the inscription reads: 'This Rose Garden was Given in Honour of the Research Workers in this University who discovered the clinical importance of Penicillin. For saving of life, relief of suffering and inspiration to further research all mankind is in their debt.' Penicillin was described and named by Alexander

Fleming in 1929 but he had not been able to make the preparation chemically stable. In 1939 Howard Florey and the Oxford team took up the challenge stimulated by the wartime need. They worked with makeshift equipment, milk churns and ironmongery from local shops, and in 1941 used penicillin for the first time on a patient in the Radcliffe Infirmary; a small plaque over a bed in one of the wards commemorates one of the greatest steps forward in medical history.

17.1 The penicillin rose garden
Designed in 1953 by Silvia Crowe outside the Botanic Garden.

The penicillin memorial garden was designed by Dame Sylvia Crowe. The donor had stipulated a rose garden and this had to be fitted in with its position on the High directly opposite Magdalen, and the historical tradition of the Botanic Garden. Although some felt that there should be an informal treatment of an area flanking the High, Sylvia Crowe was successful in pressing for formal beds, which would make a firm framework for the informal growth of the roses, and echo the traditional plots associated with the Botanic Garden through the centuries. Yew and box were the obvious choice for the framework and magnolias were introduced within the rosebeds for added interest and effect. There are very pleasant contrasts of green, especially the light whitebeam and the silver tassles of the *Garrya elliptica* against the dark yew foliage. There are stone seats at the western end of the garden under a row of stilted copper beech.

Nuffield College was the first of the post-second world war colleges. The buildings were designed in 1939 by Harrison, Barnes and Hubbard but, with the war intervening, were not begun until 1949 and finally finished in 1960. Lord Nuffield had been anxious to bridge the gap which he knew existed between academic studies and the world of practical affairs and founded his graduate college with a view to making 'easier the co-operation of academic and non-academic persons.' The site chosen was away from the main academic area but right by the old Castle mound and the old Westgate. The land had become available when the Hythe Bridge wharf finally closed down in 1937 due to a decline of canal traffic after the coming of the railway. A college built on the site of the Oxford canal basin was faced with certain difficulties; a high water table and a cliff-like eastern boundary. There could be no cellars, or underground storage for books, and the high tower, which has been an addition to the Oxford skyline, is mainly a book stack.

The unusual feature about the building of Nuffield College was that the fellows lived in it before it was finished and joined in the designing of their college as further needs and constraints emerged. One serious constraint was that the £900,000 given by Lord Nuffield in 1937 proved insufficient for a post-war college. The layout of the college became a joint enterprise between the appointed architect and the amateur architect fellows. Harrison had only worked in Tel Aviv and Cyprus and had had no experience of Oxford colleges and when a lodge was required made a tour of the colleges and with the fellows decided what was needed. In some ways the building of Nuffield College was like that of Merton, seven centuries before, where the final shape of the college was dictated by the growing needs of a community of scholars. Lord Nuffield had wanted a traditional college, built on the well-tried staircase principle, and even a cloister was considered. The buildings, first conceived in the 1930s, have something of the Cotswold period of college architecture, as seen at Rhodes House, and the quadrangle garden completes the manor house appearance as Lutyens had done for Campion Hall. The axial layout of the Nuffield garden was again dictated by the site with a lower and upper quad on different levels. The upper quad has on its lawn a bronze fountain by Hubert Dalwood, which demanded ingenuity in directing the flow of water, and the lower quad has a long narrow piece of water which evokes the previous history of the canal site.

St Peter's College in New Inn Hall Street also benefited by the closure of the canal. In 1949 they took over the elegant eighteenth century office of the Oxford Canal Company with its pedimented entrance, which formerly overlooked the canal basin, for the Master's Lodgings. It is now approached along Bulwark's Lane, one of Oxford's most picturesque lanes, too narrow for motor traffic, which runs between the old walls in sight of the Castle Mound.

The first strikingly modern college to arrive on the Oxford scene was St Catherine's, the foundation stone of which was laid in 1960, the year that the Nuffield fellows officially occupied their long-building college. There was no question of Cotswold vernacular charm in the planning of St Catherine's College by the Danish architect, Arne Jacobsen, nor were the fellows, who were in any case already housed in Linacre College, going to be allowed in before it was finished to make helpful suggestions as work proceeded. Linacre College had been built in 1936 for the St Catherine's Society by Sir Hubert Worthington by the side of Christ Church memorial garden and this was in the squared rubble Cotswold material with hipped roofs. In 1960 when the Society was about to receive full college status its governing body clearly felt ready to take the plunge into modern architecture. According to Pevsner in his *Buildings of Oxfordshire* (1974) what they got was 'the most perfect piece of architecture of twentieth century Oxford.' It is a concrete structure which allows the frame and beam ends to show and is severely geometrical. The buildings form one long rectangle, 600 feet long and there is a great deal of glass. One cannot help wondering whether the undergraduates exposed in their projecting glass cubicles sometimes hanker after a cosy den in a Tudor college or a bit of Cotswold charm. From the onlooker's point of view, on the other hand, the undergraduate clutter visible in the glass panels adds a human touch to the 'self-discipline' of Jacobsen's geometry. Pevsner felt that the architectural ideal of 'self-discipline' would counteract the 'self-permissiveness among students' and that if the undergraduates didn't like it, that was probably an argument against them rather than the college.

17.2 St Catherine's College

The first strikingly modern college in Oxford, with landscape environment designed by its architect Arne Jacobsen.

Professor Arne Jacobsen designed everything, buildings, furniture, fittings, cutlery, the bicycle shed in a perfect circle, and the gardens. College gardens, unless of the courtyard kind such as at Nuffield or Campion Hall, are usually an afterthought to the building and change as the needs of the occupants become apparent. Jacobsen decided what was needed in garden terms and gave it to St Catherine's along with the college. Blomfield had insisted that the architect should indicate the formal guidelines for the garden layout, but it was not since the days of Alberti and the Renaissance that an architect had planned a total environment, uniting the building and the garden on the drawing-board. Obviously it could not be a garden of old-fashioned flower borders and roses round the door in the Daniel manner and in Pevsner's words, 'the geometry is made to tell yet further in the paving of the paths through the garden areas inside and outside the parallelepiped, all of the same oblong slabs and never moving in an undulating way, and in the many screen walls, high or low, including those placed fin-wise to demarcate the gardens inside the parallelepiped from the more public circulation areas.' Irregularity in minor ways, was, however, apparently permitted and in describing the circular lawn between the library and the hall Pevsner comments that one tree has been planted out of axis 'because nature is nature.' Given the building, the garden, or perhaps one should say landscape architecture, of St Catherine's is remarkably successful, especially now that the college has largely replaced the original planting, which proved unsuitable for the soil. The Art Workers Guild were clearly right when they insisted that a garden designer should know the materials of his craft.

The St Catherine's site lies on part of an island between the two arms of the Cherwell and was liable to flooding. There had been a large defensive earthwork here in the Civil War and the line of the ravelin can still be seen along the college boundary fence. The earthwork itself was submerged when the land became a corporation rubbish tip just before the second world war. The present Garden Master, Dr Barrie Juniper, who has been responsible for the replanting of the landscape, laments in his *Guide to the Gardens of St Catherine's College* that 'any subsequent planting operation reveals the Marmite pots and sauce bottles of an earlier civilization.'

The most successful feature of the landscape architecture is the moat-like water garden parallel to the entrance front. There are groups of ornamental grasses on either side of the bridge and water lilies in the moat and a Hepworth sculpture on the grass in front of the water. The circular yellow brick bicycle shed is most successfully covered with *Pyracantha watereri* and the colour scheme in general is yellow, white and dark green with reds in autumn. There is an interesting version of a Bridgemanick outdoor theatre with the backdrop to the stage being a south wall of a building covered with a vine and *Hedera helix canariensis variegata.* Some of the groups of trees are chosen specially for the autumn colouring. One near the Middle Common Room garden includes *Ptelea trifoliata aurea, Acer capillipes* for its leaves and interesting bark, *Parottia persica, Cotoneaster watereri* for its berries, *Malus tschonoskii*, both for its coloured fruits and autumn leaf tints, and fruitful black mulberry.[4]

17.3 Wolfson College

The college takes advantage of its setting in the rural landscape of the Cherwell valley.

Wolfson College followed St Catherine's as a twentieth-century college by the Cherwell. At Wolfson the ground slopes down to the river and a new footbridge links the college with the water meadows on the other side of the river. Having chosen the site the College 'called in the country' and 'appropriated' the landscape in true eighteenth-century fashion, using to advantage the bend in the river and the miniature landscape as William Kent had done higher up the Cherwell valley at Rousham. Wolfson College, however, is not picturesque as seen from the surrounding countryside. The college moved from a Wilkinson house in the Banbury road with Gothic door, angle turret and all the Victorian extras to a sleek uncluttered building by Powell and Moya with traditional college quadrangles. To make up for their lack of history and the picturesque the Fellows put one of the discarded pinnacles from Magdalen tower in a part of the garden and opened up a vista to it.

Green College, the latest of Oxford's colleges is making conservationists purr with delight. As part of this new medical college includes the Radcliffe Observatory, and the entrance to the college is from the Woodstock Road, any new building would have to be in keeping with its surroundings. This has been most successfully achieved by the University Surveyor, Jack Lankester, who has been exemplary in adapting, fitting in and restoring old buildings for new uses. His own offices, built in 1956 in Tidmarsh Lane, are a malthouse conversion. The new entrance to Green College looks like a William Townesend eighteenth-century building and when the clock tower went on it, many people, even those who had lived in the district, were convinced it was a restored old building, which had been there all the time.

The climate of opinion had changed considerably since the demolition of The Mount in 1916 for the building of the new St Hugh's College by Buckland and Haywood. Even when, after the War, protection for historic buildings was given through the statutory listing, few Victorian buildings were included. Many years were to pass before Catherine Cole began her dedicated task of conserving North Oxford. Catherine Dodgson, as she then was (but no relation to Lewis Carroll) had been coached by the formidable Miss Annie Rogers for her Oxford entrance examination and after graduating took a diploma in archaeology. She went from classical archaeology to take an interest in the history of her own North Oxford Victorian suburb. She was dismayed by the lack of knowledge in the area (it was referred to as 'an architectural nightmare' still in 1948) and was particularly incensed when her old college, St Anne's, began to demolish

17.4 Green College: the gatehouse, 1981
An 'eighteenth-century' college by the University Surveyor. A Weldon
quarry was re-opened to supply the stone which matches, both in
colour and texture, the old Headington stone traditionally used in
Oxford buildings.

the fine Wilkinson houses in the Banbury Road. She became Secretary of the Oxford Architectural and Historical Society and wrote a series of articles for the St Anne's Magazine on 'Some Vanishing Houses in North Oxford.'[5] She then formed a group under the O.A.H.S. to study the history of the building of North Oxford, which painstakingly recorded the Victorian houses and, as is so often the case, the making of the inventory and the increased knowledge about the area, and particularly about its architects, led to the first steps for its conservation.

Largely due to Catherine Cole's efforts North Oxford became a Conservation Area in 1968 and wholesale demolition and alteration of the houses was halted. When the 99-year leases expired, however, the houses, now much too large for the normal staffless family, were converted into institutions, hotels or multiple dwellings. In most cases sympathetic conversions are now being made under the planning authority, but the essential character of the area which is being eroded, is its parklike quality. With the present changes of use the front gardens are being made into car parks so that the Victorian houses with their steep-pitched roofs, turrets and gables, now stand in a sea of tarmac instead of the country house setting that William Wilkinson planned for them. A leaflet has been issued by the City of Oxford with the support of the Victorian Group and the Garden History Society to encourage replanting, especially of the evergreen hedges, which are not only traditional to the red-brick suburb but have the advantage of screening cars and dustbins all the year round. A list of trees and shrubs appropriate for planting in North Oxford was given and there has been a marked improvement in front garden planting in the last few years, which greatly enhances the Conservation Area.

Gardens always suffer first when there is increased pressure for building. This was particularly noticeable when the colleges began to expand in the seventeenth and eighteenth centuries. All Souls and Oriel virutally lost all their garden space for new buildings. In recent years there has been a conscious effort to conserve space, so important to the setting of the building, and to create new space by integrating existing buildings. In 1966 Pembroke College restored a range of old houses in Pembroke Street belonging to the college but blocked up their entrance doors, extended the backs, and made a delightful quadrangle area with space behind the north range of the Chapel Quadrangle. A small garden quadrangle was landscaped by Sylvia Crowe at the Goodhart Building at University College utilising space which might have been overlooked in such a cramped area. Geoffrey Beard gave the new student accommodation for Lincoln College a delightful little courtyard pleasance made out of left over space in the arrangement of the small buildings on the scale of the town houses. These were sited so that a vista of Aldrich's All Saints' spire could be enjoyed above the neighbouring rooftops. Hertford are now making a new quad in space behind houses in Holywell Street and St Helen's passage.

Undoubtedly, the best way to preserve garden space around a building is to make any necessary extension underground, but this of course is only possible where permanent living accommodation is not required. The underground extension to the Radcliffe Science Library was made by Jack Lankester, the University Surveyor, under the grass in front of the University Museum, so that the view of the Ruskinian Gothic building and the Abbot's Kitchen chemical laboratory is unimpaired. The Picture Gallery at Christ Church was built under the Deanery Garden, an event which would surely have added another chapter to *Alice's Adventures under Ground* if Charles Dodgson had been alive. Some overground extensions have been made to look like garden pavilions on a grander scale in order to partake of the garden setting; the Morley-Fletcher garden room at Worcester College, the Garden Building accommodation at St Hilda's, and the Senior Common Room at Balliol. One of the most novel, but not necessarily successful ideas, advanced for respecting the character of existing college building is the glass range at Keble College. The theory was that a twentieth-century copy of Oxford Movement convictions would be unconvincing and that a new glass building would genuinely reflect and draw into it the philosophy of Keble's age, streaky bacon and blue sky and all, if the sun happens to be out.

The old grey Oxford walls, so beloved by Morris and

Burne-Jones, are sacrosanct and new college buildings such as the Blue Boar range at Christ Church or the Oriel Common Room have managed to poke out over the walls of Bear Lane and Magpie Lane in an intriguing fashion. The Keble accommodation which presents a mirror inward to the quadrangle turns into a medieval solid curtain wall on the Black Hall Road side of the range. New defences for the city of Oxford also appear in the new Florey Building for the Queen's College on the east side of Magdalen Bridge. In spite of Oscar Wilde's fears, it is doubtful whether anyone ever did try to buy a railway ticket at Balliol, but many visitors have understandably mistaken the Florey Building for a multi-storey car park.

Almost every Oxford college has had to spend huge sums of money on restoration in the last decades as pollution finally took its heavy toll on the soft local stone. In 1980 Magdalen tower, Merton tower and the Christ Church Wolsey tower were all under scaffolding. Oxford's gasworks lay to the south-west of the city and the prevailing wind brought pollution from them in its trail, particularly affecting the Gothic pinnacles and nooks and crannies. Many of the refaced buildings now look as they must have done in their Tudor beginnings. For a time a few voices, who were not responsible for handing on the Oxford heritage to posterity, were heard lamenting the passing of the Piranesian effects of blackened and ageing buildings.

The Victorians had believed in covering even Perpendicular architecture with ivy to give it a romantic look and many, including Dr Gunther, lamented that Oxford's Edwardian architects would have none of it. Dr Gunther maintained, not without truth, that the ivy was a protection against the sulphuric acid-laden raindrops from the industrial areas. Magdalen College apparently had long and heated Governing Body debates about the ivy on the tower. In 1892 the Bursar proposed that it should be removed but was outvoted. In 1904 he tried again but the ivy was still saved by 9 votes to 7. Finally in 1908 the two Waynflete Professors of Botany and Physiology put the case scientifically and this time sealed the fate of the ivy by 15 votes to 11. Another factor may well have influenced the decision, as the ivy's roots penetrated the vault of the wine cellar and after branching about in the sawdust, made for a cork through which some moisture was oozing, entered the bottle and drank up the vintage port. Dr Gunther still stuck up for the innocence of the plant, maintaining that it only makes for moisture and so long as the walls remain dry it would not penetrate.[6]

The lasting impression that visitors to Oxford take away with them is of its stone buildings enhanced with gardens, groves and green quadrangles. In his *English Note-books*, Nathaniel Hawthorne wrote: 'The world, surely, has not another place like Oxford; it is a despair to see such a place and ever to leave it, for it would take a lifetime, and more than one, to comprehend and enjoy it satisfactorily.' His compatriot and admirer Henry James also found that it seemed 'to embody with undreamed completeness a kind of dim and sacred ideal of the Western intellect.' It was always in the gardens that such Passionate Pilgrims found the embodiment of what they were seeking.[7]

> 'We repaired in turn to a series of gardens and spent long hours sitting in their greenest places. They struck us as the fairest things in England and the ripest and sweetest fruit of the English system. Locked in their antique verdure, guarded, as in the case of New College, by gentle battlements of silver-grey, outshouldering the matted leafage of undisseverable plants, filled with nightingales and memories, a sort of chorus of tradition; with vaguely-generous youth sprawling bookishly on the turf as if to spare it the injury of their boot-heels, and with the great conservative college countenance appealing gravely from the restless outer world, they seem places to lie down on the grass in for ever, in the happy faith that life is all a vast old English garden, and time an endless summer afternoon.'

Notes and references

Chapter 1: Medieval Oxford

1. Geoffrey Chaucer, *The Canterbury Tales*, line 293.
2. Ibid., line 3203.
3. A.E. Emden, *An Oxford Hall in Medieval Times*, 1927, p. 213.
4. *Archaeologia*, liv, pt. I, p. 166.
5. J.R. Magrath, *The Queen's College*, 1921, Vol. I, p. 85.
6. Alice Coats, *Flowers and their Histories*, 1956, p. 62.
7. See John Buxton, *New College, Oxford. A note on the garden*, 1976, for a full account of the building of the mount.

Chapter 2: Collegiate Oxford

1. For the history of New College see John Buxton and Penry Williams, *New College, Oxford, 1379-1979*, 1979.
2. R. Willis, 'Description of the ancient plan of the Monastery of St Gall,' *Archaeological Journal*, V, p. 8.
3. See Carter's *Ancient Sculpture and Painting*.
4. Z. von Uffenbach, *Oxford in 1710*, ed. Quarrell, 1928.
5. See H. Salter, *Survey of Oxford*, Oxford Historical Society, New Series, Vol. XIV.
6. A description of Wolsey's buildings (1533) after his death from *The Acts and Monuments of John Foxe* (ed. S.R. Cattley, 1838) Vol. 4.
7. W. Shakespeare, Henry VIII, Act VI, Scene 2.
8. Christ Church Order, c. 1550.
9. St John's Register. Coll. I. 231.

239

Chapter 3: Renaissance Oxford

1.   The letter containing the description of the villa garden was written to Apollinaris. It was described and drawn out in Robert Castell's *Villas of the Ancients Illustrated* 1728.
2.   H.L. Thompson, *Christ Church*, 1900, p. 20.
3.   C.G. Robertson, *All Souls College*, 1899, p. 73.
4.   By Dr Sylvia Landsberg, who has laid out a new knot garden at the Tudor Museum, Southampton by these methods.
5.   Sir Hugh Platt, *The Garden of Eden*, 1608, p. 173.
6.   Vivian Green, *The Commonwealth of Lincoln College 1427–1977*, 1979, p. 219n.
7.   Gutch, *Collectanea Curiosa*, 1781, Vol. I, p. 190.
8.   See Cambridge Antiquarian Society, Vol. IV, (1881) p. 7. On a draft of a letter proposing the formation of a Physic garden at Cambridge shortly before 1598.
9.   Bodl. Ms. Twyne 6, f. 287.

Chapter 4: Commonwealth Oxford

1.   Vivian Green, *The Commonwealth of Lincoln College 1427–1977*, 1979, p. 247, n. 3.
2.   See Gomme's plan of the defences of Oxford, Bodl. Ms Top. Oxon. b. 167 and E.G.W. Bill, *Christ Church Meadow*, 1955.
3.   J. Harvey, *Early Nurserymen*, 1974, p. 62.
4.   J. Bobart, *Catalogus plantarium Horti medici Oxoniensis*, 1648.
5.   Charles Webster, *The Great Instauration*, 1626–1660, p. 1975.
6.   Ralph Austen should not be confused with the Ralph Austen of Magdalen. The author of the *Treatise of Fruit trees* was not in the University.
7.   James Turner, 'Ralph Austen, an Oxford horticulturist of the 17th century,' *Garden History*, Vol. VI, No. 2.
8.   At Corpus 'the College of Bees', the famous bees who had greeted Ludovicus Vives, departed at the Parliament Visitation in 1648. R. Plot, *The Natural History of Oxfordshire*, 1677, p. 185.
9.   *Garden History*, Vol. VI, no. 2, p. 42 and p. 45 n. 6.
10.   R. Plot, Ibid., p. 265.
11.   Mss. Evelyn, Christ Church.
12.   John Wilkins, *An Essay towards a real Character and a Philosophical Language*, 1668.
13.   R. Plot, *The Natural History of Oxfordshire*, p. 240.
14.   *The Reformed Commonwealth of Bees.* Christopher Wren, *A Letter concerning that pleasant and profitable invention of a transparent beehive*, 1655.
15.   H.M. Sinclair and A.H.T. Robb-Smith, *A Short History of Anatomical Teaching at Oxford*, 1950, p. 14 refers to Wren's 'a Treatise of the motion of the Muscles, explaining the whole Anatomy by Models form'd in Pasteboards.'

Chapter 5: Restoration Oxford

1. *Wood's Life and Times* Vol. II, p. 479.
2. J. Summerson, *The Sheldonian in its Time*, An oration delivered to commemorate the Restoration of the Theatre, 16 Nov. 1963.
3. Trans. Medical Society London, Vol. 14, 1917.
4. For Bobarts and Herbaria see *An Account of the Herbaria of the Dpt of Botany in the University of Oxford* by H. Clokie, 1964.
5. R. Plot, *The Natural History of Oxfordshire*, 1677, p. 152.
6. Guide to the *Oxford Botanic Gardens* 1971, p. 35.
7. J.K. Burras, 'The nature of variegation,' *Journal of the R.H.S.*, Vol. XCIX, Pt. 10.
8. J. Granger, *A Biographical History of England*, 1775, iv, 88.
9. Bodl. Ms. Sherard 30.
10. H.M. Petter, *The Oxford Almanacks*, 1974, p. 51.
11. Z. von Uffenbach *Oxford in 1710*, ed. Quarrell, 1928, p. 55.
12. Bodl. ms. Ash 120a, 224-5.
13. R. Plot, *The Natural History of Oxfordshire*, p. 39.
14. John Tradescant, *Musaeum Tradescantianum*, 1656.

Chapter 6: The Grand Manner in Oxford

1. William Cartwright, 'On the Imperfections of Christ Church Buildings,' 1634.
2. John Fell's Benefaction Book. Christ Church Library.
3. Henry Thompson, *Christ Church*, 1900, p. 87.
4. M. Caroe, *Wren and Tom Tower*, 1923, p. 23.
5. See Helen Petter, *The Oxford Almanacks*, 1974.
6. See W.G. Hiscock, *Henry Aldrich*, 1960.
7. Dr Clarke's architectural library and collection of drawings was left to Worcester College. See H.M. Colvin, *Catalogue of Architectural Drawings of the 18th and 19th centuries in the Library of Worcester College, Oxford*, 1964.
8. See W.G. Hiscock, *A Christ Church Miscellany*, 1946, pp. 38-62.
9. John Buxton and Penry Williams, *New College, Oxford 1379-1979*, 1979, p. 214.
10. *Hearne's Remarks and Collections*, ed. H.E. Salter 1914, Vol. IX, p. 361.
11. See Kerry Downes, *Hawksmoor*, 1969.
12. The present Radcliffe Square was at the time full of small houses and gardens as seen in Loggan's plan. Hawksmoor would have left the square open with a large central statue. The new round library in his scheme would have been joined to the Bodleian.
   See H. Petter, *The Oxford Almanacks*, 1974, p. 49 for an illustration of Hawksmoor's 'Forum Universitatis.' The actual drawing is in Brasenose College Drawings, no. 36 and the Gibbs Collection at the Ashmolean Museum.

The drawing for the 'Forum Civitatis' at Carfax is in the Bodleian, ms. Top. Oxon a 26(R).

13.   *Hearne's Collections*, Vol. VII, p. 210.
14.   Printed by Oxford University Press, 1960.
15.   See H. Petter, *The Oxford Almanacks*, 1974, p. 54.

Another illustration is shown in *Oxonia Depicta*, Pl. 27. Hawksmoor's plan dated 1720 NH is in Worcester College Library (Colvin, *Catalogue*) nos. 65, 66.

Chapter 7: The Glorious Revolution and Dutch Gardening

1.   Daniel Defoe, *A Tour Through the Whole Island of Great Britain*, 1724, Letter 2.
2.   *The Journeys of Celia Fiennes*, edited Christopher Morris, 1948.
3.   Bodleian Mss. Eng misc b. 73 f. 7.
4.   Thomas Salmon, *The Foreigner's Companion through the Universities of Cambridge and Oxford*, 1748.
5.   Miles Hadfield, *A History of British Gardening*, 1960, p. 108.
6.   Ibid., p. 147.

Chapter 8: Addison, the prophet of natural gardening

1.   William Mason, *The English Garden*, 1772-81, Book I, lines 468-72.
2.   Pope's Essay in the Guardian 1713 condemns vegetable sculpture in a witty parody. Echoing Addison it makes a plea for informality in gardens.
'There is certainly something in the amiable Simplicity of unadorned Nature, that spreads over the Mind a more noble sort of Tranquility, and a loftier Sensation of Pleasure, than can be raised from the nicer Scenes of Art.'
3.   *The Spectator*, no. 10.
4.   Ibid., no. 1.
5.   Ibid., no. 411.
6.   The essays on the Imagination were originally a single essay which were expanded into eleven essays in *The Spectator*, no. 411-421. The original ms. Essay came to the possession of J. Dykes Campbell who published it as *Some Portions of Essays contributed to the Spectator by Mr Joseph Addison* in a limited edition at Glasgow in 1864. See *The Spectator*, ed. Donald F. Bond, 1965, p. 535.
7.   The ms. Essay: a passage not included in the description of Country Life in Spectator no. 417.
8.   *Dialogues upon Ancient Medals III*. See *Joseph Addison, Miscellaneous Works*, A.C. Guthkelch, 1914, vol. II, p. 377.

9. In a miscellany entitled *Cytherea, or poems upon Love and Intrigue*, 1723, and in *Epistle to Dr Arbuthnot*, 1735.

10. The second part of Essay no. 414 was added after he had visited French and Italian gardens and the Essay on Architecture which followed was entirely new and written after Addison's visit to Rome in 1701.

11. The Kit-Cat Club was founded early in the eighteenth century by leading Whigs, including Steele, Addison, Congreve, Garth and Vanbrugh. It included many landowners who were engaged in laying out their grounds such as Cobham, Dormer and Carlisle.

12. *Remarks on several parts of Italy*, 1705.

13. Mavis Batey, 'An Early Naturalistic Garden,' *Country Life*, 22 Dec, 1977.

14. See R.W. King, 'The ferme ornée: Philip Southcote and Wooburn Farm,' *Garden History* Vol. II, no. 3.

15. *Pope's Works*, ed. Elwin and Courthorpe, 1872. p. 324 n. 1.

16. *Congratulatory Epistle to the Rt Hon Addison*, by a Student at Oxford, 1717.

Chapter 9: The Landscape Movement

1. Mavis Batey, 'Shotover's Continuity with the Past,' *Country Life*, 29 Dec, 1977.

2. W.G. Hiscock, *A Christ Church Miscellany*, 1946, pp. 38-62.

3. A. Woods & W. Hawkes, 'Sanderson Miller of Radway,' *Cake & Cockhorse*, Vol. 4, Autumn 1968.

4. R. Dodsley, *Description of the Leasowes*, 1764. See also C. Thacker, *The History of Gardens*, 1979, pp. 199-203.

5. Radway Inclosure Act passed and Award signed May, 1757. W.R.O.

6. *The Spectator*, no. 415.

7. Ibid., no. 387.

8. Dorothy Stroud, *Capability Brown*, 1950, p. 153.

9. T.F. Dibdin, *Reminiscences of a Literary Life*, 1836, Vol. I, p. 87.

10. Garden Bills in St John's Archives.

11. Balliol Archives.

12. T.G. Jackson, *Wadham College, Oxford*, 1893.

13. Mavis Batey, 'Nuneham Courtenay: An Oxfordshire 18th century Deserted Village,' *Oxoniensia*, Vol XXXIII, 1968.

14. Mavis Batey, 'Oliver Goldsmith: An Indictment of Landscape Gardening,' *Furor Hortensis*, 1974, ed. P. Willis.

15. Mavis Batey, 'Romantic Vision in a Flower Garden,' *Country Life*, 12 Sept. 1968.

Chapter 10: The Picturesque Movement

1. *Memoirs of Dr. Richard Gilpin*, written by W. Gilpin, ed. W. Jackson, 1879.

2. Bodl Mss. Eng. misc. b. 73. f. 7.
3. See William D. Templeman, *The Life and Work of William Gilpin*, 1939, and Carl Paul Barbier, *William Gilpin, His Drawings, Teaching and Theory of the Picturesque*, 1963.
4. Bodl Mss. Eng misc c. 388 f. 137 and Mavis Batey, 'Gilpin and the schoolboy picturesque,' *Garden History* Vol. II, No. 2, 24.
5. His nephew William Sawrey Gilpin, son of Sawrey Gilpin the animal painter, did become a practitioner of picturesque gardening and published *Practical Hints on Landscape Gardening* in 1832, following the Gilpin principles extended by Uvedale Price to cover real landscape.
6. Mason-Gilpin correspondence, Bodl. Mss. Eng. misc. d. 570-1.
7. Nuneham Guide, second edition, published University of Oxford, 1979, Mavis Batey, 'William Mason, English Gardener,' *Garden History*, Vol I, No. 2.
8. *Nuneham Courtenay*, 1797 and 1806 (Simon Harcourt).
9. Magdalen Red Book dated January 1st, 1801.
10. Ms Top. Oxon b. 123, f. 105 used for the 1856 Oxford Almanack illustration.
11. Magd. Ms. cII. 3, 4.
12. Kerry Downes, *Hawksmoor*, 1959, p. 101.
13. T.S.R. Boase, 'An Oxford College and the Gothic Revival,' *Journal of the Warburg and Courtauld Institutes*, 18, 1955.
14. Julian Munby, J.C. Buckler. 'Tackley's Inn and Three Medieval Houses in Oxford,' *Oxoniensia*, Vol 43, 123.
15. R. Southey, *Letters of Espriella*, 1807, Vol II, p. 69.

Chapter 11: Horticulture in the University

1. J.C. Loudon, *The Gardener's Magazine*, Vol. 8, 1832, p. 700.
2. *Guide to the Oxford Botanic Gardens*, 1971 compiled by C.D. Darlington, Emeritus Professor of Botany and J.K. Burras, Superintendent of the Oxford Botanic Garden. Professor Darlington was Sherardian Professor 1953-1971.
3. K.L. Davidson, *Gardens Past and Present*, 1908, p. 19. There are several versions of this story.
4. R.T. Gunther, *Oxford Gardens*, 1912, p. 18.
5. W.T. Stearn, 'From Theophrastus and Dioscorides to Sibthorp and Smith: the background and origin of the *Flora Graeca*,' *Biological Journal of the Linnean Society*, Vol. 8, pp. 285-298.
6. The original sketches and master copy of *Flora Graeca* are in the University Department of Botany.
7. A Report presented to the Visitors of the Oxford Botanic Garden, 1834.
8. Rules of the Ashmolean Society, 1831.
9. R.T. Gunther, *Oxford Gardens*, p. 23.
The collection of willows first planted by Baxter is now established in a separate Salicetum across the Cherwell from the University Parks.

Also see article on Oxford Flora by E.C. Druce, *Gardener's Chronicle*, November 4th, 1871.

10. Introduction to the Duncan Ashmolean catalogue.
11. Obituary, *Jackson's Oxford Journal*, January 18th, 1868.
12. Ruth Duthie, 'Growers and Showers of Florists' Flowers in the Oxford Area up to 1820,' *Top. Oxon.*, no. 22, 1978.
13. John Rea, *Flora: or a Complete Florilege*, 1676, p. 144.
14. Ruth Duthie, 'Growers and Showers of Florists' Flowers . . .,' *Top. Oxon.*, no. 22, 1978.
15. George Crabbe, *The Borough*, 1810, Trades. Line 95.
16. First Report of the Park Delegates. O.U. Archives.
17. Ruth Duthie, 'Carnation Growing in 19th Century Oxford,' *The Year Book of the British National Carnation Society*, 1981, p. 21.
18. Ruth Duthie, 'Growers and Showers of Florists' Flowers in the Oxford Area after 1820,' *Oxfordshire Local History*, Vol. I, no. I, p. 13.

Chapter 12: Victorian Oxford

1. Matthew Arnold, *Essays in Criticism*, 1865.
2. T. James, *The Carthusian*, 1839.
3. Balliol College Archives.
4. Architecture in Oxford, Letter to Pall Mall Gazette, 3 Nov. 1874.
5. G.W. Kitchin, *Ruskin in Oxford and other Studies*, 1904, p. 47.
6. Walter Scott, The Lay of the Last Minstrel, Canto II, VIII.
7. E.T. Cook, *The Life of Ruskin*, 1911, Vol. II, p. 186.
8. *The Athenaeum*, no. 4330, October 22, 1910.

Chapter 13: The North Oxford Victorian Suburb

1. Park Town Minute Book. See Peter Howell, 'Samuel Lipscomb Seckham,' *Oxoniensia*, Vol XLI, 1976, p. 337.
2. Park Town Trust deeds. Bodleian Library.
3. E. Dodgson, 'Notes on Some Houses in the Banbury Rd,' *Oxoniensia*, Vol XXXII, 1967, p. 53.
4. The Bates nursery was formerly in Summertown.
5. E.M. Odling, *Memoir of the late Alfred Smee by his Daughter*, 1878.
6. -. Simpkin, *Within the Sound of Great Tom*, 1879.
7. *The Letters of Lewis Carroll*, edited by Morton N Cohen, 1979, p. 189.
8. First Report of the Park Delegates Minute Book 1863, Oxford University Archives.
9. *Oxford Jackson's Journal*, July 2nd, 1887.
10. Betjeman was at Magdalen 1925-8 and first knew North Oxford as a Dragon School boy 1917-20.
11. From notes by Minn. Ms. Top Oxon d. 501 in the Bodleian

Library. Also see Prof. Goldwin Smith's letter to Oxford Mag., June
21st 1886.
12.   Mary Augusta Ward, *A Writer's Recollections*, 1918.
13.   *The Story of the Unknown Church*, a contribution in the
Oxford and Cambridge Magazine, 1856.
14.   *The Works of Ruskin*, edited by E.T. Cook and A. Wedderburn, 1903, Vol. I, p. 156.

Chapter 14: Arts and Crafts

1.   William Mason, *The English Garden*, Book I, line 21.
2.   William Robinson, *The English Flower Garden* (5th edition),
1896, p. 8.
3.   Betty Massingham, *Miss Jekyll*, 1966, p. 50.
4.   Mavis Batey, 'Landscape with Flowers: West Surrey – the
background to Gertrude Jekyll's Art,' *Garden History*, Vol II, No. 2,
1974.
5.   Annie Rogers, *Degrees by Degrees*, 1938.
6.   Annie Rogers, 'Alice in Wonderland,' The Times, March 29,
1928.
7.   Jan Morris, *The Oxford Book of Oxford*, 1978, p. 289.
8.   E.S. Procter, 'St. Hugh's College Garden,' *St Hugh's Chronicle*,
no. 25, 1952.
9.   Ray Desmond, 'Victorian gardening measures,' *Garden History*, Vol. V, no. 3, 1977.
10.   From ms. notes in the Minn photographic collection, Bodl. Ms.
Top Oxon. d. 501.
11.   E.S. Procter, 'St Hugh's College Garden,' *St Hugh's Chronicle*,
no. 25, 1952.
12.   See Alan Crawford, 'New Life for an Artist's Village,' *Country
Life*, 24 Jan, 1980.
13.   Henry James, 'Our Artists in Europe,' *Harper's Magazine*,
1889, p. 58.
14.   *The Letters of Henry James*, ed. Percy Lubbock, 1920, Vol. I,
p. 273.
15.   Verity Anderson, *The Last of the Eccentrics: A Life of Ross-
lyn Bruce*, 1972, p. 88, quoted in *The Letters of Lewis Carroll*, ed.
Morton, N. Cohen, p. 1055, n2.
16.   Herbert Baker, *Architecture and Personalities*, 1944.

Chapter 15: Boars Hill

1.   'Orchards, Surrey,' *Country Life*, August 31st, 1901.
2.   G.E. Blackman, 'Cultivation and Harvesting of Sunflowers,'
Agriculture, April, 1946.
3.   Address given by Professor Harley at the Memorial Service
for Geoffrey Blackman in St John's Chapel on May 17th 1980.

4.   Bagley Wood was purchased in 1583 through William Leech who married the Founder's niece. See W.H. Hutton, *St John Baptist College*, 1898.

5.   Joseph Conrad, *Romance: A Novel*, 1903, p. 463 (last words of the novel).

6.   Joan Evans, *Time and Chance*, 1943, p. 363.

7.   Arthur Evans, *Jarn Mound*, 1933, p. 38.

8.   Ibid., p. 10.

9.   Ibid., p. 10.

10.   Ian Scargill, *The Preservation of Oxford*, 1973, p. 13. An account of the work of the Oxford Preservation Trust 1927–1972.

11.   52nd Report, *The Oxford Preservation Trust*, 1978, p. 26.

12.   A. Evans, 'The Rollright Stones and their Folklore,' *Folklore*, Vol. VI, 1895.

Chapter 16: Christ Church Meadow

1.   E.G.W. Bill, *Christ Church Meadow*, 1965, p. 31.

2.   Max Beerbohm, *Zuleika Dobson*, 1911, p. 189.

3.   E.G.W. Bill, *Christ Church Meadow*, p. 10.

4.   Ibid., p. 21.

5.   G.V. Cox, *Recollections of Oxford*, 1868, p. 145.

6.   Boswell's *Life of Johnson*, A.D. 1728, Aetat 19.

7.   Robert Southey, *Letters of Espriella*, Vol. II, 1807, p. 62.

8.   E. Bradley, *The Adventures of Mr Verdant Green*, 1853, p. 105.

9.   J.K. Burras, *Tree Planting Proposals for Christ Church Meadow*, 1976.

10.   Ibid.

11.   *Ruskin Works*, ed. Cook and Wedderburn, 1903, Vol. 35, p. 203.

12.   *The Journals and Papers of Gerard Manley Hopkins*, ed. House, 1959, p. 133.

13.   *Ruskin Works*, Vol. 27, p. 466.

14.   R. Plot, *Natural History of Oxfordshire*, 1677, p. 13.

15.   Bodl Ms. Locke c. 41.

16.   G.V. Cox, *Recollections of Oxford*, p. 23.

17.   R.T. Gunther, *Oxford Gardens*, 1902, p. 132. Article by G.C. Druce. The latest escape is a Mexican plant, *Erigeron mucronatinus*, which grows on the sunny walls in Deadman's Walk.

18.   *Botanical Exchange Club Report*, Vol. IX, 1929–31, p. 549.

19.   F.A. Bellamy, *A History of the Ashmolean Natural History Society*, 1908.

20.   D.A. Allen, *The Naturalist in Britain*, 1976, p. 249.

21.   Ibid., p. 255.

22.   *Travels of Carl Philipp Moritz in England in 1782*, 1924, p. 158.

23. Thomas Sharp, *Oxford Replanned*, 1948, p. 118.

24. Dr R.J. Newman has made a case study of *The Road and Christ Church Meadow*, 1980.

25. Ibid., p. 19.

26. G.A. Jellicoe, *Studies in Landscape Design*, Vol. II, 1966, p. 58.

27. E.G.W. Bill, *Christ Church Meadow*, p. 37. Unpublished poem by W.H. Auden.

Chapter 17: Modern Oxford

1. C.D. Darlington, *Inaugural Lecture*, 1953.

2. See *Guide to the Oxford Botanic Gardens*, 1980. The Genetic Garden pp. 32–7.

3. C.D. Darlington, Inaugural Lecture.

4. B.E. Juniper, *A Guide to the Gardens of St Catherine's College*.

5. J.C. Cole, 'Some vanishing Oxford houses', *The Ship* (magazine of St Anne's College), 1962.

6. R.T. Gunther, *Oxford Gardens*, 1912, p. 210.

7. Henry James, *A Passionate Pilgrim*, 1875.

Picture acknowledgements

Acknowledgements and thanks for the use of copyright illustrations are expressed as follows.

Black and white illustrations:

1.1 (Magdalen's medieval gardens): photograph by Alun Jones.
2.2 (Agas map): photograph by Alun Jones.
3.1 (Hovenden's map): the Warden and Fellows of All Souls College.
3.2 (Knot garden patterns): Sylvia Landsberg proposed the derivation shown at lower right.
8.1 (Joseph Addison): National Portrait Gallery.
8.3, 8.4 and 8.5: photographs by Alun Jones
9.2 (The Gothic temple): 'Country Life'.
9.5 (The Carfax Conduit): The Oxford Mail and Times.
10.1 (Worcester picturesque landscape): Oxfordshire County Libraries.
11.1 (Island flower beds): Bodleian Library P. 1713. d. 1.
12.1 (Natural art history): the University Museum.
12.2 (Ruskin's road building experiment): Oxfordshire County Libraries.
13.1, 13.2 and 13.3: 'Country Life'.
13.4 (North Oxford in 1876): H.M. Ordnance Survey.
13.5 (No. 13 Norham Gardens): photograph by Alun Jones.
14.1 (The building of St Hugh's): Oxfordshire County Libraries.
15.1 (A study in persuasion): Audrey Blackman.
16.1 (Map of Christ Church Meadow): The Governing Body of Christ Church College.
17.4 (Green College): the University Surveyor.

Colour plates:

1 ('Rosa Medicinae'): Bodleian Library Ms Bodl 362.
2 (Embroidery by Queen Elizabeth I): Bodleian Library Ms e Musaeo 242.
3 (Botanic Garden entrance): Bodleian Library G.A. Oxon b. 109b.
8 ('Flora Graeca'): Bodleian Library Ms Douce 223.
9 (Repton's Red Book): the President and Fellows of Magdalen College.
13 (The Deanery garden, by J. M. W. Turner): painting reproduced by courtesy of the Governing Body of Christ Church College; colour transparency lent by Pitkin Pictorials Ltd.
15 ('Convent Thoughts'): Ashmolean Museum.
16 (Wood Croft): photograph by J. W. Thomas.

Index

250